people's capital. *This behavioral problem is one that must be addressed to keep capitalism functioning efficiently; everyone who reads this work will come away with a strong sense of the work left to be done and the direction in which we need to go.*

Overall, I am certain that the essays collected here will add substantially to the nation's understanding of the root causes of our corporate governance crisis and to the road ahead that we must travel together."

Greg Taxin, chief executive, Glass Lewis Inc. Shareholder Advisors

"Gandossy and Sonnenfeld have brought together a provocative series of essays from individuals well informed on the issues of leadership and corporate governance. An important read for any business leader grappling with today's issues."

Roger Enrico, former chairman and chief executive officer, Pepsico

"Strong governance is not something that can alone be mandated by the SEC or the NYSE. It has to be instilled in an organization by the CEO and the board of directors. Leadership and Governance from the Inside Out *is a great opportunity for directors and CEOs to learn from others' mistakes and best practices."*

William D. Perez, president and CEO, S.C. Johnson & Son, Inc.

"At a time when corporate governance is preoccupied by legal liability and forensic accounting, Gandossy and Sonnenfeld's insightful anthology correctly places good governance and effective leadership as twin top priorities. Those who lead, or hope to lead, need to read these essays and learn their lessons."

Richard E. Cavanagh, president and CEO, The Conference Board, Inc.

LEADERSHIP AND GOVERNANCE FROM THE INSIDE OUT

ROBERT GANDOSSY
JEFFREY SONNENFELD

EDITORS

WILEY

JOHN WILEY & SONS, INC.

Library of Congress Cataloging-in-Publication Data:

Leadership and governance from the inside out / [edited by] Robert Gandossy, Jeffrey
Sonnenfeld.
     p. cm.
   Includes bibliographical references.
   ISBN 0-471-67185-1 (cloth)
  1. Leadership. 2. Corporate governance. 3. Business ethics. 4. Directors of
corporations. 5. Corporations—Corrupt practices. 6. Chief executive officers—Conduct
of life. I. Gandossy, Robert P. II. Sonnenfeld, Jeffrey A., 1954–
   HD57.7.L4314 2004
   658.4—dc22

                                                                    2004007663

Printed in the United States of America
10 9 8 7 6 5 4 3 2 1

The authors dedicate this book to their loving families,
where all good governance originates.

Bob Gandossy would like to thank Simone Gandossy, Taylor Gandossy, Dylan Gandossy, and Connor Gandossy for their support, laughter, and love. He would also like to thank James Corsetti who taught him a lot about integrity and looking for qualities in people that others don't see.

Professor Sonnenfeld would like to thank Clarky Sonnenfeld, Sophie Sonnenfeld, Rochelle Sonnenfeld, Marc Sonnenfeld, and Ann Laupheimer Sonnenfeld for their inspiration, advice, and encouragement.

CONTENTS

PREFACE

Over the centuries, social commentators have complained that "laws are like spider webs, which may catch small flies but let the wasps and hornets break through." In fact, before the writing of criminologist Edwin Sutherland in 1939, theft was widely seen as a pathological reaction to poverty. Sutherland is credited with coining the term *white-collar crime,* which refers to respected, affluent members of society who broke laws as often as did those less fortunate although their deeds often did not label them as criminals. The outrage of the financial scandals of the 1930s led to the Pecora hearings in Congress, from which new securities legislation resulted. Some financiers were even imprisoned. Nonetheless, white-collar criminals were rarely treated as genuine felons. For example, criminal violations of the Sherman Anti-Trust Act of 1890 did not lead to a single imprisonment until 1961.[1]

That all began to change in the United States in the late 1970s and early 1980s as chief executive officers (CEOs) and other top leaders became ensnarled in both the crimes and the punishment. The seeds of this book were planted at that time when our paths first crossed. Jeffrey Sonnenfeld was then teaching as a professor at the Harvard Business School and Robert Gandossy had just completed his graduate work at Yale and had begun his consulting career in Cambridge, Massachusetts. Interestingly enough, the hot topic then, as now, revolved around corporate wrongdoing and governance. Thus, a quarter century before breakdowns in corporate governance became so salient, Jeff was researching corporate scandals and price fixing beginning with the 1976 punishment of 48 executives from 22 companies in the forest products industry where 15, including CEOs, were sentenced to prison terms with the others facing stiff fines and civil penalties.[2] Meanwhile, Bob examined what was—up to that point anyway—the largest fraud ever committed in the United States, the OPM Leasing Scandal. Over a period of 10 years, OPM's principal owners perpetrated a fraud amounting to more than $200 million.[3] OPM, by the way, blatantly presaged what they were to become—OPM stood for *Other People's Money.* We recognized a shared interest, not only in subject matter, but in the whole process of research and writing; it wasn't long before we bonded, forging a professional and personal relationship, based on a common cause, not to mention mutual admiration and respect.

Over the next two decades, we came to recognize that corporate scandals come in waves. During the late 1970s and early 1980s, for example, we saw The Penn Square Bank, E.F. Hutton, The Bank of Boston, Drysdale Government Securities, Lincoln Savings, and The Bank of Credit and Commerce International (BCCI) among the financial services scandals and other revenue recognition fraud at firms like Sunbeam and Cendant. In each case—despite the number of fiduciaries involved—"no one knew" about the wrongdoing for long periods of time. Or so it seemed.

The Penn Square Bank, a small, windowless shopping mall bank in Oklahoma City, sold questionable oil and gas loans upstream to several of the largest and most prestigious banks in the country, including Chase Manhattan, Continental Illinois, and Seattle First National Bank. The person who headed the oil and gas loan department at Penn Square was Bill "Monkey Brains" Patterson who was known to drink beer from his boot and wear Mickey Mouse ears, a Batman hat, or a Nazi storm trooper helmet to work. He was also known to engage in food fights in fancy restaurants.

But for years, no one knew that the Penn Square loans were not collateralized properly. No one knew that many of Penn Square's credits were not creditworthy. No one knew about Patterson either. Not Continental Illinois, which lost several hundred million dollars on Penn Square. Not Chase Manhattan. Not SeaFirst. Not the comptroller of the currency. And not Penn Square's auditors, Peat, Marwick, Mitchell & Company.

The Bank of Boston was accused of failing to report $2 billion worth of international currency transactions. For over four years, the bank's compliance officers were apparently unaware that they were required by law to report those transactions. The bank's auditors claimed they did not know; the bank's management claimed they did not know; and the comptroller of the currency also claimed ignorance.

E.F. Hutton, at the time, the nation's fifth-largest brokerage house, engaged in a complicated check-kiting scam that involved over 400 banks and allowed Hutton the use of millions of dollars of the bank's money without ever paying interest. Again, no one knew. Not E.F. Hutton's management, not the victim banks, not Hutton's auditors, not the SEC. Everyone seemed to be so distracted by succession politics and internal political sabotage, no one seemed to know about the complicated top-level scheme, and outside legal investigator Griffin Bell failed to locate those responsible.[4]

And then there was OPM. Over the course of a decade, OPM committed its multimillion-dollar fraud against 19 financial institutions. American Express and Rockwell International were among its customers; Goldman Sachs and Lehman Brothers were its investment bankers; and Fox & Company—one of the nation's largest accounting firms—were its outside auditors. But no one knew. Not Lehman. Not American Express. Not Rockwell and not OPM's lawyers, accountants, or their own employees. At least this is what they would have us believe. In fact, many people knew about OPM's crimes or had strong reasons to suspect them, but failed to take adequate steps to put an end to the misconduct.

Later in this decade, the BCCI banking scandal revealed a massive financial criminal network involving many prominent political leaders from 73 countries where the funds of central banks were used to create shell corporations hidden by bank privacy laws. The network was also responsible for hiding tax evasion, bribery, smuggling, arms trading, and terrorist activities.[5] Arizona's Lincoln Savings scandal led by Charles Keating had links to BCCI which was later accused of political influence peddling, misrepresenting risk, fabricating earnings of over $500 million, and leading to the eventual collapse, which cost the public $3.4 billion.[6] Several other savings and loan disasters, including Neil Bush's ill-fated Silverado Savings,[7] added to the public bill. Many prominent legislators, regulators, and investment banks were deeply immersed in these S&L scandals, yet all claimed to have been surprised.

Similarly, darlings of Wall Street came crashing down to earth in the next wave, which included such firms as Al Dunlap's out-of-control Sunbeam Corporation with one-third of its earnings fabricated, misleading revenue figures from channel-stuffing manipulations, and which incurred $15 million in fines against former CEO Al Dunlap, among other penalties. Here again, a win-at-all costs, profit-at-any-price mindset led to a celebrity beyond Wall Street before the accumulated fraud brought down the enterprise.[8] After a first decade of brilliant revival, Michael Eisner's Walt Disney Company, the beacon of family entertainment, suffered high-level staff defections and political intrigue that began to engulf the enterprise. The scandal erupted when it was discovered that CEO Michael Eisner had promised his friend and right-hand man Michael Ovitz $100 million in the instance he should be fired. After just 14 months on the job, Eisner did indeed terminate Ovitz but awarded him an astounding lush severance package that paid him $7 million for each failing month on the job. Stockholder litigation in Delaware courts—challenging the *business judgment rule* protection of board members from liability—helped bring several alarming facts to light, including the fact that the Disney compensation committee had never reviewed Ovitz's final severance package and that he was, in fact, terminated for cause, having been given a harsh performance assessment by Eisner.

In the immediate aftermath of the anticipated Y2K database systems crisis and the 2000 Presidential election debacle came the most recent wave, fed by the scandal-hungry, 24-hour news networks and anger at the collapse of the technology bubble that had emerged from the greatest economic expansion in the history of the United States—but this wave of scandals seemed bolder, brasher, and more brazen. To be sure, leaders in most corporations are trustworthy, have integrity, and operate with strong ethical standards. But the minority charged with wrongdoing in this latest wave— these residents of the C-suite appeared not to give a damn about their employees, shareholders, or any of the other constituencies whose best interests they were charged with looking out for.

This most recent spate of corporate scandals began just one month after the terrorist attacks on New York City and Washington D.C., when the most infamous of the scandals first broke. That was when the public became aware that one of the world's most highly regarded energy companies, Texas-based Enron, had been hiding more than $1 billion worth of accounting indiscretions by improperly using off-the-books partnerships, manipulating the Texas power market, bribing foreign governments to win overseas contracts, and manipulating the California energy market. The leadership became intoxicated with a shared hubris and flagrantly violated basic accounting practices.

In a flash, the $70 billion company declared bankruptcy, and thousands of employees found themselves not only out of a job but also without any retirement savings. At the top, heads rolled, as executives faced literally dozens of criminal charges, including fraud, obstruction of justice, insider trading, money laundering, and filing false income tax returns. Fines of up to $1 million were levied, and once-revered leaders found themselves facing the real possibility of trading the corner office for the corner cell.

The Enron story struck a nerve among the American public, not to mention Wall Street. Granted, as the first major scandal of a fresh wave of corporate misgovernance, it received more than its fair share of attention. Then there were the purported ties to the White House and the reams upon reams of documents that Enron executives supposedly ordered shredded to cover their misdeeds. Perhaps more than anything else, people were struck by the fact that Enron had been, by all accounts, a highly admired company, right up until the scandal broke. No less a magazine than *Fortune* had branded Enron the most innovative company in America for six years running. Once again, for years, no one knew the real Enron. Even its chairman—the paternalistic but detached Ken Lay, who surreptitiously sold $80 million of stock during the secret unraveling—claims to have been in the dark.[9]

The nightmare didn't end with Enron, of course. In short order, there were Arthur Andersen; Global Crossing; Tyco; AOL Time-Warner; Adelphia Communications; and WorldCom, which declared bankruptcy on July 21, 2002 after admitting to an $11 billion accounting fraud, beating the record for the largest insolvency in U.S. history, which had been set by Enron less than eight months earlier. Andersen, once the beacon of integrity for its profession, came crashing down on charges of obstruction of justice.[10] In each of the others, there were hundreds of millions of dollars misdirected to top leadership.

In every corner of corporate America, allegations were flying as executives were accused of cooking the books, overstating earnings, establishing off-the-book partnerships, profiteering from Initial Public Offerings (IPOs) and phony or inflated stock ratings, and participating in trading misconduct in the form of market timing and late trading. Personal indiscretions, such as the filing of false tax claims, money laundering, wire fraud, inside trading, and elaborate and outrageous perquisites, made household names out of the likes of such former leaders as Enron chairman Kenneth Lay and its CFO, Andrew Fastow; Imclone founder Samuel Waksal; and Tyco CEO Dennis Kozlowski. From mid-2003 to mid-2004, dozens of top executives from such firms as Enron, Worldcom, HealthSouth, and Imclone were convicted of massive frauds and imprisoned. These were followed by the mutual fund scandal and conviction of none other than Martha Stewart.

For a country already in the throes of recession, facing high unemployment and a weak stock market—not to mention national security fears— these scandals cast a permanent shadow on corporate America. What's more, they brought into question the validity of the stock market boom of the 1990s—to what extent was some of it built on scandal, deception, and illegal practices?

As employees, shareholders, consumers, and citizens, we are comforted by the integrity of leaders. Whether one of the leaders of this nation or one of the leaders of a corporation, we expect those entrusted with *the keys to the store* to exhibit high integrity, to keep their promises, and, above all, to operate within the bounds of the law. Trust and integrity are important foundations for leaders everywhere. Yet there's been a decline in confidence in the integrity of leaders in recent years. While employees generally trust their own bosses, Gallup surveys show that CEOs in general have fallen, with roughly 75 percent of the nation believing that corporate fraud is widespread in high office. From the shenanigans of corporate leaders already discussed herein, to questions about misleading weapons of mass destruction, to intelligence evidence to justify President Bush's push for war in Iraq, to President Clinton's denial of sexual escapades in the Oval Office, the integrity of leaders—or lack thereof—is a hot-button issue that isn't going away anytime soon. High degrees of trust and integrity take years to build, yet—as we've seen numerous times in recent years—they can be destroyed in mere moments.

Executive indiscretions have a major impact on how employees, shareholders, and the public view corporate America and the people who lead it. What's more, the scandals that arise from misconduct in the C-suite are problematic not just for the wrongdoers but also for everyone associated with the organization as they find themselves tainted by the deeds of a relatively small number of people. Consider what it's like to be a former employee of Enron or Arthur Andersen. Particularly in the early postbankruptcy days, going in for a job interview with a potential employer had to feel like a scene out of *The Scarlet Letter.* Instead of wearing their stigma on their clothing, however, they wore theirs on their resume.

Recognizing that it's impossible to create vibrant, growing, dynamic businesses when trust and integrity are not present, we set out to give a complete and accurate picture of the problem in the hopes of breaking the cycle so that we're not constantly having this recurring theme. Granted, there are many ways to look at corporate wrongdoing—through the findings of academicians and through the sound bites of talking heads, who regularly pop up on broadcast news programs, expounding on the subject.

In reviewing the shifting landscape of corporate misconduct, three key elements stand out that guide this book. First, the problems are not isolated in any sector—corporate, consulting, banking, governmental, and even nonprofit leadership complicity is involved. While each professional has raced to seize moral high ground and point the fingers elsewhere, the truth is that there is no purely virtuous ground. In fact, this is not even a set of problems unique to U.S. soil as continuing scandals in Europe remind us, afflicting such global titans as Royal Dutch/Shell, Parmalat, Royal Ahold, Adecco, Vivendi, SwissAir, and Asea Brown Boveri Ltd. (ABB).

Second, there has been a sad democratization of this misconduct. World-Com founder Bernard Ebbers was a former high school basketball coach and barroom bouncer. Enron's Kenneth Lay was the son of a part-time tracker salesman–part-time preacher. Adelphia's John Rigas was the son of a Greek immigrant street vendor. Tyco's Dennis Kozlowski was the son of a New Jersey Transit cop. Where once the thieves were misguided aristocrats who had abused their positions of wealth and privilege, the current crop of corporate criminals is largely populated by upwardly mobile strivers. They had distorted the American Dream into a nightmare.

Third, the knowledge required for improving the leadership and governance is not in the exclusive domain of any profession or academic discipline. These most recent governance scandals had a wide array of relevant embedded problems cutting across fields, such as corrupt leaders, overhyped markets, short-term pressures, intentionally ambiguous accounting practices, dishonest financial analysts, weak internal audits, unscrupulous financiers and consultants, conflicted interests among board members, skill deficiencies, lax regulation, careless board supervision, improper board structure, perfunctory board processes, inadequate disclosure, misguided financial incentives, insufficient whistle-blower protection, autocratic imperial CEOs, unethical cultures, and inadequate character assessment in leadership searches. Thus, this book has solicited a broad slice of experts.

In assembling this book, we felt it was important to bring together some of the best minds from a number of different constituencies to reflect on the challenges, the problems, and yes, the potential solutions. Among them, you will find academicians and consultants, presidents and CEOs, representatives of corporate boards and regulatory bodies, accountants and psychologists, even one well-known whistle-blower, whose historic actions helped heighten the awareness of this entire issue. Brought together, their voices form a coherent picture—from the boards and regulators who bear the responsibility for protecting shareholder interests to the employees who don't know where to turn when they observe wrongdoing by occupants of the C-suite. The wide array of contributor perspectives has a common theme, but it is, nonetheless, one that encourages examination of governance failures. Through the scandals of the last three decades, there was no absence of regulation with clear purpose, no lack of accounting rules with overintentions, no lack of corporate codes of conduct, no lack of board member financial literacy, and no shortage of many of the other governance remedies that abound as panaceas. Sadly, major accounting firms, investment banks, executive suites, and corporate board rooms were filled with professionals who knew they saw wrongdoing, but failed to act. Worse, some even participated in fraud and other forms of misconduct. The original contribution of this book then is to utilize various disciplines to gain greater insight into the behavioral failings that facilitated these scandals.

Each author is also a national if not globally renowned, expert in their field. They each bring their own unique commentary and tone to this critical issue and address what can be done to possibly reroute the next wave of corporate scandals that is inevitably already positioning itself to come crashing to the shore. They have a wealth of wisdom to share. We laud their efforts and encourage you to take their candid, insightful words to heart.

—Robert Gandossy and Jeffrey Sonnenfeld

NOTES

1. Edward H. Sutherland, *White Collar Crime: The Uncut Version,* ed. Gilbert Geis and Colin Goff (New Haven, CT: Yale University Press, 1985).

2. Jeffrey Sonnenfeld and Paul R. Lawrence, "Why Do Companies Succumb to Price Fixing?" *Harvard Business Review* 56.4, July-August (1978), pp. 145–157. See also Jeffrey Sonnenfeld, *Corporate Views of the Public Interest* (Boston: Greenwood Publishing, 1981).

3. Robert P. Gandossy, *Bad Business: The OPM Scandal and the Seduction of the Establishment* (New York: Basic Books,1985).

4. James Sterngold, *Burning Down the House: How Greed, Deceit, and Bitter Revenge Destroyed E.F. Hutton* (New York: Simon & Schuster, 1990).

5. Jonathan Beaty and S. C. Gwynne, "B.C.C.I. Scandal: Too Many Questions," *TIME Magazine,* 11 November 1991. Also, "The BCCI Scandal: A Singing Sheik; Congress's Restless Republicans," *U.S. News & World Report,* 10 August 1992.

6. Stephen Pizzo, Mary Fricker, and Paul Mulo, *Inside Job: The Looting of America's Savings and Loans* (New York: Harper, 1989).

7. Steven K. Wilsen, *Silverado: Neil Bush and the Savings & Loan Scandal* (New York: National Press Books, 1991).

8. John A. Byrne, *Chainsaw: The Notorious Career of Al Dunlap in the Era of Profit-at-Any Price* (New York: HarperBusiness, 1999).

9. Bethany McLean and Peter Elkind, *The Smartest Guys in the Room: Enron: A Business Epic* (New York: Portfolio, 2003).

10. Barbara Toffler, *Final Accounting: Ambition, Greed, and the Fall of Arthur Andersen* (New York: Broadway, 2003).

Acknowledgments

Sitting at lunch at the New Haven Lawn Club one day in the spring of 2003, we began drawing parallels between the many recent business scandals and those that broke 20 years ago when we first met in Cambridge, Massachusetts. In the early 1980s, we were independently working on the rash of fraud and corporate misconduct occurring during that time. And, as is so often the case, what goes around comes around—here we are again.

We debated how these events come in waves, yet there seems to be little that is learned from one wave to the next. We wondered whether current proposals for reform would have impact or whether they would miss the mark as had earlier attempts.

These are challenging, difficult, and complicated issues. We decided it would be useful to bring together a variety of perspectives to shed light on the topic of leadership and governance. We made a list of friends and colleagues that have influenced our thinking over the years. The list included academics, CEOs, board members, and heads of regulatory commissions. We were delighted when nearly everyone we asked to contribute to this book eagerly accepted. We'd like to thank all of these exceptional contributors for exactly what we had hoped for—bold insight, clarity, and direction.

We'd also like to thank the vast majority of leaders who struggle everyday with difficult and competing demands but do so with strong values and integrity. We hope you find these pages a source of inspiration and a source of ideas to do more.

We'd also like to thank Matt Holt and his team at Wiley. We'd especially like to acknowledge Julie Offord of Hewitt. Julie kept the contributors informed and on track and maintained her sense of humor in the process. We'd like to thank Tina Kao and Shelli Greenslade for the background research and for keeping other things afloat—with Julie—while we were working on this book. Joe Micucci, Jon Hay, Kyra Ramsey, and Don Minner have always been there for us and have often been one step ahead. Thanks. We'd also like to thank Julie Cook for editing assistance under some very tight schedules.

Finally, we'd like to thank Joe DeLillo, executive vice president of the Yale School of Management's Chief Executive Leadership Institute, and Bonnie Blake, business manager of the Yale School of Management's Executive Programs, for their skillful management of our relationships to key contributors to the book.

A portion of the royalties for this book will go to City Year, and we'd like to thank them for the good they do for so many.

BG
JS

PART I

FUELING THE CRISIS

CORPORATE SCANDAL AND WRONGDOING

Forever epitomized by the megameltdown of Texas-based energy giant Enron, a series of grand-scale scandals rocked the business world from 2001 to 2003. In addition to Enron, there was WorldCom, Adelphia, HealthSouth, Global Crossing, Arthur Andersen, and numerous others. As if that wasn't enough, news also broke regarding outrageous compensation levels at the top rungs of the corporate ladder as well as rampant market timing and fee-gouging activities in the mutual fund industry. If the wrongdoers had any fear of being caught or reprimanded, it was trumped by their desire to boost their own personal fortunes, with absolutely no regard for others. Across the country, employees, shareholders, and consumers rightfully felt duped and cried out angrily for retribution, all the while uneasy that it could happen again.

The chapters in this section set the stage for the rest of the book, exploring the recent wave of corporate governance scandals. Included is the ultimate insider's view of the Enron implosion, from the point of view of the woman who blew the whistle on the company's questionable accounting practices, off-the-books activities, and excessive executive compensation packages. She argues that corporate America's current board system is seriously in need of revamping. Granted, the recently enacted Sarbanes-Oxley Act and the newly formed Public Company Accounting Oversight Board are a step in the right direction, but old habits die hard, leading her to question whether such legislation will be effective in preventing unethical business among corporate leaders.

CHAPTER 1

"I SEE NOTHING, I HEAR NOTHING"

CULTURE, CORRUPTION, AND APATHY

ROBERT GANDOSSY AND JEFFREY SONNENFELD

IN HIS testimony before the House and Senate investigation of widespread corruption at Enron, former CEO Jeffrey Skilling insisted he had no knowledge of any serious problems in the company before his abrupt resignation six months into his term and six months before the firm's collapse. Similar testimony by board members who chaired the finance and audit committees at Enron led U.S. Congressman Edward Markey to label this response the "Sergeant Schultz" defense. Sergeant Schultz was a fictional character on the 1960s TV comedy series "Hogan's Heroes," a sympathetic prison guard who routinely looked the other way when he observed rule infractions by prisoners.[1] His refrain "I see nothing, I hear nothing!" is widely used by both white-collar criminals and their compliant colleagues who are aware of the corruption but look the other way.

"If only one of the scores of lawyers, accountants, or managers had spoken up, this whole scheme would have unraveled. I just cannot understand how they could stay silent." These were the remarks made to us by a decorated veteran of Silicon Valley tech start-ups, who was recruited in the mid-1990s as the new CEO in an attempt to salvage Informix, once a close rival of Oracle. Despite its path-breaking, often superior multimedia software, Informix was felled by a greedy revenue recognition scheme that deceptively propped up international sales. The turnaround CEO was horrified by

3

the apathy of those who knew and the timidity of the board to rout out the villains once the fraud was public.

"Either these people are just plain stupid or they don't listen," a CEO cried out to us decades ago at International Paper after the company was embroiled in a large price-fixing conspiracy. Several executives at International Paper were convicted, along with over 40 top leaders from 22 firms, who moved from Babbitt-like middle-class respectability to the stigma of being convicted felons. "We have clear codes of conduct and ethics statements," the CEO continued. "Is it fair to hold the high school principal responsible because some students misbehaved?" Somehow the formal incentive systems, the intended role modeling from top executives, and the overt codes of conduct were inadequate in combating the informal culture that had taken root in this industry. But the patterns we observed in the paper industry decades ago—and the excuses, justifications, and calls for reform—are vaguely familiar today.

Whenever we enter the economic market, whether it is to seek employment, to purchase a product, or to strike a business deal, we are confident that the terms of the transaction—the promise, as it were—are exactly as they appear. It is easy to cheat if we want. Most diners can flee a restaurant, or taxi cab passengers can race into a crowded street, to skip paying—but few operate this way. In business, we rely on the words and actions of the others involved. What people say and do are moral and legal assurances to us that they are as they appear: that is, devoid of fraud and material misrepresentation. We have trust that our laws and regulations protect us against illegal business practices, and we believe violators will be discovered quickly and dealt with appropriately. We're also comforted by the trust and integrity of leaders. We expect our leaders to have high integrity, to do what they say, and to operate within the bounds of the law. We have confidence that commercial activity operates this way. Without such confidence, the economy could never have evolved as it has.

This confidence—or trust—is not always well placed, as the recent series of highly visible cases of corporate wrongdoing and malfeasance tells us. It is sometimes difficult to determine who can be trusted and who cannot. We are not omnipresent. We cannot be sure their business associates have remained within the bounds of the law. We trust that they have. In part, this trust is derived from reliance on others—auditors, lawyers, the board of directors, internal staff, and the government—to monitor and police commercial activity.

During fiscal year 2002, the Security and Exchange Commission (SEC) filed a record 163 actions for financial reporting and disclosure violations— 46 percent higher than the previous year. The Commission attempted to permanently ban 126 unfit officers and directors from corporate boardrooms—a 147 percent increase over the previous year. They filed 48 temporary restraining orders, up 55 percent from 2001, and they filed more subpoena enforcement actions than in previous years, supporting an extraordinary number of criminal prosecutions. Although the SEC cannot bring criminal charges itself, it worked in collaboration with the Corporate Fraud Task Force, established by President Bush, to bring 259 criminal actions by 30 different U.S. Attorney's offices.

A number of well-known companies were implicated in these actions, and several were once the darlings of Wall Street or revered as models of innovation and entrepreneurship. And in many cases, their wrongdoing was conducted over a period of years, under the collective noses of a bevy of outside advisors and internal staff.

The examples of missed opportunities are staggering. On January 9, 2004, the venerable Royal Dutch/Shell Group admitted to the public that its senior management had known for over two years that its petroleum reserves were overstated in excess of 20 percent. In the aftermath a tumble in market value, a shattered corporate reputation, and the ousting of the chairman and other top officers, investors and regulators wondered how this massive fraud was kept secret.[2] In the trial of John Rigas and his sons at Adelphia Communications, prosecutors charged that the family took personal trips on company jets, spent millions of dollars of shareholder money on personal real estate, hid billions of dollars of debt, stole $100 million, lied about revenue, and "borrowed" more than $1 billion to buy Adelphia securities. A decade earlier, one finance vice president questioned extravagant personal expenses, only to be demoted and let go.[3] *Where were the other voices of outrage?* At HealthSouth, five former Chief Financial Officers (CFOs) were convicted after admitting to a $2.5 billion accounting fraud that involved 11 other top executives. Reports show that auditors were tipped off five years earlier, but no investigations followed.[4] Tyco's brazen CEO, Dennis Kozlowski, and CFO Mark Swartz were charged with looting $600 million of corporate funds to support extravagant lifestyles. Questionable purchases included properties in Manhattan, Florida, and Massachusetts; multimillion-dollar relocation payments; paintings by masters of western art, like a $3.95 million Monet and a $4.7 million Renoir; a now-infamous $6,000 shower curtain; $40,000 draperies; a $2 million birthday party for Kozlowski's wife on the island of Sardinia; and other such waste, all while claiming legendary corporate frugality to investors and the media.[5] It has now been revealed that before Enron's collapse, senior executives at the nation's most prestigious financial institutions joined scams that helped hide debt and inflate earnings through fictional offshore special-purpose entities.[6]

No one knew. *Or did they?* Few if any took action. No one blew the whistle to put an end to the wrongdoing. How can it have been possible for some of the nation's leading institutions to have remained blind to such massive misconduct for so long? There are many shades of awareness and action. We might think of the state of awareness as a continuum ranging from individuals in the know—the criminals themselves, for example—to those in the dark—victims, for instance. In between the states of being fully aware and unaware are situations in which individuals have partial knowledge, a vague understanding or suspicion about the criminal activity happening around them. But what prevents people from seeing criminal acts for what they really are? What prevents people who suspect from learning more? What factors inhibit them from digging deeper?

There is no single answer to these questions, but there are several factors we've observed that interactively create situations in which individuals genuinely do not know enough to take action. In situations where they do know, there are circumstances that allow individuals to easily shift responsibility for taking action to others. First is the diffusion of responsibility for seeing and acting. Bystander apathy, the division of responsibility between specialists and organizations, obedience to the authority, and professional codes of conduct all contribute to this diffusion. These circumstances make it easy for information about and accountability for wrongdoing to slip through the cracks. The second factor is what we call *golden shackles*—a euphemism for the strong financial incentives to look the other way. These are often not explicit payments for complicity but rather a risk to a lucrative business partnership or job if too many questions are raised. Third is the lack of options for individuals who suspect wrongdoing. Where do you turn if you *suspect* but *don't really know*? Finally, there is a widespread tolerance for illegal and unethical conduct in the business community. This submissiveness to the firm, industry, or profession's culture at all costs has been termed *groupthink*. None of these factors alone explains such behavior, but together they create the conditions for otherwise ethical directors and executives to look the other way. Each of these is discussed in the following sections. Once we understand the conditions, we then turn our attention to the prospects of reform.

DIFFUSION OF RESPONSIBILITY

The terms *diffusion of responsibility* and *bystander apathy* followed the landmark studies that attempted to understand the 1964 brutal murder of Kitty Genovese in front of her two-story Tudor building in the respectable New York City neighborhood of Kew Gardens. This young woman was stabbed to death at 3:20 am on March 13, 1964. Her screams for help after several stab wounds awakened 38 of her neighbors and initially frightened away her assailant. When none of her neighbors came to her aid, the murderer, Winston Mosley, returned to finish the job. No one called police for over 30 minutes after the initial attack.[7]

The public was naturally more alarmed about the unresponsive neighbors than by the murder itself. To further understand this disturbing phenomenon, social psychologists Bibb Latane and John Darley launched a series of experiments in which participants heard the sounds of people in distress under different conditions. The studies showed that as the number of bystanders increased, the likelihood that anyone would help decreased. People were more likely to help when they were alone. When others are present, people assume someone else will act.[8]

Even individuals operating alone may be reluctant to act under certain circumstances. Research pioneered by Yale's Stanley Milgram demonstrated the willingness of adults to go to almost any extreme if they believed they were being directed or encouraged by a legitimate authority. In his studies, he found that adults of all ages and backgrounds were willing to suspend their own ethics and values and inflict what they thought was great pain on a person at the direction of authorities in a scientific research setting.[9] In extending these studies around the globe, researchers found some cultures where obedience levels were as high as 85 percent.

Financially savvy executives at Enron, Worldcom, HealthSouth, and Andersen surely fell victim to these psychological traps.[10] With so many professional experts endorsing or ignoring what each knew was professionally and ethically wrong, they discarded their own individual sense of responsibility, deceiving themselves into believing that fellow experts who allowed the misconduct might know better than they did about what was right. This diffusion of responsibility demonstrated a collective bystander apathy exacerbated by obedience to the top leaders responsible for initiating the fraudulent schemes. If the misconduct was committed by a senior executive at the top, an aura of legitimacy was wrongly conferred.

Modern businesses necessarily depend on a system of formal authority and many specialists to survive. Operating in our complex global economy can be challenging without the aid of professional and specialist firms to navigate complicated regulations, tax laws, financial and technological matters, accounting procedures, and so on. Under pressure to protect themselves from legal liability and other risks, organizations hire specialists, form alliances to reduce risk and error, and develop structures to maximize efficiency and effectiveness.

Few things are left to chance—at least nothing that really matters. By creating an interlocking network of experts, all the bases are covered. Tax lawyers examine tax shelters and write-offs. Computer specialists appraise our equipment's value and advise us on our purchases. Investment bankers tell us how to finance capital goods and corporate expansion. Auditors suggest how best to present our financial picture. And attorneys try to keep us within the bounds of the law. Suppliers, customers, and employees see these experts' presence as a sign that they approve of the organization and its business practices.

But the very structure that provides comfort creates other difficulties. Certainly, bystander apathy is one: we *assume* someone else will act. But there are other challenges as well. Organizations that come together for a particular project, joint venture, or series of transactions generally have specific and often very narrow concerns. Even within each organization, the aspects of the deal or other business activity that occupy an individual's time are further differentiated. Information is diffused and fragmented. Specialists may have only partial knowledge of a fraudulent deal, just enough to vaguely suspect or easily dismiss the suspect data. Or specialists may not see signals of impending trouble simply because experts do not know enough about the big picture to ask the right questions.

That leads to another reason specialists may not see illegal activities: in some cases, to know or act is not in their best interest, for their reputation or image may be at stake. The possibility of seeing might mean admitting they were wrong in the past. Some potential whistle-blowers may refuse to act because they are benefiting from the current way of doing things. A line from a Kipling poem captures the point: "But I'd shut my eyes in the sentry-box / so I didn't see nothing wrong."

There are times, too, when professionals know about wrongdoing but their professional standards prevent them from revealing what they know to third parties. Lawyers, for instance, would be severely handicapped as advocates for their clients if their clients were uncomfortable about revealing certain information. But more and more in society today other professionals are granting confidentiality to their clients, thereby closing off a major opportunity for outsiders to learn about improprieties being committed by companies. With such standards for support, it is often easy to shut their eyes to illegal activity or, at least, put aside suspicions. A professional standard then becomes nothing more than an ethical pretension.

Under new rules in the Sarbanes Oxley Act, internal auditors, external auditors, and even outside legal counsel must voice their concerns about misconduct. Most notable is Section 309 of this act, which requires an attorney to report evidence of a material violation of the securities law, breach of fiduciary duty, or similar legal violations to the chief legal officer and the CEO of the company. If the executives do not respond appropriately through timely investigations, the attorneys are required to continue to report up the ladder to the company's audit committee, composed of independent directors, or the full board of directors.

Of course, the systems problem is often a weapon for the perpetrators. Paradoxically, when one is surrounded by experts, the likelihood of anyone discovering wrongdoing goes down—at least, for a time.

GOLDEN SHACKLES: MISLEADING FINANCIAL INCENTIVES

Critics calling for reform have pointed to the widespread use of stock options as encouraging executives' short-term thinking and harmful, win-at-all-costs values. New reforms regarding the use of options outlined by the Financial Accounting Standards Board (FASB), and endorsed by many in the

Senate as well as Federal Reserve Chairman Alan Greenspan and investor Warren Buffet, have helped shine the spotlight on financial incentives for wrongdoing.[11] Executives are under great pressure to perform, and with large dollar amounts at stake, so the theory goes, there are incentives to cheat. Companies are at a much higher risk of corporate crime when business pressures are intensified. In difficult or highly competitive times, signals emanating from top management stress the need to generate more business—and quickly. Employees are recognized for the revenues they bring in and the dollars they save—not necessarily for being careful.

Under these circumstances, employees—even entire organizations—can easily become involved in various forms of cheating. Professionals, particularly those in the highly competitive financial industry, increasingly are compensated for their short-term performance—and the sums at stake can be millions of dollars. Managers, too, get caught up in the short-term numbers and can become dependent on apparently stable, lucrative business relationships with employers or customers.[12] It can become very difficult for managers to abruptly halt practices that contribute directly to their bottom-line performance.

When a manager feels his or her division's survival is in question, the corporation's standards of business conduct are more apt to be questioned. A convicted division vice president explained: "I think we understood it was against the law. The moral issue didn't seem to be important at the time." We found, for example, in historic industrywide price-fixing schemes, managers were encouraged, with a wink and a nod from management, to "do what it takes" to meet predetermined price targets despite difficult conditions.[13]

Investors lost several hundred million dollars in the 1987 E.S.M. Government Securities Corporation fraud. E.S.M.'s outside auditor went along with the ruse because he had missed the scheme in two previous audits.[14] Two officers from the Florida-based firm told him about the fraud two days after the auditor had been made a partner in his accounting firm. He explained his predicament to *The Wall Street Journal:* "I was 31 years old. I felt I had a terrific career path in front of me and a lot of ambition. And I agreed just to think about it. A day or two later, I felt I had gone too far. I also didn't want to face it. I didn't want to face walking in [to his superiors] and saying 'this is what happened.'"

Whenever compensation or promotion is tied directly to objective performance measures, there is a pressure to look good on the books. Suppose you were responsible for bringing in a client who provided $1 million a year in revenue to your firm. That revenue is now expected as part of your normal performance; any deviation is a reflection on you. Or, to examine another situation, suppose you were responsible for negotiating several multimillion-dollar deals that saved your company hundreds of thousands of dollars. It is quite likely, should any of these deals later backfire, that you would be held responsible.

The implications of such dependencies are clear. Too often, employees are quick to look the other way to avoid pushing hard for compliance—particularly if they are not ultimately responsible anyway. Some individuals become involved in wrongful conduct, but direct complicity in illicit activity—people on the take, for instance—is probably rare. It is far more likely that the people know or suspect illegal activity but have strong incentives to look the other way.

NOWHERE TO TURN

While heroic employees occasionally do speak out, their courage and integrity are often met with harassment, intimidation, demotion, and even termination. Famed whistle-blowers Sherron Watkins of Enron, Cynthia Cooper of Worldcom, and Coleen Rowley of the FBI were anointed TIME magazine's Person of the Year for 2002 for their selfless internal alerts. Cooper went to the audit committee of Worldcom. Watkins went to Enron CEO Ken Lay and warned him of massive internal accounting frauds, while Rowley sent a memo to FBI Director Robert Mueller alerting him to ignored warnings over Al Qaeda activity in the United States.[15] But in each case, their careers suffered. Policy experts long ago warned that the whistleblower often has nowhere to turn.[16] Our society frowns on the squealer, the rat, the tattletale. We learn very early that such behavior is considered inappropriate. To be sure, blowing the whistle on fraud or other crimes is not the same as telling on a misbehaving sibling or friend. Yet people who know about or suspect improper behavior in organizations are torn between doing what is right and confronting a system that is often not very supportive of blowing the whistle.

One senior executive who revealed a colleague's million-dollar fraud scheme reflects: "The path I chose was brutal on my family and lost me tens of thousands in income. It also meant that I'd never again work in a corporate environment. You can negotiate a 'golden handshake,' but it doesn't guarantee a reference. There is always the nuance, the raised eyebrow, the inflection that means, 'Well if you really want to know. . . .'" When this emotional tug-of-war is added to other disincentives, such as a lack of accountability and financial considerations, it becomes easy for people to ignore a crime.

MANAGEMENT TOLERANCE: GROUPTHINK CULTURE

Another reason that illegal and unethical activities can continue for years is the culture or environment created by leaders. Sometimes executives may not encourage illegal practices, but they may not actively discourage them either. For instance, managers often neutralize the seriousness of crimes through the use of language. In one case, for example, "double hocking," "double-discounted" loans, and "dipsy-doodle" leases were all euphemisms for fraud and theft. Each of these substitutions effectively lets individuals off the hook by making the subject matter somehow more acceptable.

Many executives also have failed to speak out directly against illegal conduct, thus sending the wrong signal to employees and the public. Following corporate convictions for fraud, stock manipulation, and bribery, the largest shareholder and board member of a Fortune 100 company said, "We didn't do anything wrong, but it wasn't right either." He added, "It was wrong, but it wasn't purposefully wrong." *How should managers and supervisors respond to such statements?*

Speaking in euphemistic terms or otherwise neutralizing illegal conduct hardly sends a strong signal of condemnation to employees or the wider business community. Neither does management's failure to establish mechanisms that will prevent the occurrence of misconduct. Managers who fail to check, to monitor, to audit, to speak out, and to penalize wrongdoers are communicating their values and priorities to others.

Yale psychologist Irving Janis studied group decision making in historic contents like the Bay of Pigs fiasco, the Korean War, Roosevelt's complacency and inaction just prior to Pearl Harbor, and Johnson's escalation in Vietnam. Even 40 years later, Janis's fascinating work on groupthink sheds light on how intelligent people can make such gross miscalculations and flawed decisions. Janis defined groupthink as "a mode of thinking that people engage in when they are deeply involved in a cohesive group, when the members striving for unanimity override their motivation to realistically appraise alternative courses of action."[17]

These tendencies toward concurrence seeking and poor judgment are manifested by several symptoms, according to Janis: there is often an illusion of invulnerability—Enron's Jeff Skilling believed, for example, in the inherent morality of the group, and the company's leaders were generally hostile toward what was perceived as an anachronistic energy regulation. Another common symptom is a collective rationalization. Price fixers in forest products, for instance, told us that they were only doing for themselves what legislators do for more politically protected industries such as steel and agriculture. Janis also wrote about groups holding stereotypical views of rivals. Worldcom's conventional telecom competitors, for example, were labeled as stodgy and out of step with technological advances. Self-censorship is another symptom identified by Janis. Andersen accountants presumed that a new, efficient relationship with their client Enron resolved suspicious practices. Another symptom of groupthink is the direct pressure on dissenters. In our work on price fixing, resistors to these schemes were threatened by their colleagues with termination and even physical violence.

None of these factors alone can explain why such frauds continue for so long. But when they are taken as a whole, we can begin to understand how segmented responsibilities, pressure to perform, social norms that suggest we should not rock the boat, ambiguous norms about appropriate and inappropriate behavior, and limited options for those in the know make it very easy for managers to look the other way.

THE PROSPECT OF REFORM

Following the latest wave of corruption, managers, investors, public policy makers, and scholars search for management tools and metrics to guide executives and investors. The search has often led to misguided metrics that fail to address the conditions contributing to misconduct and the lack of oversight. Instead of looking at group psychological factors and cultures that encourage conformity as catalysts to misconduct, researchers have advanced legalistic and misguided checklists. The yardsticks for measuring potential governance misconduct and the underlying recipes for reform have acquired a large following because they are easy to use, not because they are accurate and reliable.

There are several challenges to the current use of metrics for governance. The first is that some governance scoring systems are provided by institutions with commercial conflicts. A second challenge is that the metrics currently being used do not predict governance breakdowns, or their assumptions about what constitutes good governance are unsupported—or both. Myths regarding board structure, director age, the splitting of the roles of CEO and chairman, the importance of financial expertise to the board, the continued presence of the former CEO, attendance records, size of the board, and the number of independent directors are examples of the reform, but few reforms in these areas have been shown to prevent fraud, much less expose it.[18] Let's take a closer look at the issue of governance metrics and the limitations and myths that attend current proposals for reform.

HIDDEN CONFLICTS

Unlike *Consumer Reports,* J.D. Power, epinions.com, and Edmunds, which use objective metrics, many governance raters seem to think its okay to consult for the entities over which they are also providing purportedly independent evaluations to the public.[19] Ironically, this faintly echoes two of the governance problems now prohibited by the Sarbanes Oxley legislation. One is the forbidden practice of accounting firms serving as public auditors for clients of their consulting businesses. The other problem is research analysts at brokerage firms pumping the stocks of their firms' major investment banking clients.

While these governance consultants denied the existence of these conflicts when the subject was first raised, the major firms have since addressed the issue in very different ways. The influential proxy advisor Institutional Shareholder Services (ISS) has now published on web sites its board members and a statement regarding conflicts of interest. In short, they claim that they will not sit on both sides of the table that is advising institutional investors on how to launch a proxy battle while also advising the same target firm's management on how to beat such efforts. They claim to have created separation in their business by using different staffs for these efforts as well as physical separation—similar to the "Chinese Wall" once claimed by some securities firms.

Strangely, there appears to be no such Chinese Wall protecting their governance consulting services from conflicts with their governance ratings services. Thus, it seems to be the same Corporate Programs staff who rate firms including those client firms for whom "we make recommendations for improving your company's corporate governance policies or establishing a set of corporate governance principles. ISS Corporate Programs has also done advisory services work related to changes to director compensation, the institution of officer and director stock ownership requirements, and changes to a company's state of incorporation."

Some firms feel that in order to decipher the meaning of their ISS ratings they have to become clients and learn how to raise their ISS ratings. ISS CEO Jamie Heard counters, "Many companies have, in fact, significantly improved their scores without making use of our paid services."

That is not convincing enough for ISS competitors. Governance Metrics International (GMI) seems to repudiate ISS policies, although their chief operating officer was formerly the CEO of ISS. GMI claims, "We will not provide corporate governance consulting services to any company that is part of our research universe or is expected to become part of that universe within twelve months." Then, to ensure that ISS feels the slap, they add, "To do so would in our opinion impinge on our reputation for independence and credibility." Other ISS competitors, such as governance pioneer the Corporate Library and the venerable credit analysis bureau Standard & Poor's, also avoid governance advisory services attached to their ratings.

DO THE SCORES PREDICT PERFORMANCE?

While there is irony in all of this, the most important question is: Do these metrics tell us anything? One month after the fanfare of launching their new "Corporate Governance Quotient" (CGQ), ISS proudly announced that the "Adelphia Fraud May Have Been Predicted: Company's Corporate Governance Rating Is in the Lowest Quartile." They confidently proclaimed, "Clearly in the case of Adelphia and others whose poor governance practices have made recent headlines, the CGQ database would have raised a red flag for an investment manager holding or considering the stock." In fact, the ISS HealthSouth rating states that HRC outperformed 64.3 percent of the companies in the Standard & Poor's 500 and 92.3 percent of the companies in the Health Care Equipment & Services group. They congratulated Health-South on the fact that "the board is controlled by a supermajority of independent outsiders; no former CEO of the company serves on the board" (of course, there is no former CEO of this young enterprise).

These are just the sort of speculative dimensions which wrongly bring down several of the most admired U.S. firms that *Fortune* magazine's 10,000 experts and executives rate highest, like Wal-Mart, Southwest Airlines, UPS, Dell, eBay, Goldman Sachs, and Starbucks, which were all shockingly in GMI's "Below Average" categories and elevate purportedly better-governed firms embroiled in recent governance controversy, such as Health-South and Tenet Healthcare.

In fact, while ISS and GMI analyze many sensible dimensions, others, such as the presence of the former CEO, the separation of the chairman role from the CEO, and the number of outside directors are not indicators of better corporate governance, nor are they shown to improve company performance. In fact, research in progress suggests little relationship between these items and corporate performance.[20]

Accordingly, Securities and Exchange Chairman William Donaldson recently commented:

"Such a 'check the box' approach to good corporate governance will not inspire a true sense of ethical obligation. It could merely lead to an array of inhibiting, 'politically correct' dictates. If this was the case, ultimately corporations would not strive to meet higher standards, they would only strain under new costs associated with fulfilling a mandated process that could produce little of the desired effect. They would lose the freedom to make innovative decisions that an ethically sound entrepreneurial culture requires."[21]

JUDGMENT OR CHECKING BOXES?

One governance rating firm, the Corporate Library, collects a tremendous amount of data but avoids the lure of conflicting consulting services. Like good financial analysts, they also avoid simplistic quantitative ratings. Once all the numbers are analyzed, companies are assigned a qualitative grade from A to F. The Corporate Library previously gave HealthSouth an F.

Finally, the credit rating agencies Standard & Poor's and Moody's are developing governance practice areas. Moody's claims that its new governance practice area will not publish scores, while it admits to a plan for scoring firms. According to Kenneth Bertsch, head of this new practice area at Moody's, "We do plan to publish written Corporate Governance Assessments, but will not assign a grade. . . . At this point, we also are unconvinced of the value of such a score given the nature of the subject."

Their competitor, S&P, has carefully worked directly with corporate managers of firms to avoid cookie-cutter governance templates based on uniform rules, instead allowing for broad principles that accommodate globally sensitive standards. According to George Dallas, S&P's director of governance practices: "The Standard & Poor's approach to governance analysis benefits from direct interaction with those governing the company. This provides important new information and insights, and allows for more nuanced, and less rigid, weighting of analytical factors . . . to interpret individual company governance structures and practices through the overarching lens of principles such as fairness, transparency, accountability and responsibility."

To James Heard, the CEO of ISS, this intensity, judgment, and customization is not needed. "Our ratings . . . are based on objective criteria. A board either has a majority of independent directors (according to our very strict definition of independence) or it doesn't. It either has independent audit, compensation and nominating committees or it doesn't. . . . Each company is scored . . . on a scale of 1 (low)–100 (high) and all 5000 companies in the database are ranked regardless of whether they want to be or not. . . . The only way for a company to improve its CGQ score is to improve its governance practices."

BEYOND THE RECIPES

If corporate life were only so simple, we could program robots to be our executives. Good leadership is not recipe driven. Again in the words of SEC chief Donaldson,

> I believe we should go slowly in mandating specific structures and committees for all corporations. . . . [T]here are vast differences in the function, structure and business mandate of the thousands of corporations struggling with the issues of good corporate governance. I believe that

> these differences dictate that once the board determines the ethical cul-
> ture that is to prevail, each company board should be afforded a level of
> flexibility to create their own approach to its structure . . . . [T]o insist
> on one rule for all belies the dynamics of the fast changing business and
> corporate environs and the nature of varied business situations.

In fact, our research on ISS-like governance dimensions confirms Donaldson's caution regarding uniform structures. Utilizing the database of the
Corporate Library, we examined the peer-adjusted five-year shareholder returns of 2,000 public firms, comparing them against such dimensions as the
following: whether the CEO is also the chairman; the number of independent directors; the existence of ethics codes; the tenure of directors; the number of directors; and Delaware incorporation. No individual or combined
relevance was found. In fact, contrary to ISS scoring, the age of directors was
actually a positive predictor of corporate earnings!

Even the S&P principles, while less rigid as governance dimensions, are
still legalistic and ignore the prevailing impact of the culture or social system
of the board. This neglects such issues as director preparation, breadth of
board roles, depth of group discussion, the foundation for trust and open-
ness, evidence of tolerance for dissent, and effective evaluation. By contrast,
SEC chief Donaldson has pushed for far broader criteria that will "look
beyond the traditional methodologies and include not only a study of law
and business practices, but also an examination of the interpersonal human
dynamics that influence a board and its decision making. One of the most
interesting evaluations of a board that I ever read was not done by a lawyer
or an MBA, but by an organizational behaviorist."

It seems that the more adaptive approaches of the Corporate Library's data
and the interviews of S&P are headed in the right direction. The next stage
should include more understanding of the underlying business cultures,
leadership styles, and group processes rather than adding easy-to-measure
but misleading recipes.

THE HUMAN SIDE OF GOVERNANCE

While groups can pathologically suppress problem-solving skills through
diffusions of responsibility, groupthink, and other dysfunctional responses,

they can additionally react pathologically once the resulting crisis breaks, through misguided attempts to contain the damage or circle the wagons. Even after scandals at Enron, Worldcom, and Freddie Mac surfaced, forcing the exit of the chairman and CEO, the sophisticated boards of these firms turned to install the next in line fully knowing that this individual was also tainted.[22] In response to reform-minded calls for greater roles for independent directors, James Minder, 74-year-old independent director of Smith & Wesson, the nation's second-largest gun maker, was elevated to the role of chairman until it was revealed that he had spent 15 years in a Michigan prison for eight armed robberies. This poor choice was possible because the board did not really know each other and Minder merely proudly offered that he did not have any past securities violations. Several directors sought to retain him as chairman, and he remained on the board after stepping down.[23] The challenge of these situations shows that the remedies often have more to do with human processes than simple rules and regulations alone. A critical part of corporate diligence has to do with group process at the top for the culture of the board.[24]

Create a Climate of Trust and Candor

There is a classic asymmetry of information between the management, which has the core facts, and the board, which needs to learn them. Often boards are managed by executives who see them as obstacles to circumnavigate rather than as trusted business partners. Critical information should be shared with directors in time for them to read and digest the facts. Polarizing factions and in-groups should be discouraged. Long-service and newer directors should be mixed together and not allowed to drift into separate circles. This can help break down the illusions of groupthink.

Foster a Culture of Open Dissent

Dissent is not the same thing as disloyalty. One prominent corporate director warned that "no one wants to be seen as the skunk in the lawn party." Safeguarded channels for whistleblowers in management should supplement new Sarbanes Oxley protections and audit committee solicitation of concerns. The CEO and the board can set a tone that welcomes internal feedback so that problems can be identified and corrected before they become major integrity, financial, and public relations disasters.

Utilize a Fluid Portfolio of Roles

Managers and corporate directors must avoid getting trapped into rigid or typecast positions. To stimulate debate and avoid the stereotypes of being the fire-the-bastards person, the harmonizer, the big-picture person, or the governance whiner, people should take turns as enthusiasts and devil's advocates. Managers should be asked to develop alternative scenarios to evaluate strategic decisions. This can challenge the blind obedience to authority structures and break the group's tendency to avoid reality testing in favor of preserving group coherence.

Ensure Individual Accountability

To escape the quicksand of bystander apathy, managers and directors can be required to report on strategic and operational issues the company faces. These tasks should involve the collection of external data, interviews with customers, anonymous mystery-shopper visits, and the cultivation of links to outside parties critical to the company's future.

Create More Opportunities for the Board to Assess and Develop Leadership Talent[25]

At the world's top companies, the board is actively involved in assessing talent. At Procter & Gamble, Home Depot, and GE, the board regularly visits facilities and meets with managers and customers to learn and observe operations and talent firsthand. Board members at Procter & Gamble often come in early to board meetings to meet with and coach emerging leaders. Board members at top companies also teach at the company's leadership development initiatives. These boards have a direct, unfiltered feel for the business and are less likely to be blindsided by unscrupulous business practices.

Evaluate the Board's Performance

It is impossible to learn without feedback from the environment on our success, and yet many in top management and half of all boards do not provide performance appraisals. Everyone else in the enterprise can be assessed, but somehow the more senior players find excuses to not collect this often discomforting information.

While these interventions can help improve the group process of the board collectively, the SEC is encouraging more direct nominations of directors from shareholders, by-passing self-perpetuating board nominating committees. While shareholder activists and corporate executives battle over the legal definitions of the triggering events that should lead to such bypasses of the board, the criteria for identifying more diligent directors have been left on the sidelines. To improve the likelihood of identifying more diligent directors, we suggest the steps outlined in the following sections.

Seek Knowledge Rather Than Names

An excess of enthusiasm for the branded names preferred by directors and search consultants has led to a pathological fixation on marquee names. Many of the prominent public figures on troubled boards, like Enron, Worldcom, and Freddie Mac, probably would have been endorsed by all parties in advance. Corrupt CEOs, such as John Bennett of the fraud-ridden philanthropy New Era, love to hide under the reflected glory of star-studded boards, knowing that investors will be impressed and the directors themselves—like John Whitehead and Sir John Templeton—will be too busy to roll up their sleeves and ask the tough questions.[26] A great chief technology officer from another firm may be more valuable than five former U.S. ambassadors. Imagine how much better off Global Crossing would have been if instead of hiring former U.S. Ambassador of Singapore Steven Green, they had hired lesser-known (at that time) Michael Capellas, then company CEO and formerly its chief technology officer. It's almost a rule of thumb these days that the bigger the scandal, the bigger the director names that have been soiled. Consider Enron, whose board included Robert Jaedecke, the former dean of Stanford's Business School, former top commodities regulator Wendy Graham, and Alliance Capital Chairman Frank Savage; or Worldcom, which included Clifford Alexander, the chairman of Moody's, and Judith Areen, the dean of Georgetown Law School.

Focus on Character More Than Independence

Independent-mindedness is not the same thing as independence, but many shareholder activists are pushing for supermajorities of independent outside directors with the ultimate goal of having the CEO the only insider. One of the most courageous voices on the Enron board was a renowned scientist, Charles LeMaistre. But today, LeMaistre—despite his courage—would be suspect because his institute, MD Anderson Cancer Center, received Enron funding. Similarly, having some inside directors who know the business can help inform the outside directors by reducing the filtering of knowledge through the sole voice of the CEO. Certainly some insiders can feel intimidated or obligated to echo the CEO. At the same time, independent directors may also lack courage in a desire to be accepted. There is no research that shows greater performance with more independent directors—or fewer scandals, for that matter. Wisely, firms like GE, Berkshire Hathaway, Dell, and UPS are determined to retain inside voices on the board.

Ruthlessly Purge Those with Hidden Commercial or Social Agendas

Boards and management committees should not resemble city council meetings. Sometimes unrevealed conflicts become more apparent in later actions, and sometimes the conflicts are not even financial but rather political and personal. Forest products, pharmaceuticals, and media firms are especially exposed to public-issue advocacy groups. Board candidates who are primarily anchored in single-issue causes are not likely to be legitimate representatives of a broader group of shareholders.

Find People with a Passionate Interest in the Business

Sadly, many people seek board posts for power and the gratification of vanity, but have little interest in the industry or culture of the enterprise they have joined. Sometimes directors will even admit that they do not fully understand the acronyms on the charts in PowerPoint presentations.

Avoid Joiners Who Collect Boards Like Trophies

Until the forceful reform efforts of shareholder activists a decade ago, it was common to find directors serving on more than a dozen boards and frequently attending fewer than 75 percent of the meetings. With a single board post now easily requiring 200 hours per year of preparation and meetings, four boards is becoming a common limit for otherwise employed directors. Shockingly, in an effort to clean up tainted governance practices, the new and improved NYSE board has selected for its board a Rensaleer university president, Shirley Jackson, who already sits on eight boards.

Ignore False Recipes from Governance Consultants

Many of the proposals put forth go against conventional wisdom, like head-hunters who used to screen out those who salt their food before they taste it or those who use handrails walking up stairways. There is a growing witch-craft of good governance that avoids noble directors who may have crossed an arbitrary retirement age. Enterprises such as Corning, Delta, Boeing, and even the SEC have wisely sought energetic elder statespersons, like Jamie Houghton, Jerry Grinstein, Harry Stonecipher, and Bill Donaldson to lead them through troubled times. Similarly, admonitions against former CEOs on the board should be invoked only in those prominent rare situations where the former CEO and the current CEO have unresolved agendas be-tween them. Many former CEOs, such as Andy Grove of Intel, Bill Gates of Microsoft, Michael Dell of Dell, Jim Kelly of UPS, and Herb Kelleher of Southwest Airlines, have hugely helpful roles to play on the board.

For reformers, the situation is akin to the dog that finally caught the car it chased for years: now that we have it, what do we do? It's time to shift the debate from rules and procedures to focus on what we really know about people and their character.

NOTES

1. Kevin Maney, "Skillings Sgt. Schultz Defense Peeves CEOs," *USA Today,* 12 March 2002.

2. Jim Peterson, "The Perils of Ignoring the Big Thing," *International Herald Tribune,* 27 March 2004.

3. David Voreacos, "Witness Says He Warned Rigases about Spending," *Bloomberg,* 23 March 2004.

4. Bill Berkrot, "First HealthSouth Sentencings Set for Wednesday," *Reuters,* 11

November 2003. Craig Schneider, "Did Auditor, Regulators Ignore HealthSouth Warning?" *CFO.com,* 23 May 2003.

5. Christopher Mumma, "Kozlowski Judge Denies Mistrial Request in Tyco Trial," *Bloomberg,* 29 March 2004.

6. Bethany McLean and Peter Elkind, *The Smartest Guys in the Room: The Amazing Rise and Scandalous Fall of Enron* (New York: Portfolio, 2003).

7. Martin Gansberg, "37 Who Saw Murder Didn't Call the Police," *The New York Times,* 27 March 1964, p. 1; A. M. Rosenthal, *Thirty-Eight Witnesses: The Kitty Genovese Case* (Berkeley: University of California Press, 1999), Part 2, pp. 68–69.

8. Bibb Latane and John Darley, *The Unresponsive Bystander: Why Doesn't He Help?* (New York: Appleton-Century-Crofts, 1970).

9. Stanley Milgram, *Obedience to Authority* (New York: Harper, 1974).

10. Bill Berkrot, "First HeathSouth Sentencings Set for Wednesday," *Reuters,* 11 November 2003.

11. Jonathan Weil, "FASB Unveils Expensing Plan on Option Pay," *The Wall Street Journal,* 1 April 2004, p. C1.

12. Jeffrey Sonnenfeld and Paul R. Lawrence, "Why Do Companies Succumb to Price Fixing?" *Harvard Business Review* 56.4, July–August (1978), pp. 145–157.

13. Robert P. Gandossy, *Bad Business: The OPM Scandal and the Seduction of the Establishment* (New York: Basic Books, 1985), and Robert P. Gandossy and Rosabeth Moss Kanter, "See No Evil, Hear No Evil, Speak No Evil: Leaders Must Respond to Employee Concerns about Wrongdoing," *Business and Society Review* 107, no. 4 (Winter 2002), pp. 415–22.

14. Donald L. Maggin, "The Repo Men—Scandals in the Bond Market," *Management Review,* January 1986.

15. "The Whistleblowers: Persons of the Year," *TIME,* 22 December 2002.

16. Alan F. Westin, *Whistleblowing: Loyalty and Dissent in the Corporation* (New York: McGraw-Hill, 1981).

17. Irving Janis, *Victims of Groupthink* (Boston: Houghton Mifflin, 1972).

18. Jeffrey Sonnenfeld, "Good Governance and the Misleading Myths of Bad Metrics," *Academy of Management Executive* 18, no. 1 (2004): 109–13.

19. Adam Lashinsky, "ISS Want Business Both Ways: The Firm That Got Its Start Saving Shareholders Is Now Catering to Big Business, *Fortune,* 3 June 2003. Monica Langley, "ISS Rates Firms—and Sells Roadmaps to Boosting Scores," *The Wall Street Journal,* 6 June 2003. Jeffrey Sonnenfeld, "Meet Our Corporate Governance Watchdogs," *The Wall Street Journal,* 11 March 2003, p. B2.

20. Jeffrey Sonnenfeld, "Good Governance and the Misleading Myths of Bad Metrics," *Academy of Management Executive* 18, no. 1 (2004): 109–13.

21. William H. Donaldson, "Corporate Governance: What Has Happened and

Where Do We Need to Go, Business Economists," Address before the National Association of Business Economics, Washington Economic Policy Conference, 24 March 2003.

22. Jeffrey Sonnenfeld, "Hit the Road, Mac," *The Wall Street Journal,* 26 August 2003, p. B2.

23. Vanessa O'Connell, "Smith & Wesson Chairman Quits as Past Armed Robberies Surface," *The Wall Street Journal,* 27 February 2004, p. A1.

24. Jeffrey Sonnenfeld, "What Makes Great Boards Great," *Harvard Business Review,* October 2002.

25. Robert Gandossy and Marc Effron, *Leading the Way: Three Truths from the Top Companies for Leaders* (New York: John Wiley, 2004).

26. "New Era Fiasco: A Debacle for Charities' Credibility," *The Chronicle of Philanthropy,* 1 June 1995, pp. 1, 24–30.

CHAPTER 2

TWENTY-FIRST-CENTURY CORPORATE GOVERNANCE

THE GROWING PRESSURE ON THE BOARD TOWARD A CORPORATE SOLUTION

SHERRON S. WATKINS

FOR BETTER or worse, I will probably always be known as the Enron whistleblower, and my former employer, Enron Corporation, as the byword for corporate scandal. I have learned a number of lessons from my days at Enron and have formed strong views about the state of our capitalist system and what is required to repair it.

The most disturbing aspect of the Enron meltdown is the willful blindness of so many to the warning signs that were often as loud as tornado sirens. From Enron's boardroom to its executive suite to its investor relations and legal groups, from Wall Street's research analysts and the country's largest commercial banking institutions to the financial press—all seemed stuck on the same song and dance, best summed up in the following press release issued by Enron on February 6, 2001, ten months prior to its bankruptcy:

> Enron Corp. was named today the "Most Innovative Company in America" for the sixth consecutive year by *Fortune* magazine.
>
> "Our world-class employees and their commitment to innovative ideas continue to drive our success in today's fast-paced business environment," said Kenneth L. Lay, Enron chairman and CEO. "We are proud to receive this accolade for a sixth year. It reflects our corporate culture which is driven by smart employees who continually come up with new ways to grow our business."

Enron placed 18 overall on *Fortune*'s list of the nation's 535 "Most Admired Companies," up from 36 last year. Enron also ranked among the top five in "Quality of Management," "Quality of Products/Services," and "Employee Talent."

Enron's bankruptcy filing on December 2, 2001, was the largest in U.S. history until WorldCom's filing just a few months later. It spawned more than a dozen congressional investigations and endless press coverage, starting with the *New York Times* and the *Wall Street Journal* and ending with the *National Enquirer.* All dissected the scandal, its villains, and its victims. The primary concern was how we were all duped and by whom, followed closely by an angry cry for retribution, fused with a touch of fearful unease that it could all happen again.

What exactly did happen at Enron? I offer my (initially) anonymous letter to Ken Lay, delivered to him the day after his anointed replacement, Jeff Skilling, resigned after less than eight months at the helm:

> Dear Mr. Lay,
>
> Has Enron become a risky place to work? For those of us who didn't get rich over the last few years, can we afford to stay?
>
> Skilling's abrupt departure will raise suspicions of accounting improprieties and valuation issues. Enron has been very aggressive in its accounting—most notably the Raptor transactions and the Condor vehicle. We do have valuation issues with our international assets and possibly some of our Enron Energy Services' Mark-to-Market [EES MTM] positions.
>
> The spotlight will be on us, the market just can't accept that Skilling is leaving his dream job. I think that the valuation issues can be fixed and reported with other goodwill write-downs to occur in 2002. How do we fix the Raptor and Condor deals? They unwind in 2002 and 2003, we will have to pony-up Enron stock and that won't go unnoticed.
>
> To the layman on the street, it will look like we recognized funds flow of $800 million from merchant asset sales in 1999 by selling to a vehicle (Condor) that we capitalized with a promise of Enron stock in later years. Is that really funds flow or is it cash from equity issuance?
>
> We have recognized over $550 million of fair value gains on stocks via our swaps with Raptor, much of that stock has declined significantly—Avici by 98 percent, from $178 million to $5 million, The New Power Co by 70 percent, from $20/share to $6/share. The value in the swaps won't be there for Raptor, so once again Enron will issue

stock to offset these losses. Raptor is an LJM entity. It sure looks to the layman on the street that we are hiding losses in a related company and will compensate that company with Enron stock in the future.

I am incredibly nervous that we will implode in a wave of accounting scandals. My eight years of Enron work history will be worth nothing on my resume, the business world will consider the past successes as nothing but an elaborate accounting hoax. Skilling is resigning now for 'personal reasons,' but I think he wasn't having fun, looked down the road and knew this stuff was unfixable, and would rather abandon ship now than resign in shame in two years.

Is there a way our accounting gurus can unwind these deals now? I have thought and thought about how to do this, but I keep bumping into one big problem—we booked the Condor and Raptor deals in 1999 and 2000, we enjoyed a wonderfully high stock price, many executives sold stock, we then try and reverse or fix the deals in 2001 and it's a bit like robbing the bank in one year and trying to pay it back two years later. Nice try, but investors were hurt, they bought at $70 and $80/share looking for $120/share and now they're at $38 or worse. We are under too much scrutiny and there are probably one or two disgruntled 'redeployed' employees who know enough about the 'funny' accounting to get us in trouble.

What do we do? I know this question cannot be addressed in the all-employee meeting, but can you give some assurances that you and Causey will sit down and take a good hard objective look at what is going to happen to Condor and Raptor in 2002 and 2003?

After receiving my memo, Ken Lay turned to his chief financial officer and my direct superior, Andy Fastow, and his chief accounting officer, Rick Causey, for advice. Fastow responded via a phone call with the standard party line: all was fine because Enron's outside auditor, Arthur Andersen, had blessed the accounting structures in question. Causey responded with the following e-mail:

Question regarding Raptor and Condor:
NOTE: I would not read this question [at the all-employee meeting]. I would simply state that there was a question submitted regarding structured transactions and the use of contingent Enron equity (that is equity that might have to be issued in the future).
RESPONSE: "We do from time to time use contingent Enron equity in transactions. However, to the extent that the current economics of

such a transaction would imply that we would issue that equity in the future, we must count that equity as issued and outstanding currently. To state it more clearly, all transactions that use Enron equity currently or in the future are fully accounted for today. All future commitments have been considered and reflected in calculating earnings per share and shares outstanding today."

I was shown Causey's e-mail response on August 20, 2001, five days after I had identified myself as the anonymous letter writer and two days before I met with Ken Lay. I was asked if Causey's response satisfied my concerns. My response was visceral—I thought Causey's rather technical-sounding response was akin to a man accused of beating his children who, when confronted, insists nothing is wrong because he's got their future college tuition fully funded. *Huh?* What about the $500 million of hidden losses on the income statement in 2000? On a pretax basis, the fraud exceeded 50 percent of Enron's net income for the year. Where was a discussion of *that* problem?

Enron's culture went horribly wrong. Nearly 30 officers and board directors sold over $1 billion worth of Enron stock and options in the company's final years. Shareholders lost over $60 billion in Enron's final two years of prebankruptcy existence. Very simply, greed won out over any fear of being caught or reprimanded.

Have we learned any lessons from Enron? Has the system been fixed by the recently enacted Sarbanes-Oxley Act, the oversight of the newly formed Public Company Accounting Oversight Board, and the helpful guidance of Bill Donaldson (current head of the Securities and Exchange Commission [SEC]) and the ever-diligent watch of New York's Attorney General Eliot Spitzer?

Only time will tell, but I remain concerned that the old ways may still be the status quo. Rick Casey, a columnist for the *Houston Chronicle,* recently wrote an article on Bill Donaldson's new SEC proposal to allow qualified shareholders to nominate a small percentage of board members to public company boards. Casey's February 6, 2004, column noted the following about the powerful efforts to end Donaldson's proposal:

> In the wake of Enron and other corporate scandals, the Securities and Exchange Commission has proposed a new rule that would attempt to open up corporate boards just a crack to more independent board members. The notion is that self-perpetuating boards tend to become captive to management and to self-serving instincts.

The proposed rule is hardly radical. It would not allow bands of ethereal nuns bent on saving the world to buy a few shares and put themselves on the board. A stockholder or group of stockholders would have to own at least 5 percent of a corporation's stock for two years to nominate a board member. This would mostly mean large pension funds.

Even with that many shares, an investor group couldn't guarantee getting a candidate on the ballot. Other rigorous thresholds would have to be met to place the outside nominee on the ballot. And only about 15 percent of any board could be named through this process.

The proposal has drawn a record 12,000 comments. Of the 11,000 that generally favor the proposal, many complain the reforms didn't go far enough.

[Wendy] Gramm, on the other hand, thinks they go too far. (Gramm was a long-term member of the Enron board, sitting for a time on its audit committee.) Writing from her post as director of the regulatory studies program at the Mercatus Center (a free-market think tank at George Mason University that received $50,000 from Enron before its collapse), she joins the group of corporate CEOs and corporate lawyers that opposes the change.

As always, Gramm puts her faith in markets rather than regulation, even a regulation that simply and weakly attempts to open up board nominations.

"Boards who consistently operate at variance with shareholder interests . . . will see the values of their firm's shares fall, other things equal," she writes, adding that this will result either in a takeover or bankruptcy.

"Indeed, the recent spate of corporate scandals has, if anything, provided vivid testimony as to how quickly and efficiently this market process works in practice," she concludes with no evident sense of self-irony.

Those of you who lost your life savings in Enron stock (after Gramm cashed hers out for $300,000) can appreciate the quickness and efficiency of the current system.

We need a revamped board system in this country. Bill Donaldson's efforts at the SEC are to be lauded, but are they enough?

For illustrative purposes, I have outlined below a mathematical model for preventing unethical behavior in our business leaders. The model and its definition are presented directly from an article entitled "Moral Hazard: The

Figure 2.1
Model for Determining Moral Hazard

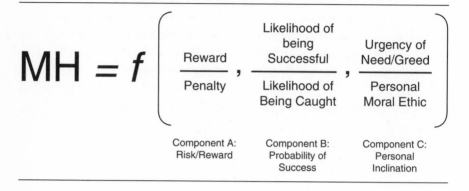

Assassin Lurking Within Energy Trading Organizations" by Duncan L. Cobb that appeared in *Platts Energy Business and Technology*, July/August 2003. Mr. Cobb, a graduate of Yale University, studied this issue in a 1970s course entitled "The Economics of Corruption." Although Mr. Cobb's report focused on energy-trading outfits and the problems of errant traders, its application for the executive suite is apt. According to Mr. Cobb's observations, *moral hazard* is defined as "people doing bad things," and the model for moral hazard has three components: (1) risk/reward, (2) probability of success, and (3) individual inclination. Within each component are competing factors: for the first, the potential reward versus the potential penalty; for the second, the likelihood of success versus the likelihood of being caught; and for the third, the urgency of the individual's need/greed versus his or her higher personal moral ethic. For each component, the denominator is the disincentive for bad behavior, and the numerator is motivation in favor. The objective in managing moral hazard is to keep the potential incentive for bad behavior (the numerator) from overwhelming the disincentive (the denominator). Figure 2.1 depicts this model.

For chief executives, the reward drivers are more money, more power, more influence, and a long-lasting, highly regarded legacy. For business leaders with a very strong personal moral ethic, the temptation of putting personal interests (rewards) ahead of those of the company's customers, employees, and shareholders is rarely, if ever, an issue. For those business leaders less ethically inclined, however, the chance for wrongdoing is generally higher, since the likelihood of being caught and/or suffering any reprimand diminishes the higher the position within an organization.

In the past, executives who lacked an internal moral compass were often kept in line by shareholder activists. Embarrassing questions on hard-to-defend activities acted as a wonderful deterrent, particularly in the executive pay area. Auditors and the financial press offered some deterrent as well.

In the '90s, we lost the benefit of shareholder activists, while the market gained a new type of investor, the day trader. Day traders are not to be confused with hedge fund managers, but the two groups often encouraged the same unwelcome behavior in company management, an extremely myopic focus on the stock price. With the explosive growth in mutual funds, the majority of stock market investors no longer hold individual stocks, owning mutual fund units instead. With web-based, people-free shareholder meetings and institutional investors that lean toward rubber-stamping proxy statements, modern watchdogs are limited to basically two groups: the regulators and boards of directors.

Once the regulators find a moral hazard problem, the jig is up and it's usually too late to save shareholders, employees, and customers from less-than-ideal circumstances. That leaves the board of directors, a group woefully ill equipped to prevent unlawful, unethical, egregious, or just plain embarrassing executive actions.

Take for instance the retirement package of GE's former CEO, Jack Welch. In 2002, a rather nasty divorce proceeding brought to light what otherwise probably would have remained well hidden: Each year, until death, Mr. Welch would receive approximately $2.5 million in various perks, ranging from use of GE's corporate jets and a Manhattan apartment to tickets to sporting and cultural events and complimentary dining and flower tabs. Welch's initial explanation for this bounty was that the terms were part of a negotiated compensation package from several years ago. With the board's blessing, he had given up current compensation for postretirement perks. (Current disclosure requirements do not cover retired executives; maybe the SEC should add one to ensure that shareholders understand what their company is truly paying its top executives.) In the end, pressure from others or concern for ruining what had previously been a stellar reputation forced Welch into giving up or paying for all of the retirement services.

The controversy over Welch's retirement package is trivial in comparison to the grand-scale scandals of 2001–2003, which included corporate mega-meltdowns like those at Enron, WorldCom, Aldelphia, and HealthSouth; outrageous compensation levels epitomized by the $188 million pay package for Richard Grasso, the CEO of the New York Stock Exchange; and trust-destroying market-timing and fee-gouging activities in the mutual fund industry, to name just a few. The Welch example is made only to illustrate the importance of that age-old ethical litmus test: If you don't want something discussed on the front page of *The Wall Street Journal,* then you'd best not do it.

In Enron's case, senior executives were driven to meet earnings targets no matter what ethical compromises were made in the process. In fact, certain stock grants and performance bonuses not only had the potential to create several dozen multimillionaires, but also contained vesting triggers based upon Enron's relative stock performance over a three- to five-year period that accelerated the potential payoff. The cliff-vesting options heightened the sense of urgency to grow earnings and reap the rewards, which far outstripped any perceived dangers of being caught and penalized. Any vestiges of personal moral ethics that might have served as a disincentive to cheat went out the window.

When complex accounting structures no longer solved all problems, Enron set up its chief financial officer in outside investment partnerships that were then used to fill the gaps in earnings or cash flow. That same chief financial officer has pled guilty to a number of criminal counts and is headed to prison for 10 years; his wife (who aided and abetted him in a few of his schemes) is headed to prison for at least five months. To date, the Enron scandal has produced nine felons, 16 indictments, and a team of Department of Justice prosecutors promising more.

Where was Enron's board during this time? The directors have denied wrongdoing, claiming they were misled. A July 2002 report issued by the U.S. Senate's Permanent Subcommittee on Investigations, *The Role of the Board of Directors in Enron's Collapse,* disagreed, however, listing 61 pages of signals willfully ignored by Enron's board members.

To use the Senate's conclusions:

The Enron board of directors failed to safeguard Enron shareholders and contributed to the collapse of the seventh-largest public company in the United States by allowing Enron to engage in high-risk accounting, inappropriate conflict-of-interest transactions, extensive undisclosed off-the-books activities, and excessive executive compensations. The board witnessed numerous indications of questionable practices by Enron management over several years but chose to ignore them, to the detriment of Enron shareholders, employees, and business associates.

Frankly, Enron's board was outmatched. Ralph Ward, author of *Saving the Corporate Board,* likens our current board system to volunteer fire departments: an effective safeguard if the company is small, but once a company is the equivalent size of, say, Cincinnati or Albuquerque, the only way the volunteer fire department can be successful is if there are no fires.

If management has a strong personal moral ethic (i.e., if they're good firefighters), the board oversight function works. But if management is not very effective in preventing and fighting fires—or, in the case of Enron, Tyco, Aldelphia, WorldCom, and HealthSouth, if management has become arsonists—the board is in no position to stop a conflagration.

Compounding the problem are the governance gurus that rate a company by counting the number of fire trucks, ladders, and hoses. Most governance graders ranked many of the recent scandal-plagued companies in the top category for corporate governance procedures.

Even without scandals and meltdowns, certain unchecked executive behavior can lead to unwelcome executive upheavals. American Airlines' board approved million-dollar pay packages for CEO Don Carty and his executive team while Mr. Carty was busy winning 15–23 percent, five-year pay concessions from his union workers. The board failed to see the employee and public relations nightmare that would arise from his actions; they believed Carty's assurance that union officials knew of the executive packages when they did not. As a result, American Airlines lost a person many considered to be an otherwise outstanding airline CEO.

In my simplistic modeling example, just how can our capitalist system strengthen the denominators in the moral hazard function? We cannot legislate moral ethics, but we have increased the criminal penalties with the passage of the Sarbanes–Oxley Act. The risk of being caught in illegal activities is higher as long as Eliot Spitzer is the attorney general for New York, but is that enough? What of the reputational risk and resultant stock price penalty for the exorbitant pay package disclosure, the significant customer problem (Boeing and the Air Force), the self-dealing discovery (Richard Strong), and the asset devaluation (Shell's reserves)?

Our board system needs a serious revamping. Its role as the ultimate fiduciary for shareholders does not work and, I would argue, if unchanged will never work. Boards should be selected by shareholders from a pool identified by the company and qualifying shareholders. A two-tiered system is needed: one focusing on the company, its strategy, its management, and the other focused on shareholders and oversight of the first group. In other words, this two-tiered system would function as a good cop–bad cop team, when necessary.

It is tough to be a business leader. Not only do we expect top-notch industry expertise, but we also demand leaders that have the ability to motivate, to challenge, and to innovate. Those attributes are comparatively easy to measure and monitor.

It is much tougher to evaluate morality. We want business leaders who inspire ethical behavior in others in the same manner that they demand it of themselves. Without a strong combination of denominators in the moral hazard function, the system fails to stop the numerator influences. A stronger board system is urgently needed to restore balance in our capitalist system.

PART II

THE ROLE OF THE LEADER

The success or failure of any great enterprise depends on the quality of its leadership and, more specifically, on the quality of the decisions made by the occupants of the C-suite. By their actions, as well as their inactions, executives can enhance the lives and the wealth of both their employees and their investors. By the same token, they also have the power to destroy assets or an entire organization, for that matter. In recent years, we've seen a number of previously well-performing companies brought to their knees by the tragically ill-advised—not to mention selfish—decisions of those at the top.

While the establishment of sound governance principles certainly won't hurt the situation, there are deeper, underlying issues that also must be addressed. In this section, the authors set out to help organizations curb the problem of runaway executives by examining the factors behind the leadership and governance decisions that precipitated the decline of Enron, Tyco, and other once-revered companies. They also scrutinize the relationship between capitalism and morality, provide strategies for fighting narcissism in the executive suite, and suggest guidelines for encouraging upward challenge to preserve corporate integrity.

CHAPTER 3

HOW LEADERS
RESTORE CONFIDENCE

ROSABETH MOSS KANTER

FOR THOSE who like happy endings, this chapter offers an optimistic perspective on leadership. But as in all great dramas, first we must wrestle with the forces of evil before the good side can emerge triumphant. There may not be a Santa Claus (sorry, Virginia), but there are still honest CEOs and exemplary leaders, and they will be the ones to save the capitalist system from rot from within.

How the mighty have fallen. After the lionizing of celebrity CEOs in the 1990s, after corporate chieftains became admired household names and their success at the pursuit of wealth and power became role models praised in countless books and taught at leading business schools, the very label "chief executive" is tarnished. But business is not alone. Mounting corporate scandals have joined crises in other major institutions—from the Catholic Church to public schools and national governments—to undermine confidence in dominant organizations and their heads—I dare not call these failed executives "leaders."

In business, hiding bad news from stockholders and creditors while offering rosy forecasts to make managers look good is not a recent invention of Enron, Tyco, and Parmalat, or of the Royal Dutch/Shell chiefs who

---

overstated oil and gas reserves. In the 1960s and 1970s, "creative account-ing" was found to be a factor in the bankruptcies of British companies. In 1994, before the company's successful turnaround, a former COO of Con-tinental Airlines was shocked to discover that the previous finance staff had inflated profit projections by plugging in overly optimistic revenue estimates.

The problem is also not confined to business. The temptation to skirt the truth, cover up mistakes, and deny problems has long infected public life in many countries. Sex and spy scandals in Britain in the 1960s started with War Minister John Profumo's denials and ended up bringing down the Tory government. The Watergate scandal in the 1970s eventually caused U.S. President Nixon to resign. Senior members of government in Japan in the 1970s and 1980s were implicated in denial-ridden bribery scandals in which they tried to recast bribes as donations. Denial of an affair led to U.S. Presi-dent Clinton's impeachment hearings in the 1990s. Financial scandals pro-voked the resignations of Japanese Prime Minister Yoshiro Mori, economic minister Fukushiro Nukaga, and others in the early 2000s. In the spring of 2004, both President George W. Bush's administration in the United States and Prime Minister Tony Blair's government in the United Kingdom were under investigation for allegedly misleading the public in their intelligence reports about the existence of weapons of mass destruction in Iraq.

Failures of leadership to confront problems honestly occur even in sectors dedicated to teaching morality, such as schools and religious institutions. In the 1970s, public school officials hid data on declining enrollments or on school dropouts. More recently, the Houston school district, once a national model, became mired in scandal when it appeared that test scores were signi-ficantly lower and student dropout rates were significantly greater than had been claimed. It was reported in 2003 that administrators pushed out kids who would skew test scores, then entered codes indicating that students had transferred somewhere else, reducing the official dropout rate to near zero not by real actions, but by false data. The superintendent of the highly-regarded Everett, Massachusetts school system was indicted in March 2004 for bid rig-ging and illegal kickbacks of school construction and maintenance contracts. The Catholic Church saw leaders fall from grace following revelations that abusive priests had been protected by church leaders and the pattern of abuse covered up for many years. Discovery of the problem began in the United States and soon reverberated in Catholic countries around the world. The

Boston Archdiocese, a division of the world's wealthiest religious establishment, had to sell its property, including the former Cardinal's residence, to pay for an $85 million settlement to victims. In Ireland, the government was helping the Catholic Church with a $200 million victims' settlement.

IMPERIAL CEOS AND THE PROBLEMS OF EMPIRE

Today, corporate chief executives seem almost as likely to be featured in courtrooms as feted at charity dinners. That's an exaggeration, of course, but it shapes public perceptions. A March 2004 report by Public Agenda based on national focus groups found that both business leaders and citizens see a general decline in values contributing to recent scandals. But what angers respondents the most is seeing some executives enrich themselves while allowing their companies to decline. And some (including business leaders themselves) sound a sour note about executive compensation, proposing that it has ballooned out of proportion. According to studies sponsored by the Institute for Policy Studies and United for a Fair Economy in Washington, the wage gap between CEO pay and average worker pay in the United States in 1982 was 42:1. In 2000, the ratio of CEO to worker pay peaked at a gigantic 531:1 before falling to a mere 282:1 in 2003.

The pay gap is just one manifestation of the rise of the imperial CEO. "Business is the last monarchy," the head of a large New York company frequently told his staff, as he issued commands and brooked no arguments.

The arrogance of success is well known. Powerful people who are driven to turn their domains into empires begin to feel that they are above the rules, that what applies to ordinary people does not apply to them, and they can use their power to suppress criticism and force their will on others, whether employees, customers, suppliers, or external watchdogs. Consider the story of the Coca-Cola Company, owner of perhaps America's best-known global brand. As *New York Times* reporter Constance Hays told it in her deeply researched book, *The Real Thing,* vanity blinded Coca-Cola's leaders to vulnerabilities accompanying the unbridled exercise of corporate power. The Coke said to run in executives' veins went to their heads, and they became drunk with power.

Roberto Goizueta, who became chief executive in 1981, was much admired for moving the company close to its dream of world domination. He took Coke to lucrative international markets and rewrote contracts to push the secret-formula syrup on increasingly captive bottlers, "launching an engine of wealth unparalleled in the American corporate world," Hays wrote. Intense loyalty was demanded from everyone. Analysts were discouraged from publishing anything negative about the company. Goizueta worked out his bonus privately with a director, and enormous pay packages were presented to a compliant board as a fait accompli. Despite the New Coke debacle, he was "treated more like a pontiff than a chief executive," Hays said.

Then Goizueta died unexpectedly, and Douglas Ivester became CEO at Coca-Cola's zenith in stock price, market share, and prestige. Soon dreams of world domination became nightmares because of world events, and far from controlling a submissive empire, Ivester found himself fighting wars of rebellion for which he was not prepared. He faced globalization woes (emerging market problems in Asia, devaluation of the Russian ruble); anti-American sentiment in Europe and unwelcome attention from European antitrust officials, egged on by Pepsi; and product safety issues, including the largest product recall in Coca-Cola history after the illness of Belgian schoolchildren (traced to contaminated shipping pallets). Ivester fumbled communication about the Belgian children, then made another public relations gaffe when he touted technologically sophisticated vending machines that could raise prices when thirst increased. Under his watch, the company lost a race discrimination suit initiated years earlier, and the highest-ranking black executive resigned.

Practices that had brought Goizueta admiration undermined Ivester, as the evidence from Hays' research makes clear. Viewed with today's post-Enron lenses, some practices hover in ethical eyebrow-raising territory. The formation of a "super-bottler" in Coca-Cola Enterprises enabled the Coca-Cola Company to shift debt off its balance sheets, and though the company never owned more than 49 percent of any bottler, it exercised control through directorships. (When an accountant at a small investment firm investigated these relationships, his boss stopped him out of fear of retribution; his next target was Tyco.) The company used its clout to get exclusive deals with retailers; it was found guilty in a Texas antitrust suit brought by Royal Crown distributors. Coca-Cola bottlers were pushed to seek volume regardless of market demand or their own profitability, because the company made most of its money from selling Coke syrup to the bottlers. Bottlers who had consolidated under Coca-Cola influence felt the company had pushed them too far and started pushing back, whispering discontent to Ivester's detractors.

Boardroom maneuvering culminated in Ivester's removal after just over two years as CEO, Hays reported. Douglas Daft became chief executive in 2000, just as business conditions worsened. Turnaround struggles through 2002 included awkwardly executed layoffs, strategic floundering, a failed deal to buy Quaker Oats to get Gatorade, and the use of a feng-shui expert to bring better luck to headquarters. The one thing that Hays did not report Coke executives doing was questioning their own practices with a dose of humility. Where was the impetus to change the organization from a closed empire to a more open, collaborative marketplace of ideas?

Lapses from efficient, rational, law-abiding, virtuous, or otherwise functional behavior are a constant danger in organizations—sometimes because of flawed people, but more often because of complex changes and ambiguous situations that require juggling competing demands (pay raises for employees or price cuts for customers?). When lapses or fumbles occur, denial is tempting, especially when people are pressured to promise strong results regardless of circumstances. Fear of failure can lead to distorted numbers and ineffective actions—such as the unfortunate practice of trade loading at the end of a quarter, in which manufacturers push their inventory on retail customers regardless of consumer demand, just to show strong sales, but do it by discounting. Such practices, which I have seen in businesses as different as cosmetics and industrial demands, make the problem worse in the next quarter, when customers are loaded with too much inventory and know they can wait until quarter's end for an even better deal.

In every sector, the typical pattern has become depressingly familiar and leads to a downward spiral, as I show in my new book, *Confidence: How Winning Streaks and Losing Streaks Begin and End*. Mistakes and failures are covered up rather than confronted, information is distorted or restricted, communication externally, as well as internally, becomes defensive, contact among organization members is minimized, and initiative shuts down, stifling dissent and problem solving until it is too late. A small mistake for which a simple apology might suffice then mushrooms into a huge crisis.

Imperial CEOs flourish in closed system lacking self-scrutiny, accountability, dialogue, and dissent. When those chiefs themselves do not break rules, they still create circumstances in which the people below them feel so desperate to please the domineering boss that they cut corners, hide information, and make deals with the devil. The ultimate failure of leadership is that those at the top have stifled the initiative and innovation of those below. People begin to feel helpless to do anything to solve problems or influence change.

Transforming these sick systems involves more than improving governance at the board level; it involves changing the culture of the entire organization.

HOW CEOS CAN RESTORE CONFIDENCE

Turnarounds are when leaders matter most. That's when good leaders step in to shift downward cycles of cover-up and passivity to more productive cycles of dialogue and innovation. Such leaders prove that values-based leadership in an empowering system is not just a way to regain public trust: it is a better way to run a company.

Jim Kilts is one of those leaders, and he is a star of my book *Confidence,* because he shows how to rebuild it. Kilts was appointed chairman and CEO of Gillette early in 2001, the first CEO from outside the venerable consumer products company in over 70 years. Gillette had slipped from winning streak to decline cycle around 1996 or 1997, as earnings were flat and sales and market shares were declining in categories other than blades and razors. There were many potential reasons: a troubled acquisition (Duracell), uneven performance of product categories outside of shaving systems, unrealistic sales targets that led to costly end-of-quarter discounts, sloppy internal practices, a confusing organization structure that made it easy to duck responsibility. Some of the company's historical strengths had become weaknesses, and the foundation for high performance had crumbled.

On Kilts's first day as CEO, he convened his direct reports and made his expectations clear. Kilts described himself as open and straightforward—what you see is what you get. He said he was action oriented—fair but somewhat impatient. He wanted outstanding performance. He wanted integrity. He did not want competition between functions. Some of his words on that first day became slogans for the new Gillette culture:

- Expect excellence; reward the same.
- Often wrong; never uncertain.

- Contribute before decisions made; support decisions once made.
- Don't make dumb mistakes, don't punish smart mistakes, don't make smart mistakes twice.
- Never overpromise, always overdeliver.
- A promise made is a promise kept.

"If something bothers you, I want open dialogue," he said. "And I hate anyone saying: 'Jim said' or 'Jim wants' as the reason for doing or not doing something. Things are done—or not—based on rigorous assessments and considered deliberation." How refreshing! How simple! Look at the facts, tell the truth, run a company by integrity.

Kilts expressed his determination to set and achieve realistic targets. He outlined a disciplined process for setting annual and quarterly objectives and providing structured feedback, through weekly operating committee meetings, quarterly two-day meetings away from the office, and weekly email postings from the next layers of management around the world. Meetings, he said, would feature fact-based management, open communication, simplicity, and collaboration. Attendance was required, meetings would start on time, there would be no gossip, he wanted full attention and active listening, he strived for consensus, and he expected preparation.

Kilts' emphasis on honesty and integrity was manifested in his early actions. As CEO, Kilts was not afraid to say "We were wrong." He reiterated the Board's earlier decision to stop issuing earnings advisories before the end of a quarter, one of the first U.S. companies to do so. And he told investment analysts that Gillette would lower its quarterly targets to make them more realistic.

This was the shot heard round the world. Everyone in the company talked about it as a symbol of a new day dawning. I was told about Kilts's action in London, Singapore, Boston, and Shanghai. Seeing Kilts stand up to Wall Street was the moment that Gillette managers and employees believed a turnaround was possible. "I began to believe that Kilts had the courage to make the needed changes when he told us to forget Wall Street, we were going to deal with the trade loading," David Bashaw recalled from his office at European headquarters. And over the next nine months, the company virtually ended trade loading and the associated promotions and discounts; this increased funds that could be invested in improving the businesses.

Kilts's turnaround was characterized by open and abundant information, honest communication, facts on the table, and efforts to foster cooperation and active collaboration across all parts of the company. Executives saw each others' numbers and grades on a report card of goals achieved. Even performance appraisals became honest and realistic. Previously, nearly all managers were given the highest ratings—reminding me of radio humorist Garrison Keillor's fictional town of Lake Woebegone, in which "all of our children are above average." Kilts reduced grade inflation—facing some grumbling at first, but gradually the noise ended, as people came to appreciate the honesty as well as the bonuses that came from improved company performance.

Gillette managers were also graded on their leadership skills; employee feedback was solicited and published. And as financial and strategic problems too easily denied in earlier eras were confronted and solved, the emphasis of Kilts's changes shifted to what he called Total Innovation—empowering people to seek and implement imaginative new ideas for products or processes. In March 2004, I toured Gillette's first Innovation Fair with Jim Kilts to judge the winning exhibits from the 25 entries submitted by every department and business unit in North America. The grumbling when the fair was announced (why add another task when we have so much to do?) had been replaced by the excitement of team competition. People staffing each exhibit created team colors and costumes, built displays and created videos, and enjoyed showing off their accomplishments to Jim Kilts, complete with honest, audited data about results.

After the hundredth or so handshake that day, I thought that there was nothing imperial about this CEO. His low-key, matter-of-fact style might not even be called charismatic; it was a model for a humbler style of leadership, in which the institution was larger than the person. Kilts is not alone. When researching my book *Confidence*, I could find many leaders using similar principles, from Gordon Bethune of Continental Airlines or Akin Ongor of Garanti Bank in Turkey. Domination and denial are not inevitable, even if they are always a temptation.

The essential task of leaders—whether the goal is to improve corporate governance or to improve the performance of the whole organization, is to reinforce the foundations for confidence—to demonstrate that they will be accountable to stakeholders, work with them more collaboratively, and empower people inside the organization to speak up, speak the truth, and take initiative. For example, they can:

- Model straight talk, based on facts and data.
- Make information abundant and accessible.
- Structure collaborative conversations across the organization.
- Encourage mutual respect and inclusion.
- Identify shared goals and joint definitions of success.
- Open channels for new ideas and for communication from every level and function.

These behaviors and practices make it more likely that mistakes will be confronted and corrected, that people will speak up about ethical lapses, that cover-ups will soon be exposed, and that people in top positions will not be able to bend the organization to their will or use it for their own private purposes.

Leaders face the Humpty-Dumpty problem—that it is very easy to break the egg but very hard to put it back together again. Once promises are broken, it can take many years to believe any promise again. It can take much longer to restore confidence than it does to solve financial and operational problems. This is hard work, but it is not impossible. And behaving with integrity does produce benefits beyond keeping CEOs out of jail: it is a better way to run a company.

Rising to Rising Expectations

Finding better ways is increasingly important today, when "do no harm" is not enough to restore the image of business. Financial investors are joining customers, consumers, and the general public in holding leaders to ever-higher standards. Avoiding ethical lapses is a minimum standard; companies are increasingly expected to make positive contributions to improving the state of the world.

Consider these facts: over 90 percent of 25,000 citizens of 23 countries reported on a Millennium Survey that they want companies to focus on more than profitability. Two-thirds of American consumers, in another survey, said they felt more trust in a product aligned with social values. By the end of 2003, over $2.14 trillion was invested in the United States in social investment funds, representing a growth of 6.5 percent from 2001, while the broader universe of all professionally managed portfolios declined 4 percent in the same period of the stock market bust. Criteria for investments included screens for alcohol, tobacco, gambling, defense/weapons, animal testing, environment, human rights, labor relations, employment equality, community investment, and community relations. This was a global trend, in advanced market economies. Japan's Keidanren, the Japanese Federation of Economic Organizations, issued a Charter for Good Corporate Behavior. In October 2001, the Association of British Insurers, whose members control one-quarter of the U.K. stock market, published new guidelines asking companies to disclose any significant risks to short- and long-term value from social, environmental, and ethical factors. The *Financial Times* called this a significant shift for investors that had traditionally seen social responsibility as an extraneous distraction.

Organizations associated with values increasingly gain goodwill benefits that contribute to financial performance, from brand enhancement to employee recruitment and retention. This is why cause-related marketing is a growing phenomenon, as companies parade their philanthropy and compete to ally the best nonprofit organizations. But it is also important to note that some of the worst corporate crimes have been committed by companies with good track records of philanthropy.

Confidence cannot be bought through external giveaways; it must be earned through internal excellence. It is earned not through side activities but at the core of the enterprise—how the money is made or victory secured in the first place. Trust is earned through the actions of leaders in guiding the daily work of the organization, in carrying out its core business. The presence of accountability, collaboration, and initiative increases external confidence that problems will be solved, crises resolved, external disasters contained. The absence of those cornerstones of confidence erodes public trust.

I promised a happy ending. That is made possible by excellent leaders in organizations with a tradition of meeting high standards, who also steer their organizations to contribute to society—for example, IBM, known for its path-breaking initiative called Reinventing Education for public schools, is also a perennial highly-ranked company on *Business Ethics* magazine's list of the best firms in terms of ethics and integrity.

But I cannot fully guarantee a happy ending, because the story of returning to values-based capitalism is only just beginning. Anyway, we live happily ever after only in fairy tales. In real life, true leadership requires continuing hard work, not magic wands or magic bullets. It requires humility, faith in other people, and the willingness to face facts and admit mistakes. And in real life, leadership is made possible not just because individuals have the right values, but because organizational systems have the right checks and balances, including abundant opportunities for dialogue and dissent.

CHAPTER 4

Greed, Vanity, and the Grandiosity of the CEO Character

Manfred F. R. Kets de Vries
and Katharina Balazs

If one has no vanity in this life of ours, there is no sufficient reason for living.

—*Leo Tolstoy*

Introduction

The possession of unlimited power has a transforming effect on most people. If the opportunity arises, even the gentlest person may try to reincarnate him- or herself into a living god. In that transformation, he or she loses the ability to distinguish between fantasy and reality.

Among chief executive officers (CEOs), a flight into grandiosity, vanity, and greed certainly is no exception. The more outrageous ones include Vivendi's J6M: Jean-Marie Messier, Moi-Même Maître du Monde—which, roughly translated, means "master of the world"—who, through acquisition mania, transformed a 150-year-old refuge and sewage operation into a media company. Under Messier, Vivendi spent close to $100 billion acquiring interests in film, music, publishing, and the Internet. His leadership riddled this newly constructed company with close to $19 million in debt, leading some investment analysts to postulate that it would be more valuable if sold in pieces.

After he had managed to destroy most of the value of a number of formerly successful, independent companies with his reckless ambition and his lack of operational aptitude, he found other people to blame. And even after so much value destruction, his greed did not dissipate: Messier claimed an exorbitant sum of money as his right when departing.

Another dismal illustration of narcissistic behavior is Global Crossing's chairman, Gary Winnick, whom *Fortune* named "the emperor of greed." Winnick cashed in $735 million in stock over four years, while leading his company into bankruptcy. And let us not forget ImClone's CEO Sam Waksal. Once he learned that the firm's anticancer drug was not going to be accepted by the FDA, Waksal broke multiple insider-trading laws—alerting his family, dumping his own stock, and contacting celebrity friend Martha Stewart, who did the same—leaving common investors holding the bag.

Among this illustrious group of greedy executives, we also find Enron's chairman, Kenneth Lay, who, along with his CEO, Jeffrey Skilling, and his financial wizard, Andrew Fastow, succeeded in bringing his company crashing to the ground, leaving thousands of employees without a job. Then there is the great Tyco robbery by toppled titan Dennis Kozlowski, who has been charged with looting his own company to the tune of $600 million. For good measure, we shouldn't forget Bernard Ebbers, the former CEO of WorldCom, who turned a small Mississippi long-distance operator into one of the world's biggest telecom providers, then succeeded in creating the biggest bankruptcy in U.S. corporate history by engaging in questionable accounting practices.

In the face of these dramatic examples of greed, it's no wonder that corporate governance suddenly has become a hot topic in business circles. But is a lack of solid governance structures the main culprit? Is the establishment of a set of sound governance principles the true answer? Are there no deeper issues we should be aware of? The answer to this final question is a resounding yes.

The well-meant solutions of business pundits typically address key principles of corporate governance—the need for a specific listing of board responsibilities and required director qualifications; appropriate executive and director compensation mechanisms; improved board performance evaluation procedures; healthy audit processes; and well-thought-out CEO succession planning processes, for example. However, what we are really dealing with is the mystery of human nature. We must tackle the questions of how to help senior executives keep a trace of humility and how to help CEOs retain their sense of proportion in the larger scheme of things and stay sane, given the insanity of the CEO position.

Behind all the hoopla concerning corporate governance, we are really faced with the problem of excessive narcissistic behavior by people at the top, a pattern that is endemic in modern-day society, where the Me Generation increasingly focuses on the achievement of personal gratification and self-fulfillment. Media reports of the rise and fall of CEOs demonstrate what grandiose behavior, coupled with greed, can do to an individual, to an organization, and to a society. Given the impact that people corrupted by excessive narcissism have on others' lives, it is important that we attempt to understand the vicissitudes of narcissism. Perhaps if we are able to make sense out of its origins and its destructive impact, we will be able to find ways to prevent its cancerous spread.

Like the mythological figure Janus, narcissism has two faces. Some self-love is required for survival; without concern for the self, the organism dies. On the other hand, too great a preoccupation with the self can actually become self-destructive. Narcissism in limited doses is necessary for the maintenance of self-esteem and self-identity, contributing to positive behavior patterns, such as assertiveness, confidence, and creativity. However, the darker side of narcissism—with its egotism, self-centeredness, grandiosity, lack of empathy, exploitiveness, exaggerated self-love, and the absence of any boundaries—can cause serious grief to self and others.

So where do we draw the line between healthy self-esteem and a compensatory, inflated sense of self? That is never an easy call to make. As a general rule, though, we can differentiate between *more healthy* narcissists and *less healthy* narcissists on the basis of interpersonal skills, the possession of a genuine interest in the ideas and feelings of others, and a willingness to take personal responsibility for one's behavior when things do not work out.

THE VICISSITUDES OF NARCISSISM

The essential characteristics of narcissism are a need for grandiosity, a persistent search for admiration, and a lack of empathy. Narcissists are preoccupied with dreams of glory, power, status, and prestige. Restless and bored when they are not in the limelight, they are flagrant attention seekers.[1] Because they overvalue their personal worth, they see special treatment as their inalienable right and believe that the rest of the world owes them something. Considering themselves above the rules that others are expected to follow, they disregard the conventions of social structure and are often arrogant, haughty, and disdainful. Determinedly self-involved, narcissists have difficulty recognizing the desires and subjective experiences and feelings of others. Even when they *do* recognize a desire contrary to their own, they believe that their own wishes take precedence over everyone else's, making their interpersonal relationships quite exploitative. All these traits tend to alienate people who have to work or live with narcissists.

As indicated earlier, we all show signs of narcissistic behavior. In fact, a modest dose of narcissism is necessary to function effectively. Among individuals whose character structure contains some of the aforementioned qualities we find many who are very talented and have made great contributions to society. Those who gravitate toward the extreme of the various qualities, however, give narcissism its pejorative reputation. They exhibit excesses of pomposity, arrogance, envy, rage, vindictiveness, and discomfort in dealing with the external environment. If they are leaders in the business arena, they are likely to engage in grandiose, unethical behavior—believing, for example, that obscene financial payouts are their God-given right.

VARIETIES OF NARCISSISTIC EXPERIENCE

Given their need for power, status, prestige, and glamour, it is not surprising that many narcissistic personalities eventually end up in leadership positions. Narcissists' ability to manipulate others and their capacity to establish quick, often shallow relationships serve them well in moving up the organizational ladder. Such people can be quite successful, despite what might be termed their handicap, particularly in areas that allow them to fulfill their ambitions of greatness, fame, and glory. Unfortunately, in many instances, power, prestige, and status are more important to these people than a serious commitment to goals and performance. Their primary concern usually remains the preservation of their own greatness and specialness, as evidenced by a contemptuous disregard for others. Because their eyes are turned inward rather than toward their business, much of their claimed success turns out to be mere smoke and mirrors, having very little substance in reality.

Like all people, leaders occupy a position somewhere on a spectrum that ranges from healthy narcissism to pathological grandiosity. In determining what makes narcissism dysfunctional for some and beneficial for others, it is helpful to distinguish between *constructive* and *reactive* narcissism.[2] *Constructive narcissism* develops in response to good caregiving from parents who offer their children a lot of support, recognize the tolerance level of their children, and thus limit frustration to what is age appropriate. By providing a proper holding environment for their children's various emotional reactions, they produce offspring who are well balanced and possess a solid sense of self-esteem.

Due to the kind of parenting they receive, such individuals possess a high degree of confidence in their abilities and are highly task and goal oriented. These people are willing to take ultimate responsibility for their decisions, not blaming others when things go wrong. Although at times they may come across as lacking in warmth and consideration—replacing reciprocity in relationships with abstract concerns, such as "the good of the company" or "the welfare of all"—their sense of inner direction gives them the ability to inspire others and create a common cause, transcending petty self-interests. Among narcissists of this ilk we find people who are labeled charismatic, individuals who have the ability to attract others to whatever cause they are pursuing. Given their realistic, positive outlook on life, they are highly successful at whatever endeavor they undertake.

Reactive narcissism, on the other hand, develops in people who have been wounded in one way or another. Having faced as youngsters serious developmental hurdles—parental overstimulation, understimulation, or non-integrative stimulation—they did not get the kind of attention needed for a smooth developmental process. The two important spheres of the self—built upon our tendency to obtain reassurance through mirroring (reflecting ourselves in the other) and our tendency to feel more powerful through identification—are poorly integrated in this type of narcissist. Reactive narcissism takes root when phase-appropriate development is interrupted, frustrating experiences are poorly handled, and parents are distant and cold or overindulgent and admiring. In that unhealthy environment, children acquire a defective, rather than well-integrated, sense of identity, and they subsequently have difficulty maintaining a stable sense of self-esteem.

Individuals with this reactive orientation frequently distort outside events to manage anxiety and to prevent a sense of loss and disappointment. To cope with such feelings, they create for themselves a self-image of specialness. As adults, reactive narcissists continue to behave like the hungry, whimpering infants they used to be—they haven't been heard and they want attention. Consciously or subconsciously, they feel a strong need to make up for the perceived wrongs done to them at earlier periods in their lives.

Having been belittled, maltreated, or exposed to other hardships as children, they are determined as adults to show everyone that they amount to something. If that determination stops at wanting—and working—to be valued or extends to making reparation, reactive narcissism can bear healthy fruit. If it turns into envy, spite, greed, grandiosity, and vindictiveness, the fruit is sour indeed.

As stressed earlier, a certain degree of narcissistic behavior is essential for leadership success. In some cases, narcissism can be a strength in a leader. In addition, people with a narcissistic predisposition are frequently very talented. Many of them have had successful academic careers and an exemplary early work history—achievements that contribute to a sense of superiority. A moderate dose of grandiosity and idealization, transformed into self-confidence about one's capabilities and expressed in the ability to identify with senior executives and the organization, contributes to effective organizational functioning.

In such instances, the excitement generated by the narcissistic leader can have a great positive impact. The self-confidence and purposefulness that a constructive narcissistic leader radiates can be extremely contagious. In a faltering organization, these strengths may foster goal-directedness, group cohesion, and alertness to internal and external danger signs. An excessive dose of these strengths, however, can lead to psychological impairment and destructiveness. At what point constructive forces turn into destructive ones depends on the situation. Determining the turning point is rarely an easy matter.

Unfortunately, the sense of excitement generated by narcissistic leaders tends to be temporary and easily wears off. Far too often—and far too soon—the dark side of narcissistic leadership behavior overshadows the initial benefits. With time and testing, narcissistic leaders reveal their lack of conviction and their tendency to resort to political expediency at the cost of long-term goals. Their actions, originally interpreted as bold and imaginative, are gradually exposed for what they really are: pure short-term opportunism. In extreme cases, their inability to accept a real interchange of ideas; their tendency toward self-righteousness; their lack of genuine problem-solving abilities; their intolerance for positive criticism; and their inability to compromise impair organizational functioning and prevent organizational adaptation to internal and external changes send the organization into a downward spiral.

One of the important roles of a leader is to address the emotional needs of his or her subordinates. Leaders pushed by the forces of excessive (reactive) narcissism seem to be unable to handle this task. They disregard their subordinates' legitimate dependency needs and instead take advantage of the loyalty of the people dependent on them. They behave callously, offering deprecation rather than support. Overly competitive, they allow envious reactions to color their behavior toward others. These leaders don't walk the talk, nor do they set the example of value-driven behavior. On the contrary, their behavior fosters submissiveness and passive dependency, thus stifling the critical functions and reality-testing skills of employees. Their lack of commitment to others; their blithe discarding of subordinates when they are no longer needed for selfish purposes; their pursuit of narrow self-interest; and their search for new alliances preclude a creative, innovative organizational culture. Indeed, these traits all but guarantee organizational self-destruction.

SURVIVING THE NARCISSIST

Given the proliferation of grandiose, vain, and greedy CEOs, many boards of directors have not been as effective as they might have been—or as they were perceived to be. Vivendi, Enron, Tyco, ImClone, Global Crossing, and WorldCom are only the most glaring examples of companies whose boards inadequately fulfilled their governance function. On rare occasions, a board will act to disempower a narcissistic leader who is harming the organization's interests. Far more often, though, board members fail to recognize danger signs, either in the form of the behaviors previously detailed or psychological pressures on the CEO. In the worst cases, board members are drawn into collusive behavior with a narcissistic CEO. But organizations need not be helpless in the face of reactive narcissistic leadership. They can take action, both preemptively and after a problem surfaces. Strategies include distributing decision-making duties and putting up boundaries against runaway leadership; improving selection, education, and evaluation of board members; and offering coaching and counseling to executives showing signs of excessive narcissism.

The first of these strategies—putting boundaries around leadership—is best handled via structural mechanisms, a system of leadership checks and balances, if you will. This entails clear and specific detailing of the role of the CEO and the board. Given human nature's tendency to fall into the trap of narcissism, the separation of the roles of chairman and CEO is a no-brainer. Combining these two roles with the intention of unifying command and expediting decision making is all too often an invitation to disaster. There are very few Renaissance leaders among us, people who can resist the seductive chant of the sirens of power. History has shown that too strong a concentration of power—in organizations and society alike—almost inevitably leads to disastrous consequences. Lord Acton's statement, "Power tends to corrupt, and absolute power corrupts absolutely," has a timeless quality.

The second narcissism-fighting strategy focuses on those who work with the CEO. To prevent pathological behavior from coming to the fore, organizations must have structures in place to guide the selection, education, and evaluation of board members. They must also look to employees and shareholders, establishing systems of accountability to encourage their participation in corporate decision making and to balance the power equation. Actively involved shareholders, particularly institutional investors, are likely to help solve many corporate challenges. Moreover, such a restructuring of roles will prevent the emergence of extreme oligarchic corporate structures, where CEOs completely control the agenda and manage (at least in the United States) to be paid 500 times the wages of their average employee. Corporations that are willing to establish such countervailing powers will be better equipped to create wealth, compete in global markets, and solve the highly complex problems of the third millennium.

Most important, however, board members need to become more aware of the potential for destructive narcissistic behavior by CEOs. They need to recognize that latent narcissistic tendencies, suppressed by a young, high-potential executive or put on hold during the climb upward on the career ladder, are likely to blossom when that person reaches his or her ultimate goal of a corner office and the pressures from peers and superiors lose their power. In the case of CEOs, predisposition and position often collude: the symbols of the power of the office work with the presence of excessive narcissism in the CEO to make a monster out of what until recently seemed to be a very reasonable human being. Even constructive narcissists, set free from proper countervailing powers, can easily go astray, although reactive narcissists are more prone to succumb. Board members need to be continuously on guard against danger signs of collusion between predisposition and position and draw boundaries—dismissal of the CEO being the ultimate boundary—when executive behavior warrants it.

In addition to these more structural corporate governance measures of dealing with the problem of runaway CEOs, counseling and coaching by members of the board can often modify potentially destructive behavior. If that fails or if the board feels unequal to the task, the wisest option may be to recommend professional outside help for the troubled executive. Unfortunately, the CEO may not be willing to hear, let alone consider, that alternative. Few overly narcissistic executives are willing to accept professional help. Their reluctance to recognize personal imperfections and their capacity for blaming others make them reluctant to expose their vulnerability and reach out. Too often, they continue to live with the delusion that they are able to solve their problems by themselves.

If they decide to look for professional help, it will likely be their own personal pain that drives them. The pull that enables such people to consult a specialist may be vague complaints about dissatisfaction with life, feelings of futility, lack of purpose, and even a sense of being fraudulent. They may speak of the absence of meaningful relationships, a lack of excitement at work, and the inability to step out of their routines. Mood swings (excitement and rage followed by depression) and hypochondriacal concerns may be other themes. Frequently, however, the driving force is a major life event, such as separation, divorce, or setbacks at work, that precipitates a depressive episode. It is important that the executive and the board recognize what such complaints stand for, because they are the cornerstones on which the individual and the concerned parties can build their change effort.

Since narcissists have a tendency not to take personal responsibility for their failures, an intervention by a coach or psychotherapist is likely to be an uphill struggle. Too often, such individuals argue that various others are the source of all their problems. Those others, whom they eagerly denounce as being motivated by envy and other unsavory emotions, are at fault for setting unrealistic goals, making even realistic goals unreachable, and otherwise putting a stick in the spokes. Whatever their argumentation, the sense of specialness, of personal infallibility, that excessive narcissists exhibit is not an easy pattern to change. Such individuals have a great capacity to draw the therapist or coach into a collusive relationship, attempting (sometimes successfully) to persuade him or her that the problem is not their responsibility. They can be masterfully seductive at inducting the therapist or coach into their own mutual admiration society, all the while criticizing others for their stupidity.

Another hindrance to psychological intervention is excessive narcissists' hypersensitivity to negative feedback. Comments or suggestions that others would perceive as constructive feedback are perceived by narcissists as humiliating criticism. When framing interventions, therefore, the therapist or coach needs to be very careful not to spook the client. Narcissistic individuals need time to learn to tolerate constructive feedback about their behavior and actions. They need time to realize that most human imperfections are not catastrophic, that they are signs of simple fallibility rather than total failure and worthlessness. They need time to shift from an all-or-nothing proposition to a more realistic middle ground. Finally, narcissists need time to learn to become more other-directed, more sensitive about how others feel, and more willing to not only accept but also seek out cooperative forms of social behavior, with the understanding that reaching out to others can contribute to more gratifying experiences in the long term.

The key challenge for the therapist or coach is to enable such people to recognize their own responsibility, regardless of the mess they find themselves in, and to make them aware of the primitive defensive processes they are engaged in. Narcissists have to understand the destructive nature of their defensive behaviors and reduce their reliance on infantile fantasies of unlimited success and glory, replacing self-serving rationalizations with authentic reality testing. They need to be weaned off of unproductive glorious fantasies, which result in an overblown self-image, and helped to construct more realistic, attainable fantasies, which help in the building of self-esteem. Looking outward, they need to become more sensitive to and understanding of other people's feelings. Because the process of personal reevaluation can be painful, psychopharmacological intervention may be needed to ward off depressive feelings.

If the coach or therapist successfully resists being drawn into collusion with the narcissist, if he or she is able to focus on the reality of the situation while demonstrating an empathic understanding of the narcissist's weaknesses, the client may finally realize that something is wrong and that he or she has a personal responsibility in the matter. With that groundwork, the therapist or coach can then help to expand the CEO's capacity to care for others without the fear of rejection and humiliation. That process involves the establishment of a more secure sense of self-esteem and the lessening of the need for grandiosity and idealization through the establishment of more benign inner images. The bolstering of a fragile sense of self eventually creates a greater cohesiveness of inner imagery: internalized images gradually lose their archaic malevolent content and become more in tune with outer reality. A secure sense of self-esteem also tames feelings of inner rage and envy of others and makes for conviction, purpose, and creativity.

As improved self-esteem allows for more personal intimacy, relationships of trust become building blocks for the development of empathy, creativity, humor, and wisdom—all of which in turn form a base for effective leadership. However, there is no quick fix for the narcissist's trauma of having been deceived, exploited, or manipulated at some critical early developmental period. Healing is a lengthy and difficult process. But if narcissistic behavior can be channeled into these more positive directions—if it can be bounded and made constructive—it can be the motor that drives a successful organization. If not, employees and shareholders, along with the defeated narcissist, may have to pay the price in disillusionment and broken dreams.

NOTES

1. American Psychiatric Association, *Diagnostic and Statistical Manual for Mental Disorders, DSM-IV* (Washington, DC: American Psychiatric Association, 1994); O. Kernberg, *Borderline Conditions and Pathological Narcissism* (New York: Aronson, 1975); M. F. R. Kets de Vries and S. Perzow, *Handbook of Character Studies* (New York: International University Press, 1991); H. Kohut, *The Analysis of the Self* (New York: International University Press, 1971).

2. M. F. R. Kets de Vries, *The Leadership Mystique* (London: Prentice Hall, 2001).

CHAPTER 5

THE ESSENCE OF LEADING AND GOVERNING IS DECIDING

MICHAEL USEEM

ENRON'S 2001 bankruptcy and Tyco's 2002 travails came to epitomize a spike in corporate corruption in much the same way that Salomon's 1991 near collapse symbolized an earlier surge. Though disastrous for those involved, the scandals of both eras sent an invaluable message to managers elsewhere: the success or failure of great enterprise depends on the quality of their leadership and governance. If that message had not always been clear when well-built companies were faring well, it became unequivocal when they faltered or fell.

The quality of company leadership and governance depends first and foremost upon the quality of the decisions taken by those serving in the executive office or on the governing board. By their actions and inactions, executives and directors have brought otherwise well-performing companies, such as Enron and Tyco, to their knees. Different decisions at the top could have driven very different histories below.

We define leadership decisions as those moments when executives and directors face a relatively discrete opportunity to commit company resources to one course of action or another. Inaction in the face of such an opportunity also should be seen as a decision. Taken well, these decisions can provide the essential platform for a company's growth and success; taken poorly, they can produce the opposite.

REVEALING DECISIONS

Although good decisions are among the most important functions of leadership and governance, they are also among the least visible since they are almost always made behind closed doors. "Most of the work done by a board takes place in the privacy of the boardroom," two observers noted, and thus, "rarely, if ever" does information about its actions "escape to the outside world."[1] The relative invisibility of top decision making is one reason that academic research on corporate governance has long focused on the composition and policies of the board, rather than on the directors' decisions themselves. Many of the decisions in the executive suite never reach the outside world either. That is a reason, another analyst has suggested, that company boards have often been forced to recruit chief executives more for their personal charisma—the aura of leadership—than for their past decisions.[2]

Although most leadership decisions are taken in private, they nonetheless define the quality of leadership far better than most public actions or displays. U.S. President John F. Kennedy inspired a nation with his inaugural rhetoric, "Ask not what your country can do for you—ask what you can do for your country." But his decisions inside the Oval Office during the 13-day Cuban missile crisis more profoundly characterized his presidency.[3] The same was true for the executives and directors who presided at Enron and Tyco: whatever their public facade, their misguided private decisions were far more consequential.

If we are to appreciate the essence of corporate leadership and governance, then we must find ways of peering inside the private rooms where critical decisions are made. Although company doors are rarely opened voluntarily, calamities often force them ajar. Regulators, reporters, and whistle-blowers have ways of revealing what ordinarily would never come to light. As with Civil War battles and space shuttle missions, the best public records often emerge from the most ruinous events.[4]

While in receivership after its bankruptcy on December 2, 2001, Enron's reconstituted board investigated what had gone wrong. With unrestricted access to company records, it took the unusual step of issuing a hard-hitting identification of the ill-advised decisions that had brought on the energy giant's failure. With the power of subpoena, the U.S. Senate published its own blunt investigation of the decisions that had hastened Enron's fall. Similarly, Tyco released its own investigation of accounting malfeasance, and the

2003–2004 criminal trial of its former chief executive exposed further details on his decisions.[5]

Drawing on such inside-out records of Enron, Tyco, and other troubled companies, this chapter seeks to extract the factors that facilitate good leadership and governance decisions through examination of notoriously bad ones. All organizations have an interest in ensuring that their decisions are optimal, especially those by their executives and directors. Yet company managers tend to fall recurrently into what two investigators have termed "decision traps," and a host of reasons for suboptimal managerial decisions has been identified by a range of investigators.[6] What have been little investigated are the factors that facilitate optimal decisions among those who lead and govern large-scale enterprise.

Three factors emerged from our assessment of the now publicly available sources on Enron, Tyco, and other distressed companies that help explain many of the most unfavorable leadership and governance decisions that precipitated their decline. By implication, mindfulness of these factors should help executives and directors elsewhere reach more optimal decisions for their companies in the future.

The first factor is *transcendent dedication,* an overarching commitment to the goals of the enterprise, regardless of the directors' and executives' personal benefits. A second is *vigilant attention,* a vow by directors and executives to remain alert and analytic in reaching decisions. And a third factor is *decisive realization,* a dedication by directors and executives ensuring that their high decisions are executed well below.

TRANSCENDENT DEDICATION

Most personal decisions are framed around private utility: what individual gains and losses are associated with one outcome or another? Most managerial decisions are similarly structured around divisional purpose: what benefits and costs accrue to a division if one product is launched rather than another?

Leadership and governance decisions necessitate a distinct framing since they are taken for the unique purpose of advancing the entire enterprise, regardless of personal concerns or divisional interests. They depend upon a capacity to transcend private agendas and parochial objectives. And that capacity must be exercised even though—and especially when—self-interest conflicts with what the organization requires.

It was the absence of transcendent commitment that nearly brought down Tyco International in 2002. A public prosecutor charged that its chief executive, L. Dennis Kozlowski, had avoided taxes on art purchases of $13 million through the use of phony invoices. On June 4, 2002, the state asserted that, in acquiring six paintings, including two by Monet and Renoir, the chief executive officer (CEO) had retained $1 million in his private pocket that should have gone to a public coffer. It was small change for a big executive, but the CEO's indictment was so discrediting that he was compelled to resign from Tyco a day before the charge was publicly announced.[7]

Under new management, Tyco executives worked with investigators and regulators to determine if the former CEO had also misappropriated Tyco funds. Three months later, government prosecutors indicted Kozlowski and his chief financial officer for misusing $600 million of Tyco's assets for private purposes.

In the subsequent trial of Tyco's former CEO, the prosecutors asserted that he gave primacy to his own welfare when it conflicted with company purpose in decision after decision on issues ranging from private parties to forgiven loans. The state charged that Kozlowski had drawn $12 million from the company to acquire his personal art; $17 million to buy a New York apartment; $29 million to purchase a Florida estate; and $58 million to award himself a bonus. The director of enforcement for the U.S. Securities and Exchange Commission (SEC) said that Tyco executives had simply "put their own interests above those of Tyco's shareholders."[8]

The absence of an unswerving dedication to transcendent purpose reached Tyco's boardroom as well. Nonexecutive director Frank E. Walsh Jr. had facilitated Tyco's $9.2 billion acquisition of the large commercial finance firm The CIT Group in 2001. For his service, the outside director asked for and accepted a $20 million fee from the chief executive, an unreported payment that he would later be forced by the SEC to return. In barring Walsh from ever serving again as a director or officer of a publicly traded company, the SEC associate director of enforcement held the former director to the transcendent standard: "Mr. Walsh served as chairman of Tyco's compensation committee and a member of Tyco's corporate governance committee," he said. "Shareholders entrusted him with the responsibility of watching out for their interests in Tyco's boardroom and executive suite. Instead, Mr.

Walsh himself took secret compensation and kept those same shareholders in the dark."[9]

The vigorous pursuit of personal self-interest may be optimal for some positions and purposes, but it is suboptimal for decisions by executives and directors if they are to effectively lead and govern the enterprise. This dedication to transcending self-interest is undermined and even countermanded by the self-maximizing precepts that run so deeply in the culture of capitalism.[10] The transcendent dedication is consistent, however, with the conclusions reached by Jim Collins in his study of why 11 firms rose from good to great performance. He found that the great performers had become so because they were led by executives who consistently placed enterprise interests ahead of their own.[11]

Thus, the challenge for those who lead and govern is to prepare themselves to resist the siren call of personal self-interest when faced with critical decisions. Their decisions are to be judged by whether they consistently transcend individual concerns to put collective purpose first. To this end, a company's leadership would do well to embrace a concept akin to what the U.S. Marine Corps makes central to its culture of leadership: "The officer eats last."[12]

VIGILANT ATTENTION

Many personal decisions are taken with calculating forethought—or at least they should be. Are the alternatives clear? Is the information complete? Are the consequences understood? Yet here, too, the decisions of executives and directors require special framing. By virtue of their responsibilities, executives and directors are obligated to be especially vigilant. Taken well, their decisions can enhance the livelihood of hundreds of employees and the wealth of thousands of investors. Taken poorly, their decisions can destroy those assets or even the company. Compared with other managers, careless actions by executives or directors are far more momentous.

At the same time, the intense time pressures faced by executives and directors because of their demanding responsibilities militate against devotion of the special attention required by each of the actions. Dozens of critical decisions cross their desk, limiting the time they can take from their grueling schedules to devote to any single one. Thus, leadership and governance necessitate a capacity to remain especially alert in taking vital decisions when time constraints would dictate otherwise.

This is precisely where the Enron board went wrong in mid-1999 when its chief financial officer (CFO) Andrew Fastow asked for approval of an independent partnership called LJM. The company's preexisting, board-approved ethics code stipulated that "even the appearance of an improper transaction must be avoided" and that no employee could receive any "financial gain separately derived" from service with the company. The board's charter also called for the audit committee to oversee management compliance with the ethics code.[13]

Enron's governance policies implied that the audit committee should review Fastow's request before it went to the full board. That would be particularly critical in this instance since the partnership was structured in such a way that the CFO represented both sides of it. He would be the voice of the company in negotiations with the partnership, but he would also be the voice of the partnership in its negotiations with the company. The arrangement had all the markings of an "improper transaction" from which the CFO might indeed derive "financial gain."

Yet the Enron audit committee, best positioned to make a fine-honed recommendation on Fastow's request for the partnership and suspension of the ethics code, did not review the request before it went to the full board, nor had the board's finance committee reviewed the financial implications. In fact, the unvetted proposal arrived in the directors' fax machines just three days before a special board meeting to be held by teleconference on June 28, 1999.

The agenda for the June 28 board meeting was filled with other important matters as well: authorization of a stock split, placement of more shares in a compensation plan, purchase of a corporate jet, and investment in a Middle Eastern power plant. CEO Kenneth Lay also intended to review an important reorganization of the company already under way. With no real discussion of the ethics suspension feasible, a motion to enact the suspension was seconded by the audit-committee chair and then promptly ratified by the directors. They wrapped up the conference call in just an hour. The risky consequences of the partnership could barely have been aired at the time. Later, it and partnerships like it would prove central to Enron's downfall.

Company directors, the Senate investigation revealed, also fell short in acquiring the essential information for making the vigilant decisions required by their oversight role. In 2001, for example, the board's compensation committee approved pay plans that gave 65 Enron executives a total of $750 million for their work in 2000, a year in which Enron's total net income was only $975 million. When directors were later asked by a Senate investigator why they had approved such exceedingly generous packages—an average of $11.5 million for each of the more than five dozen executives—they confessed that the $750 million had come from several distinct incentive programs and that nobody on the compensation committee had thought to add up the numbers before approving the programs.

Underscoring the importance of vigilance in governance, scandals at two other companies stemmed, in part, from much the same shortfall in director attention. WorldCom declared bankruptcy on July 21, 2002, after admitting to an $11 billion accounting fraud, beating the record for the largest insolvency in U.S. history set by Enron less than eight months earlier. An acquisition binge contributed to its foreclosure, and a study by a bankruptcy examiner found that WorldCom directors had approved several of the multi-billion-dollar acquisitions with no analysis of their financial implications and less than 30 minutes' deliberation.[14]

A similar oversight at the Walt Disney Company resulted in a less devastating—but nonetheless costly—mistake. In 1995, Disney CEO Michael Eisner had hired friend Michael Ovitz as his new No. 2, promising Ovitz $100 million if he ever fired him. Fourteen months later, Mr. Eisner did just that. The severance was astonishing: For each failing month on the job, Ovitz was sent off with $7 million—$340,000 per day. From stockholder litigation against the company, it emerged that the Disney compensation committee evidently had devoted just minutes to the CEO's proposed hiring of Ovitz and had never reviewed the final severance package. The directors gave their assent to the extraordinary package in what may have constituted a decision, said a Delaware judge, that was "consciously indifferent."[15]

Insufficient director vigilance contributed to an expensive mistake at Disney and fatal mistakes at Enron and WorldCom. The directors of World-Com had approved billion-dollar acquisitions with the briefest of reviews, while Disney's directors had evidently approved an off-scale severance package with conscious indifference. Similarly, Enron's directors did not secure the information they needed to ensure that their CFO did not enrich himself from the partnerships. Instead, they allowed themselves to enter meetings underprepared to make fateful choices and permitted deliberations to be so brief as to negate any possibility of informed decision-making.

These experiences serve as tangible reminders that leadership and governance decisions are usefully judged against the standard of whether they are taken with vigilant attention. The lack of vigilant attention is modestly consequential for positions of modest duties, but for those that carry great responsibilities, the absence can be devastating. Governing bodies and company headquarters require experienced people and appropriate incentives, but whether the directors and executives are consciously concerned or passively indifferent when they take key decisions is the real test of whether they are the right people with the right incentives.

Decisive Realization

Leadership and governance decisions require a host of subsidiary actions for their successful realization. The secondary decisions are what translate the lofty intentions of the grand decisions into tangible consequences on the ground. They are the essence of what Ram Charan and Larry Bossidy have termed "execution."[16]

Frontline managers who fail to execute are usually not long for this world, but executives and directors who do not implement often remain in power due to lack of hands-on oversight. Directors have no superiors to notice their dereliction except the shareholders, who are too removed to notice. Executives might suffer the hot glare of their board, but the latter is usually too removed from daily operations to notice either.

Consider what Enron's directors did not do after they approved the risky partnerships proposed by the CFO. In the wake of the board's suspension of the company's ethics code—which allowed CFO Andrew Fastow and his subordinates to sit on both sides of the table in negotiating transactions between the LJM entities and Enron—the board insisted on several safeguards. It required, for instance, the preparation of a Deal Approval Sheet prior to each new transaction between Enron and the partnerships. The transactions were to be described in detail, and the approval and signature of at least two executives were mandated before proceeding. On at least 13 separate occasions, Enron executives representing each of the two sides of a transaction reported directly to the CFO, making the deal sheets particularly salient since there was an obvious conflict of interest. Yet for many of the deals, the sheets were never prepared, never signed, or never written until after the transaction was completed.

Similarly, Enron's directors became at least vaguely aware that CFO Fastow was realizing a personal windfall from the partnership transactions. (It was later revealed that he drew $30 million from them in 1999–2000.) Consequently, the board's finance committee asked the compensation committee to examine Fastow's income from all sources. The chair of the compensation committee, Charles A. LeMaistre, well understood the request, since he had attended the finance committee meeting and subsequently asked Enron's top compensation official, Mary Joyce, for data on the outside income of all of Enron's top officers. To avoid setting off alarm bells within the company, LeMaistre did not single out Andrew Fastow in his request, although it was Fastow's partnership earnings that drove the request. As it turned out, Mary Joyce, the seniormost compensation executive at the firm, did not deliver the requested data, and when LeMaistre asked her again and failed to receive the data a second time, he simply dropped the matter. The directors saw a red flag rising above the partnerships that they had approved, but they never probed further to learn why it was rising.

The absence of decisive realization often leads to the swift dismissal of front-line managers, since superiors are quick to notice and intervene. However, executives and directors have no immediate supervisors who are in a position to readily appraise their implementing decisions. Thus, the absence of follow-up actions to execute their grand decisions may go unnoticed until well after the damage is done.

Here too, then, company leadership and governance require a distinctive mindset in decision making. Since there are so few immediate sanctions for failing to follow through, executives and directors must be personally determined to execute their major decisions through the numerous secondary actions that must follow.

Tyco's executives had allowed their own self-interest to trump shared purpose, while Enron directors had permitted themselves to take decisions with scarce analysis and scant follow-through. Such decisions may be shocking, but they should not be entirely surprising. After all, the mindset in private enterprise is to maximize self-interest, and the time demands upon those who run private enterprise foster quick decisions and limit follow-up. Given that the natural proclivities of those in high positions are not necessarily those of transcendent dedication, vigilant attention, or decisive realization, the challenge for advocates of good leadership and governance is to create devices for ensuring them.

The SEC, New York Stock Exchange, and a number of other institutions in the United States and abroad have pressed for improved leadership and governance of publicly held private enterprise in the wake of the failures at Enron, Tyco, and other companies.[17] The thrust of their policies and proposals—ranging from more independent directors to more assiduous audits—should be seen for their underlying purpose: the creation of unbiased, informed, and decisive decisions when the directors and executives convene behind closed doors.

Naturally, directors and executives must maintain the appearance of effectively governing and leading their company, for that is an essential part of sustaining investor and customer confidence in the company. But appearances are only a side part of the foundation. The center stone is the quality of the decisions they reach when nobody is looking. The essence of leading and governing is making quality decisions, and that depends on whether the company has established a culture that demands transcendence, vigilance, and decisiveness.

NOTES

1. Colin B. Carter and Jay W. Lorsch, *Back to the Drawing Board: Designing Corporate Boards for a Complex World* (Boston: Harvard Business School Press, 2004).

2. Rakesh Khurana, *Searching for a Corporate Savior: The Irrational Quest for Charismatic CEOs* (Princeton, NJ: Princeton University Press, 2002).

3. Graham T. Allison, *Essence of Decision: Explaining the Cuban Missile Crisis* (New York: HarperCollins, 1971).

4. For decisions in Civil War battles, see Stephen W. Sears, *Gettysburg* (Boston: Houghton Mifflin, 2003); for Space Shuttle missions, see Columbia Accident Investigation Board, *Report* (Washington, DC: National Aeronautics and Space Administration and Government Printing Office, 2003).

5. William C. Powers, Jr., Raymond S. Troubh, and Herbert S. Winokur, Jr., "Report of Investigation by the Special Investigative Committee of the Board of Directors of Enron Corp.," 1 February 2002; U.S. Senate, Permanent Subcommittee on Investigations of the Committee on Governmental Affairs, "The Role of the Board of Directors in Enron's Collapse," 8 July 2002 (Washington, DC: U.S. Senate,

2002; http://news.findlaw.com/hdocs/docs/enron/senpsi70802rpt.pdf); Tyco International Ltd., Form 8-K, 30 December 2002; Mark Maremont and Laurie P. Cohen, "Tyco's Internal Report Finds Extensive Accounting Tricks," *Wall Street Journal,* 31 December 2002, p. 1.

6. Edward Russo and Paul J. H. Schoemaker, *Decision Traps: Ten Barriers to Brilliant Decision-Making and How to Overcome Them* (New York: Simon & Schuster, 1990); Kenneth R. Hammond, *Judgment Under Stress* (New York: Oxford University Press, 2000); J. Edward Russo and Paul J. H. Schoemaker, *Winning Decisions: Getting It Right the First Time* (New York: Doubleday, 2002); Gary Klein, *Sources of Power: How People Make Decisions* (Cambridge, MA: MIT Press, 1998).

7. *State of New York v. L. Dennis Kozlowski,* 3418/02, 4 June 2002 (http://news.findlaw.com/cnn/docs/tyco/nykozlowski60402ind.pdf); District Attorney, New York County, News Release, 4 June 2002.

8. *State of New York v. L. Dennis Kozlowski and Mark H. Swartz,* 5259/02, 12 September 2002 (http://news.findlaw.com/hdocs/docs/tyco/nykozlowski91202ind.pdf).

9. U.S. Securities and Exchange Commission, "SEC Sues Former Tyco Director and Chairman of Compensation Committee Frank E. Walsh Jr. for Hiding $20 Million Payment From Shareholders: Walsh Had Secret Agreement With L. Dennis Kozlowski To Receive Payment for 'Finder's Fee' in Tyco's Acquisition of The CIT Group Inc," Release 2002-177, 17 December 2002 (Washington, D.C.: U.S. Securities and Exchange Commission, 2002; http://www.sec.gov/news/press/2002-177.htm).

10. See, for instance, George Soros, *The Crisis of Global Capitalism: Open Society Endangered* (New York: Perseus Books, 1998).

11. Jim Collins, *Good to Great: Why Some Companies Make the Leap . . . and Others Don't* (New York: HarperBusiness, 2001).

12. David H. Freedman, *Corps Business: The 30 Management Principles of the U.S. Marines* (New York: Harper Business, 2000); Jason A. Santamaria, Vincent Martino, and Eric K. Clemons, *The Marine Corps Way: Using Maneuver Warfare to Lead a Winning Organization* (New York: McGraw-Hill, 2004).

13. The account of Enron draws upon William C. Powers, Jr., Raymond S. Troubh, and Herbert S. Winokur, Jr., "Report of Investigation by the Special Investigative Committee"; U.S. Senate, Permanent Subcommittee on Investigations of the Committee on Governmental Affairs, "The Role of the Board of Directors in Enron's Collapse"; Mimi Swartz and Sherron Watkins, *Power Failure: The Inside Story of the Collapse of Enron* (New York: Doubleday, 2003); Bethany McLean and Peter Elkind, *Smartest Guys in the Room: The Amazing Rise and Scandalous Fall of Enron* (New York: Portfolio, 2003); Stuart L. Gillan and John D. Martin, "Financial En-

gineering, Corporate Governance, and the Collapse of Enron," Working Paper, Center for Corporate Governance, University of Delaware, 2002 (http://www.be .udel.edu/ccg/research_files/CCGWP2002-1.pdf); Michael Useem, "Corporate Governance Is Directors Making Decisions: Reforming the Outward Foundations for Inside Decision Making," *Journal of Management and Governance,* 7(2003): pp. 241–253.

14. U.S. Bankruptcy Court, Southern District of New York, *First Interim Report* of Dick Thornburgh, Bankruptcy Court Examiner, 4 November 2002; Dennis R. Beresford, Nicholas deB. Katzenbach, and C. B. Rogers, Jr., *Report of Investigation by the Special Investigative Committee of the Board of Directors of WorldCom, Inc.,* 31 March 2003 (http://www.edgar-online.com/bin/irsec/finSys_main.asp?dcn=0000931763-03-001862&x=120&y=20).

15. Court of Chancery, State of Delaware, The Walt Disney Company Derivative Litigation, C.A. No. 15452, 28 May 2003 (http://courts.state.de.us/chancery/opinions/15452-126.pdf).

16. Larry Bossidy and Ram Charan, *Execution: The Discipline of Getting Things Done* (New York: Random House, 2002).

17. The Sarbanes-Oxley Act of 2002 (http://news.findlaw.com/hdocs/docs/gwbush/sarbanesoxley072302.pdf); Final NYSE Corporate Governance Rules, 4 November 2003 (http://nyse.com/pdfs/finalcorpgovrules.pdf).

CHAPTER 6

VIGOROUS COMPETITION, CARDINAL VIRTUES, AND VALUE CREATION

ROBERT W. LANE

AS THE final battles of the first World War were being won, the CEO of a Midwestern farm implement company was preparing to wage his own battle—launching his company on a new course with a new product line. Bringing considerable skills of persuasion to bear, he convinced John Deere's corporate directors to purchase the Waterloo Boy Gasoline Engine Company, one of several businesses that were experimenting with an exciting new concept—a mechanized horse, also known as a tractor.

The technology had yet to be proven, and it wasn't clear at the time that the tractor even had what it took to replace the horse. Still, the risk was considered worthwhile because it had the potential to accomplish great good—for the farmers who would be the consumers of the product, for the craftsmen who would earn their living manufacturing it, and for the investors who wanted an honest profit on the capital they had invested in the corporation.

At the same time, across the globe, Lenin and his communist collaborators were taking a risk of their own, imposing an economic system based on forced collective sharing and centralized control upon a nation of farmers. Consequently, the enormous potential of that dark, rich soil was never realized because of a system that was fundamentally flawed.

Granted, the history of John Deere doesn't even begin to approach the same magnitude as the history of communism. However, John Deere is an excellent example of a company emerging to global scope in the soil of democracy, under the rule of law, and in a culture of competition—in other words, the antithesis of communism. Over the course of just a few decades, a competitive environment made possible the production of an excess of food for the United States. In the same decades, the process of collectivization, as one historian described it, produced a case of purely man-made famine elsewhere in the world.[1]

Capitalism can suffer from the same failure to account for human nature. Like democracy, capitalism is far from perfect, and its successes over the past century do not mean that all is well in our world. Among others, Pope John Paul II, who grew up personally experiencing the bankruptcy of socialism of Central Europe and was a key catalyst in ending it, has expressed concern over unbridled capitalism and its potential for rapacious greed. In spite of the enormous wealth spread out across the globe, as many as three billion people live on less than $2 per day. Even though American farmers have the ability to produce considerably more food than Americans can consume, the sale and delivery of this abundance to the hungry remains a significant and troubling problem. Indeed, the seemingly eternal trio of human poverty, hunger, and unemployment remains with us.

Thomas Hobbes once wrote that life in the state of nature is "solitary, poor, nasty, brutish and short."[2] All too often, we forget that this is the nature of man and we avert our minds from the reality that surrounds us. Considering the chilling events of the twentieth century—the most brutal one hundred years ever lived—not to mention the grim events that marked the early years of this century, we can only again reach the unpleasant conclusion that humans are not angels. Without moral, social, legal, and economic constraints, humans will overpower, dominate, abuse, and enslave one another.

Granted, this dour view of mankind is not the complete picture, as humans also have great potential for goodness. Over the centuries, we have produced a wide array of institutions that have made life communal, prosperous, secure, noble, and long. These include schools, universities, churches, synagogues, mosques, hospitals, libraries, orchestras, and courts. What's more, many publicly owned corporations provide abundant means for men and women to earn an honorable living by producing goods and services necessary for human flourishing. The fundamental purpose of such economic activity can be a means to the advancement of human dignity, the promotion of human freedom, and the ultimate triumph of truth over false-hood.

A competitive marketplace (i.e., a free market) possesses the wondrous ability to produce great material and social benefits. Providers of goods and services compete in a way that delivers profits sufficient to attract, compensate, and retain needed capital. This is not easy, but when it happens, it creates shareholder value and solid jobs, not to mention quality products and services that meet consumer needs. In light of the human potential for both bad and good, however, this power must be checked. The single most powerful and successful check for the discipline of capitalists and the simultaneous benefit of human beings is competition.

Clearly, the most effective counterweight to entrenched economic power is the structuring of society to unleash pro-market forces. A pro-market society is organized to benefit human beings by forcing businesses to compete with one another. A merely pro-business society is organized to encourage and promote governmental intervention on behalf of and in support of business enterprises and industries. It does not encourage or offer incentives for the free movement of capital to support new ideas or encourage new entrepreneurs and businesses that might threaten established enterprises. Whatever honorable motives there may be initially for merely pro-business actions, the outcome is almost invariably selfishness, incompetence, and corruption. Given human nature, unconstrained greed can severely damage the marvelous engine of pro-market competition.

Ironically, vigorous competition is precisely what many individuals and corporations would prefer to avoid. Throughout his epic *Wealth of Nations,* Adam Smith implied that capitalists would prefer to collude rather than compete.[3] Collusion, after all, is much easier than competition. What's more, being merely pro-business is much easier than being pro-market. In their book *Saving Capitalism from the Capitalists,* University of Chicago professors Rajan and Zingales argue that "in their continuous quest for government protection from competition, the [capitalists] often turn out to be Capitalism's worst enemies."[4]

Of course, recent governance scandals have made it clear that capitalism can go horribly wrong. This raises the question of the relationship between capitalism and morality. In his lecture "The Morality of Capitalism," Professor James Q. Wilson concluded that capitalism assumes the existence of a moral order in that it requires trust and self-command.[5] Within that moral order, pro-market competition will drive corporations that aspire to create long-term shareholder value to work in classically virtuous ways. These virtues, while not sufficient for prosperity, are necessary for sustaining it, as their practice gives corporations the ability to create shareholder value, both in the short and the long run. When a corporation survives over time, it can contribute to human flourishing by providing goods and services that add value to the quality of life, an honorable way to make a living, the potential for wealth generation for those willing to risk investment, and, through the paying of taxes, direct support of public and social needs.

With incentives and regulations in place, great corporations have the capacity to perform a role in society that not only produces great material benefit for human beings but also exemplifies and enhances the four cardinal virtues of mankind—fortitude, temperance, prudence, and justice. While a virtue is a voluntary observance of recognized moral laws, the word *cardinal* comes from the Latin, meaning "hinge." Thus, a cardinal virtue is fundamental in that everything turns on it. In a rigorously competitive market, virtue is necessary for sustained value creation.

SUSTAINED VALUE CREATION REQUIRES FORTITUDE

The virtue of fortitude is *unyielding strength in the endurance of adversity.* Vigorous competition creates a perpetual state of adversity that, in turn, requires corporations to exercise fortitude if they are to prosper and survive in both the short and long term. At John Deere, this means a journey to create a business as great as its products. While short-term financial performance could be improved rather easily by cutting research and development, environmental protection, employee safety, and investments in new products, that would not serve Deere well in the long run.

While it's true that Deere is focusing on asset reduction and cost control in its drive to be a great business, the company continues to invest heavily. Investing would not require fortitude if we had the luxury of reading the future. But since we can't, there is no substitute for the practice of fortitude. In keeping with the goal of sustained value creation, John Deere continues to introduce a record number of new products, providing new value to its customers. What's more, it continues to invest in improving operations and emerging businesses in, for example, India, China, and Russia, even though an adequate financial return on a stand-alone basis may be many quarters down the road.

SUSTAINED VALUE CREATION
REQUIRES TEMPERANCE

Temperance is rational self-restraint, moderation in the use of anything. Vigorous competition requires a corporation to exercise self-restraint if it is to survive. Many competitors in Deere's industry have not demonstrated this virtue and have failed as a result. Naturally, Deere is not immune.

Results at Deere have also lagged partly because Deere did not restrain its asset levels. Inventory and receivable levels were higher than needed to serve its customers at a consistently high level. To survive and prosper, therefore, Deere is now learning to build products that are much closer to what customers want, learning to produce them much closer to the time they want them, and learning to do so with much smaller inventories. In short, if Deere is going to compete successfully in the long term in a market free of collusion, fraud, and monopoly, it must exercise temperance—rational self-restraint.

SUSTAINED VALUE CREATION
REQUIRES PRUDENCE

Sometimes called "practical wisdom" or "discretion," prudence is the ability to discern the most suitable or profitable course of action.

Wanting to survive and prosper, Deere is attempting to be more prudent. In 1997, for example, its construction and forestry division manufactured about 25 percent of its annual production each quarter, for a relatively flat production cycle. The problem was that customer demand was lumpy, with seasonal peaks and valleys.

Because Deere was manufacturing products at a level rate during peak demand, it often wasn't getting the right machines to the right customers fast enough. During the low points in the demand cycle, Deere was laden with excessive assets, manufacturing goods that were not the right products, and experiencing a lack of waiting customers. Through prudent, leaner manufacturing, all that changed. As a result, the time it took from order to delivery and payment was reduced from 255 days to 79 days, while the time it takes to build a complete machine was reduced to six days from 33. The competition of a free market motivated Deere to make these difficult changes in its operations.

SUSTAINED VALUE CREATION REQUIRES JUSTICE

In Book V of his *Nicomachean Ethics,* Aristotle quoted a proverb: "In Justice all virtue is summed up."[6] In his mind, justice is the supreme virtue because it involves "relationship with someone else." He wrote, "justice is the only virtue that seems to be another person's good . . . for it does what benefits another."[7]

In 1837, the founder of Deere & Company produced a watershed invention—the first self-scouring plow, a tool that enabled farmers to cut through sod and shed the sticky soil of the Great Plains without manual scraping. The plow benefited both the farmers who used it and the general population for whom food was produced. In sending this tool into the free market, it is reported that Deere himself said: "I will not put my name on a product that does not have in it the best that is in me." Surely Deere's point in articulating this standard was his belief that the best products produce the greatest benefit for consumers. This is a demanding standard that Deere continues to impose on itself in everything it does. But it is also the competition of the marketplace that imposes on Deere the requirement that it act for the benefit of others if it is going to create sustained value.

At a recent dinner held to recognize suppliers who were deemed "the best of the best," one long-term supplier told me, "Deere would not be considered supplier friendly, but it is supplier fair." If his characterization is correct, then despite the high demands that Deere places on its suppliers, it is acting justly toward them. Deere seeks to build similar fair relationships of mutual long-term benefit with employees, dealers, customers, and the communities in which it operates. This is no doubt an intrinsically good thing, but it also makes Deere a more competitive corporation.

CONCLUSION

Pro-market success will continue to grow in importance as our global society faces the seemingly intractable problem of feeding, clothing, and housing a world that will likely grow from six to nine billion people in the next 50 years. Though not the proverbial "silver bullet," pro-market policy is demonstrably a powerful force for good. Free financial markets challenge corporate sluggishness, open borders, and keep political and economic elites in check.

This remarkable, though imperfect, performance of vigorous pro-market capitalism is one that can and must be expanded. It will permit great corporations, as they demonstrate the four cardinal virtues, to create value on an enduring basis and thereby contribute to the overarching good of human flourishing.

NOTES

1. Robert Conquest, *The Great Terror: Stalin's Purge of the Thirties* (London 1969), p. 22, quoted in Paul Johnson, *Modern Times: The World from the Twenties to the Eighties* (New York: Harper & Row, 1983), p. 272.

2. Thomas Hobbes, *Leviathan,* Cambridge Texts in the History of Political Thought, ed. Richard Tuck (Cambridge: Cambridge University Press, 1991), p. 89.

3. Adam Smith, *The Wealth of Nations,* pp. 69–70.

4. Raghuram G. Rajan and Luigi Zingales, *Saving Capitalism from the Capitalists* (New York: Crown Business, 2003), p. 311.

5. James Q. Wilson, "The Morality of Capitalism," The Fourteenth Annual John Bonython Lecture, 15 October 1997, www.cis.org/au/Events/JBL/JBL97.htm.

6. Aristotle, *Selections,* trans. Terence Irwin and Gail Fine (Indianapolis, IN: Hackett Publishing, 1995), p. 393.

7. Aristotle, *Selections,* p. 393.

CHAPTER 7

CHALLENGE UP

A KEY TO ORGANIZATIONAL INTEGRITY

MARSHALL GOLDSMITH

"WE WANT people to challenge the status quo!"

"We encourage constructive dissent!"

"We need people who let us know when we are headed in the wrong direction!"

Enron's leaders did a wonderful job of preaching the value of challenging the system . . . so did Andersen's . . . so did NASA's. Everyone seems to know that encouraging upward challenge is a key to maintaining corporate integrity. This is relatively easy to understand; it is just hard to do. After corporate meltdowns, it is amazing how many people claim that they knew there could be huge problems. It is even more amazing how few people effectively expressed these concerns before the problems were reported in the news.

Warner Burke has pointed out that "knows how to influence up in a constructive way" scored last place on managerial effectiveness in all items when people evaluated their managers in NASA—immediately before the Columbia space shuttle exploded.[1] While lack of effective upward challenge was not the only cause of the explosion, it was a clear contributing factor. The same story is true in almost all organizational disasters and examples of corporate wrongdoing.

In this chapter, I will suggest organizational guidelines aimed at encouraging upward challenge and preserving corporate integrity. None are a reinvention of the wheel, and they certainly are not all-encompassing, but I have seen them work in highly respected companies and I hope they can provide you with a good discussion point for reviewing your own organizational processes. While some of them may seem extreme, the organizational cost of integrity violations is—and should be—huge. If the last two years have taught us anything, it should be that ethical violations can kill even the most successful companies. The cost of preventing ethical problems will never exceed the cost of dealing with ethical problems.

SUGGESTED GUIDELINES FOR MANAGERS AND EMPLOYEES

If you are ever asked to do anything that you believe may be unethical, it is not your right to express your concern—it is your responsibility.

One of the world's most highly respected service companies clearly communicates this guideline to all employees, and it is a major message in their new employee orientation. I cannot think of any organization that should not communicate this same clear message, yet very few do.

When managers are asked why they implemented decisions that were unethical, the typical response is the Nuremberg defense: "I thought that this may have been wrong, but my boss told me to do it. I was just following orders."

No one should be allowed to pass the buck on ethical issues. All employees need to know that expressing ethical concerns is a key part of their job. It is never an option.

Another excuse for executing unethical decisions is "I had some concerns about this direction, but who am I to question the opinion of people that are supposed to know more than I know?" All employees need to express their concerns if the decision *may be* unethical. In many cases directives that *appear* to be unethical are just that. Even the perception of an ethics lapse can be damaging to the entire company. Therefore, employees at all levels need to take responsibility to ensure that their organization engages in ethical business practices. After all, managers cannot read their employees' minds.

Employees who are not satisfied with their manager's response to any ethical challenge should have the responsibility to take this challenge to the next level of management.

In some cases, issues that seem to involve ethical concerns may simply be the result of a misunderstanding by the employee. After a discussion with the immediate manager, the employee may feel comfortable that the decision is indeed the right thing to do. In other cases, the issue may be merely a misunderstanding of the situation by the manager. In these instances, the manager should simply reverse the decision and let the other employees know that an honest mistake was made.

If a resolution cannot be reached with the immediate manager, the employee should continue to challenge upward. This type of challenge should not be viewed as an indictment of either the manager or the employee. Honest, well-meaning people can have very different views of the ethical dilemmas that surround the same decision.

Any manager who threatens concerned employees or knowingly discourages upward challenge should be fired.

If only one employee is punished for honestly expressing ethical concerns, the word will quickly spread throughout the organization. Honest upward communication cannot be treated as an option. It needs to be a requirement. Managers at all levels need to understand that there are severe and immediate consequences for blocking the flow of vitally needed information.

Integrity violations should be cause for dismissal and have nothing to do with job performance.

One of the organizations that I respect the most has a clear rule: "All employees who knowingly lie, cheat, or steal will be immediately dismissed, regardless of their performance on the job." In this organization, every employee is taught that even the best performer, if found to have committed an ethics violation, will still be fired. They use historical case studies, illustrating how top salespeople have been dismissed for knowingly lying about small amounts of money on expense accounts. Their logic is simple— if we allow small amounts of lying, where do we draw the line? Many of the well-publicized corporate scandals happened not merely because of one event. They happened because of the creeping dishonesty that can occur when small violations are ignored and increasingly corrupt practices evolve over time.

New York City did an amazing job of reducing the city's crime rate. One of the major causes of the success was the enforcement of laws against so-called small crimes. When citizens get the message that breaking the law on minor offenses will be tolerated, their infractions begin to escalate and they become much more likely to break the law on major offenses. When citizens learn to respect all of the laws, the crime rate goes down.

As an executive coach, I have a simple guideline—don't *coach* people who commit ethics violations; *fire* people who commit ethics violations. I have been very disappointed when I have read of leaders who make up the numbers and are then given executive coaches to help them deal with ethics violations. This sends the wrong message about both the cost of integrity violations and the reason for executive coaching.

When all employees know that they will be fired, even for small ethics violations, and when all managers know they will be fired for discouraging honest upward communication, the company's ability to quickly deal with ethics concerns is greatly increased. Conversely, the company's need to deal with ethics concerns is greatly decreased.

Employees who do not feel comfortable using the normal chain of command should be provided with an alternative mechanism for upward communication.

In spite of the best corporate guidelines, the best training, and the best intent, some individual managers may still be very intimidating. All employees need a way to go around the system when they feel threatened by line management. They must be trained on how and when to use these alternate channels.

Many organizations have ombudsmen, whose sole job is to deal with concerns about ethics and values. Typically, these people do not report through the line organization but constitute a separate staff. They have the responsibility to investigate concerns while simultaneously protecting employees. In some organizations, these people have the authority to communicate directly with the board on cases that involve upper management.

By providing an alternate mechanism for upward communication, the organization helps eliminate the excuse of employees who blame their failure to communicate on intimidation from their management chain.

Managers should proactively ask for suggestions on how to improve the organization rather than passively waiting for employees to express concerns.

As Peter Drucker has said, "The leader of the past knew how to tell. The leader of the future will know how to ask."[2]

Over the past 20 years, managers have begun asking their direct reports for ideas on how things can be done better. By consistently asking for input, they create an environment that fosters open communication. If employees don't feel free to openly communicate business concerns, it is highly unlikely that they will feel free to openly communicate ethical concerns. If they have an open dialogue about business concerns, any ethical concerns will probably emerge as part of the ongoing conversation.

Both managers and employees should be trained in how to encourage and provide upward challenge.

Once the rules are in place, leaders need to be able to execute them. One organization that was a role model in turning around a poor ethical situation trained all managers in how to create an environment that encouraged upward challenge. Employees were also trained in how to challenge upward in a positive and constructive way that was designed to provide true benefit to the organization.

Providing traditional ethics training may be a waste of time for many employees. The vast majority of employees are probably ethical in the first place! They merely need to learn how to recognize potential integrity issues and effectively communicate these in a way that can prevent ethics problems.

The corporate scandals of the last few years have resulted in a lack of trust for major organizations. The conditions that led to ethics issues will not be remedied by having employees attend training programs or listen to motivational talks. Organizations that establish and implement clear processes for encouraging upward challenge can do a great deal to prevent problems involving ethics, integrity, and values. Trust is easy to lose and hard to regain. For many employees and for the public at large, it may take years of concerted effort to rebuild the credibility of large corporations. From both a business and values perspective, however, it is worth it!

NOTES

1. Marshall Goldsmith, "Ask, Learn, Follow-Up and Grow," in *The Leader of the Future,* ed. Hesselbein, Goldsmith, and Beckhard (New York: Jossey-Bass, 1996).

2. W. Warner Burke, "Some Key Examples of Knowledge Management," in *Leading Organizational Learning,* ed. Marshall Goldsmith, Howard Morgan, and Sandy Ogg (New York: Jossey-Bass, 2004).

CHAPTER 8

ENRON ET AL.

THE MARCH OF FOLLY

WARREN BENNIS

But I'd shut my eyes in the sentry box, so I didn't see nothin' wrong.

—*Rudyard Kipling*

SHORTLY AFTER the spectacular fall of Penn Central over 30 years ago, one of its directors admitted, "I don't think anybody was aware that it was that close to collapse." Around the same time, Gulf Oil's board members said that they were "clearly embarrassed" by their company's illicit payments and other criminal actions. But the embarrassment of earlier boards pales next to the shame rightfully felt by the board of directors of Enron, whose collapse has led to a stream of congressional hearings and media outrage. Unfortunately, all the sound and fury about Enron tends to obscure a more basic problem that is ubiquitous in corporate life today.

Let us deal with the board issue first. Yes, most board members still are willing dupes of management. Too many are expensive, impotent, often frustrated rubber stamps. Dogged by the constant threat of litigation, boards are selected solely by their subordinates, the company officers. They seldom understand their function and are prone to meddle too much or, more dangerously, not to meddle enough. Three of the six directors who served on Enron's auditing committee—the people responsible for double-checking Enron's bookkeeping—were ultra-busy chief executive officers (CEOs) of their own firms in the faraway locales of Hong Kong, Brazil, and the United Kingdom. You can guess how much time they had for the vigilant oversight required of an effective audit committee.

In addition to his annual director's fee of $50,000, the U.K. director, Lord Wakeham, was also pulling down $6,000 a month to advise the company "on European issues," whatever that means. And like too many other boards of directors, some of them had served too long—the chairman of the Enron audit committee since 1985. How Enron's directors could give license to the company's top executives to cash out one billion dollars in company stock when the market was at its peak and to overlook the fact that nearly 600 employees, deemed critical to Enron's operations, received more than $100 million in bonuses as late as November 2003 is simply unfathomable and probably subject to criminal litigation. In light of the magnitude of their failure, it is no surprise that so many of the directors say they are "deeply shocked" or have pleaded the Fifth Amendment.

But as I said earlier, it's not only about the boards. The Enron collapse is emblematic of a problem that is far more imbedded, more intractable, and, alas, far more universal than the tragic board failures and malfeasances of a single company. In any one case, you can always fire the CEO and top leadership, reconstitute the board, and file for bankruptcy. That's the easy part. The hard part inheres in the very nature and design of large-scale organizations, whose ethos and leadership too often create mindlessly corrupt cultures with ineffective boards and other vacant sentry boxes. Unless the leadership and the social architecture of these behemoths change, I promise you that congressional regulations will get tighter, the Securities and Exchange Commission (SEC) will get more vigilant, and the problems will get worse.

The basic difficulty in most organizations today, both public and private, is that they are created to suppress truth and transparency. Most are conveniently designed so that everyone seems to know what's wrong but nobody tells anyone else. When I consulted for the Department of State over two decades ago, I quickly learned that junior Foreign Services officers often decided not to tell their bosses what they had learned in the field because they believed the bosses would not accept it. In fact, the bosses often felt exactly the same way but kept silent for fear *their* bosses would disapprove. One State Department panjandrum told me that they gave their fledgling diplomats three rules to live by: (1) never tell a lie, (2) never tell the whole truth, and (3) never miss a chance to go to the bathroom. Think of the Challenger disaster, when most people in the know were aware that the O-Ring was problematic, but the truth never got to NASA. Unfortunately, the more tragic news is that the Columbia disaster was a vivid carbon copy of the Challenger debacle.

It is never easy speaking truth to power, but it is always vital. Look at what happened to heroic Sherron S. Watkins after she blew the whistle at Enron. Chief Financial Officer Andrew S. Fastow tried to fire her. History contains dozens of cautionary tales on the subject, perhaps none more vivid than the account of the murder of Thomas Becket. "Will no one rid me of this meddlesome priest?" Henry II is said to have muttered. The four barons who overheard Henry's grievances promptly murdered Beckett in the cathedral. Just as all the Enron subordinates and their complicit Arthur Andersen accountants later testified, the barons were "just doing what their leaders wanted them to do."

Unlike Henry II and top management at Enron, exemplary leaders reward dissent. They encourage it, listen to the bad news, and understand that whatever momentary discomfort they experience as a result is more than offset by the fact that reflective backtalk increases a leader's ability to make honorable and informed decisions.

Executive compensation should go far toward salving the pricked ego of the leader whose followers speak their minds. Perhaps the ultimate irony is that the follower who is willing to speak out shows precisely the kind of initiative that leadership is made of. It is no wonder that organizations fail when decision-making is based on feedback from yes-men. Ken Lay's real crime is not simply his myopia or cupidity or incompetence. It is his utter failure to create a viable organizational culture open to reality, his failure to institute intelligent reforms to get the truth. No organization can be honest with the public if it is not honest or straight *within*. That is Lay's cardinal sin and Enron's tragic folly.

The question remains: how did the credibility of corporate leadership fall so far so fast? The main causes were greed, dishonesty, and corporate malfeasance by a few people at the top. But one reason corporate leadership was so vulnerable in the first place was its wholesale failure to create a culture of candor.

It is not easy to welcome criticism, however honest and tactful. But the willingness to do so is one of the indispensable qualities of authentic leaders. Sidney Harman, CEO of Harman International Industries, understands that candor is key to a successful corporate enterprise. On his desk he keeps a plaque that reads, "In every business there is always someone who knows exactly what is going on. That person should be fired." The plaque is ironic, of course. Like other first-rate executives, Harman is aware that nothing is more valuable to him than the wisdom of his employees and their willingness to speak the truth to his power. Harman invites feedback and seriously weighs it. No, he doesn't always take his critics' advice. But the employees of Harman International know that their candor is not just welcomed: it is expected. In too many corporations, a dangerous kind of quietism is the norm. People know what is wrong; often, they know how to fix it; but they are afraid to speak out for fear of reprisals. Consider Hollywood mogul Samuel Goldwyn, who could garble a truth with the best of them. He once gathered his yes-men together after the studio had suffered a string of box-office flops. Then he barked, "I want you to tell me what's wrong with MGM even if it means losing your job!"

We laugh because we hear the ring of truth. The same is true of a cartoon in my growing collection of corporate gallows humor. It shows a bigwig surrounded by his underlings, proclaiming, "All those opposed, signify by saying, 'I quit.'" It is not enough, as a corporate leader, to say you want to hear the truth. You have to be ready to promise your followers a form of immunity, a promise that they won't necessarily be rewarded for their truth telling but that they will never be devalued or punished because of it either.

Few corporate leaders are willing to make that promise, and instead they create a culture of compromise. The CEO says he or she wants honest input, but the company's truth tellers are marginalized, if not driven out. The employees quickly come to understand that the CEO's call for candor is essentially Orwellian, that what he or she really wants to hear is not the truth but the half-truth that reinforces the status quo. In such an atmosphere, even the most courageous followers are not willing to do the right thing and buck the system. And yet, over and over again, we see the cost to organizations of not listening to their Cassandras.

We may love whistle-blowers in the abstract and on the screen—take Erin Brockovich, for example. But when actually confronted with someone who articulates a painful truth, corporate leaders (and leaders of other organizations as well) too often hate them. And that's almost always the organization's loss. Until the ugly headlines appear and the consequences are unavoidable, companies too often forget that they will suffer far more for ignoring their principled dissidents than by giving them a hearing. It is clearly wrong for companies to ignore an employee's warning that their new trucks are liable to explode or that their new drug has a rare but deadly side effect. But besides being wrong, the company's decision to turn away is ultimately bad business. Whatever the cost of fixing the problem now, it is almost always less than the cost of dealing with the aftermath—monetary and ethical—of exploding trucks and dying patients. Whenever I read of some company that has tried to suppress some bitter truth, I am reminded of the lines of W. H. Auden: "Every farthing the cost/All the dreaded cards foretell/Shall be paid." Where would Enron or Arthur Andersen be today if either firm had squarely faced Enron Vice President Sherron Watkins's warning about accounting irregularities, instead of exiling her to a windowless office? Wouldn't the FBI have been better off listening to Colleen Rowley or WorldCom to Cynthia Cooper? Every time a whistle-blower makes headlines, it is evidence of a leader's failure to recognize that internal dissent is not itself a crisis but, rather, priceless insurance *against* disaster.

However nettlesome, internal critics are the most valuable employees of all—the ones who keep a company honest and help preserve its most important asset, its good reputation. As a corporate leader, you can mutter to yourself about them, but ignore them at your peril. As for the candid follower, you may lose your job, but you have shown the kind of fearless integrity that is properly called leadership.

PART III

THE ROLE OF THE BOARD

As scandal after scandal broke across corporate America, legions of directors surely must have been asking themselves, "Would I have been smart enough to see this coming in time to take action and head it off?" After all, the boards at each of the troubled companies were composed of highly respected, intelligent, influential people. How did they fail so miserably to ensure that management was operating in the best interests of shareholders, employees, customers, and communities? Did they have an inadequate understanding of their fiduciary duties? Did they lose sight of whom they were charged with representing? Did they see what was going on and just look the other way?

In this section, the authors explore these and other critical questions regarding the role of the board in preventing future corporate governance transgressions. They argue that the failure of directors was, in part, due to a lack of independence and substantial equity ownership. What's more, they say that proposed legislation, had it been in place prior to the most recent wave of scandals, would not have prevented the problems plaguing corporate America today. It falls to the board to learn to recognize—and heed—warning signs that signify a catastrophe may be in the making. They offer their hard-earned knowledge to help boards take the initiative to strengthen corporate governance internally before more Draconian steps are taken to address it externally.

CHAPTER 9

SEEING AROUND CORNERS

NORMAN R. AUGUSTINE

Spotting problems before they become catastrophes is a special talent that directors have always needed and will need even more in the future.

DURING THE years I had the privilege of teaching in the engineering school at Princeton, I began the first class session of every semester by announcing that someone had invented a new product that virtually everyone in the world would want to have—a product that would create millions of new jobs and greatly improve the quality of most people's lives. Furthermore, as luck would have it, this person was seeking investors. When asked, most students expressed significant interest in investing in the endeavor (at least hypothetically—after all, they were students!). But when I added, "Oh yes, there is one other thing; his invention will kill a quarter of a million people each year," and then asked if they would still be interested in investing, no one showed any interest in such a reprehensible product. Furthermore, most said that any such product should be banned outright. I then told them that the inventor's name was Nicholas Joseph Cugnot, and his invention was the automobile.

Suppose you are a young, up-and-coming manager in a large corporation. One day, the chairman of the firm indicates that he is impressed with your work and is going to propose that you be elected to the board of directors. He goes on to say that there will be one condition: "You will always vote ex-

---

actly as I tell you." What should you do? In this case, the "you" is Herb Krannert, and his answer was simple: "I quit." The following day, six of his colleagues showed up at his front door, saying they heard what happened. They, too, had quit, and they wanted to go work for *him*. Together, they formed the Inland Container Corporation.

Corporate America has recently been faced with a number of similar ethical quandaries. As a result, it is probably safe to say that more than a few organizations have been deemed bad apples. Enron, Rite-Aid, Waste Management, Sunbeam, WorldCom, ImClone, Xerox, Tyco, Adelphia, Global Crossing, Computer Associates, Cendant . . . the list goes on. What is this trend about and why are business leaders struggling with these ethical issues?

First, it is not always easy to recognize that an issue or decision has ethical connotations. Second, even then, it is often difficult to determine the ethical thing to do. Third, even when this has been determined, acting ethically often requires superhuman fortitude. And, finally, doing the ethical thing often does not lead to the desired outcome, at least not in the short term.

The problem is not so much associated with the Ivan Boesky school of ethics—Boesky once told students at UCLA that "greed is good"—as it is with the Charlie Brown school of ethics. One day, Charlie Brown's peripatetic friend, Lucy, observes him shooting an arrow at a fence and then drawing a target around the spot where the arrow landed, with the point smack in the bull's-eye. Needless to say, Lucy becomes hysterical over Charlie's behavior. Her frame of mind is not helped when Charlie calmly explains; "But if you do it my way, you never miss." Supreme Court Justice Potter Stewart once defined ethics as "knowing the difference between what you have a right to do and what is the right thing to do."

The overwhelming majority of CEOs and directors whom I have known over the years have been competent, honorable, dedicated individuals, yet the growing list of troubled firms makes it increasingly difficult to argue that there is not a broad, even systemic problem affecting American business today. Of particular concern is the fact that the troubles of these and other firms—which go far beyond the consequences of normal business risks— have caused many individuals in other nations to question the fundamental premise of America's free enterprise system. Add to this the downward pressure on the stock market due to loss of investor confidence, the damaged reputations of CEOs and directors as a whole, and the impact on the personal lives of many employees and investors, and one has the makings of a world-class crisis.

Virtually every director in America is asking, "Had I been serving on the board of one of these companies, would I have been smart enough to have seen this coming in time to have done something about it?" The truth is that there actually are not all that many arrows in a director's quiver. However, a few of those arrows have extremely sharp points. In fact, to a very considerable extent, a director has but three principal lines of defense in protecting, as appropriate, the interests of shareholders, employees, customers, communities, and other stakeholders. First and foremost among these is the integrity of the senior management, especially the CEO, a person whom the board itself put in place. The second is the competence and diligence of the outside auditor—a firm that the board itself had the authority to put in place. And the third is the director's own knowledge and instincts.

When the first two break down, the director had better have a superhuman ability to see around corners.

AN ENLIGHTENED APPROACH

There must be consequences for wrongdoing—if for no reason other than fairness to those who do ethically and legally manage their company's affairs and to their shareholders. In cases where there is clear wrongdoing, the wrongdoers must be vigorously punished, but—and this is worth emphasizing—not their neighbors. Destroying an audit firm that provides employment to 85,000 individuals because of the misdeeds of a relatively few—coupled with a *laissez-faire* attitude on the part of senior management—seems like a case of gross overkill.

A permissive attitude admittedly seems to have pervaded much of Arthur Andersen's organization. However, it is still questionable whether the proper approach for the government was to attack the entire firm or whether the purpose of good governance would have been better served to single out those specific individuals who broke the law and punish *them*—including sending them to jail, if appropriate. It is not at all clear that it was beneficial to contribute to the destruction of an entire institution, disrupting careers and further contributing to the damage done to the savings of tens of thousands of employees, only to ferret out a few or even a few handfuls of wrongdoers. If we could, would we fire every citizen in a city whose city council has been found with its hands in the till?

Some years ago, I was asked by *Directors and Boards* to write an article projecting future corporate governance trends.[1] Many of my predictions have actually proven to be true—but in the face of today's environment, they did not go far enough.

THE PAST IS PROLOGUE

Among other things, my article suggested that very few inside directors would be allowed to sit on boards; meeting fees would be replaced with a simple retainer, augmented with some form of stock ownership; board self-assessments would become commonplace; staggered boards would pass from favor; CEOs would not sit on board committees; boards would become smaller; there would be more women, minority, and international members of boards; and much more time would be devoted to board and especially committee meetings.

The editor of the article, in a burst of prescience, chose to highlight the following passage: "As board service becomes more onerous, corporations will likely encounter increasing difficulty in finding strong board members. This, in fact, could turn out to be the preeminent problem facing the 21st Century board." Indeed, given the growing time demands of board service, the liabilities attendant thereto—not only financial but, more importantly, reputational—and the diminishing intangible benefits associated with corporate directorship, one of the principal challenges to be faced, once the dust from the current upheaval settles, will be to assure that this prediction proves incorrect. Not helpful at all are such well-intentioned but misguided ideas as providing for direct election of directors through a corporation's proxy.

THE 3-6-3 BOARD

Some years ago, reference was occasionally, if jokingly, made to the "3-6-3 board." Attributed to the banking industry, this phrase referred to the board's responsibility to set the interest rate on savings at 3 percent, on borrowing at 6 percent, and be on the golf course by 3:00 p.m. Those days, if they ever did exist, are over.

Additional changes that seem appropriate beyond those forecast in my earlier article include prohibiting many types of nonauditing work for audit clients by outside auditors (a step which has now been taken); eliminating the conflicts of interest whereby investment bankers receive a contingent fee and also provide fairness opinions on the transaction; preventing outside compensation firms from performing work for both management and the board; creating formal orientation programs conducted outside the company for new directors; mandatory expensing of stock options on the P&L statement; having much longer vesting periods for stock options; requiring far more timely reporting of related-party transactions as well as stock purchases and sales by insiders; making clear that the outside auditor works for the shareholders (via the board) and not for management; limiting the use of pro forma accounting; prohibiting financial transactions between directors and the firms they serve; and providing prison time for those who intentionally cook the books.

Unfortunately, in the current environment, it is likely that some overreactions will also take place. As Lee Iacocca once said about economy cars, "The American public wants economy so badly it will pay almost anything to get it." As important as it is to reform accounting and auditing practices, the problem is that legislation does not, and cannot, attack the root cause of most of the problems that have been encountered—only boards of directors can do that. The root problem, of course, is that a few CEOs and their subordinates have forgotten that theirs is a fiduciary responsibility and that the money isn't theirs. Every businessperson knows how to run up short-term profits (cut back on maintenance, reduce capital expenditures, eliminate research, delay accounts payable, sell assets, etc.). The issue is whether boards of directors will place such individuals in positions of authority. Clearly, the first and foremost criterion in electing a CEO is that individual's character.

It is noteworthy that many of the more constructive changes in corporate governance in America are not the consequence of new regulations or laws. For example, the Procter & Gamble board, on which I have the privilege of serving, decided a few years ago to terminate the practice of having formal presentations at its meetings—presentations which had traditionally been read to the board by an individual standing at a podium. Further, in an effort to enhance two-way discussion during these challenging times, the board decided to abandon the boardroom in which it had met for as long as anyone can remember. Instead, board meetings were held in a conference room around a relatively small table at which the speaker was also seated. Very little prepared material was presented at the meeting itself—having been provided to the directors in advance—and the actual board meeting took the form of an informal, two-way discussion increasingly focused on strategic issues and accountability. I believe that all involved would say that this more informal approach further enhanced the already very respectable quality of information exchange that took place between the company's directors and its executives.

THE NEXT SHOE TO DROP

If directors themselves do not take the initiative to appropriately strengthen corporate governance, it is likely that far more draconian steps will be imposed externally. These may include mandatory rotation of outside auditing firms every five years (indeed, the Sarbanes-Oxley Act is a start down this road with its requirement that the lead audit partner and reviewing or second partner must rotate at least every five years); the use of assigned outside auditors paid not by the corporation but by the government from a "tax" on exchanges of shares (sort of a public utility); blanket prohibition of employees moving from outside audit firms to the firms they audit; elimination of *all* activities by firms that audit public companies other than pure audit functions; prohibiting individuals from serving as directors whose employers provide legal, consulting, banking, vending, or similar services to the company; elimination of virtually all "golden parachute" severance benefits; *unqualified* certification by CEOs and CFOs that financial statements are accurate; requiring separation of the positions of CEO and chairman (a terrific idea in theory—a terrible idea in practice, except during brief transitions); biannual "licensing" of directors; imposing personal liability on directors for certain failures, such as excessive pay of executives (as is already the case for not-for-profit boards); requiring shareholders to (somehow) annually approve CEO remuneration packages; prohibition of CEOs and directors from exercising stock options until three years after retirement; and opening the proxy to direct election of board members by special interest groups.

We are already on a path where management and directors may be so occupied with documenting, certifying, approving, defending and providing depositions that they are in danger of forgetting they have a business to run.

HEEDING THE WARNING SIGNS

A principal task of a director, even given the plethora of new protective regulations, remains that of "seeing around corners." Based on my observation of many corporations over the years, including service on an independent public board addressing and seeking to prevent corporate auditing failures, clear patterns emerge when one searches for signs of impending difficulty. I have reduced these patterns to "The 50 Warning Signs," presented in a checklist format below. This collection is not derived from parchment diplomas; it is the result of scar tissue.

A fundamental question to be asked about the Sarbanes-Oxley measures and all the additional proposals now being implemented or proposed by the SEC, the New York Stock Exchange, the Business Roundtable, the Congress, and others is: would they have prevented the kind of problems which have been experienced by the firms listed earlier in this article? Unfortunately, in many cases the answer is likely to be "no." But by heeding the warning signals in the checklist, a director can certainly enhance the likelihood that problems will be spotted before they are permitted to become catastrophes. As Warren Buffett once told his son: "It takes years to build a reputation—and five minutes to ruin it. If you think about that, you'll do things differently."

MANAGING BUSINESS RISK

50 Warning Signs of Impending Trouble

1. Management with questionable ethical standards
2. Arrogant, autocratic, or highly risk-taking management
3. Start-up business or recent rapid growth

4. New products or processes
5. Recent mergers, acquisitions or impending plans to sell business
6. Operations or investments in politically/economically unstable countries
7. Business in fields of rapid technological advancement
8. History of management turnover
9. Recent reorganization
10. High financial leverage; demanding covenants
11. High multiple; volatile stock price
12. Declining margins
13. Speculative investments in facilities or inventories to support future growth or evidence of starvation of reinvestment
14. Large off-balance-sheet debt or transactions; failure to appropriately expense costs
15. Declining market demand; small or declining market share
16. Aggressive financial positions (leveraged derivatives, futures, etc.)
17. Inadequate reserves or history of misapplying reserves (e.g., smoothing earnings)
18. Hazardous processes or products
19. Inadequate insurance
20. Highly regulated business
21. Significant insider stock sales, imminent vesting date for options
22. Dependence on few suppliers, customers or products
23. Lack of formal delegations of authority
24. Weak, changing, or unverified control systems, especially IT
25. Diversification into new markets or geographical locations
26. Business characterized by episodic major events
27. Activities (including past acquisitions) affecting the natural environment
28. Significant pending litigation
29. Lack of successors for key employees
30. Poor or deteriorating credit rating
31. Frequent nonrecurring events; end-of-quarter or complex booking of revenues
32. Large fixed-price contracts, especially R&D
33. Militant labor force
34. Susceptibility to natural disasters

35. Weak or untested management; management with spotty track record
36. Outside directors who do not meet alone on regular basis
37. Vulnerability to fraud
38. Inadequate cash resources; consuming cash
39. Subject to external events outside control of management
40. High public visibility
41. Lack of internal checks and balances
42. Significant near-term debt payments
43. More than one or two inside directors; CEO selects directors; large board
44. Assets vulnerable to devaluation; frequent write-offs
45. Disputes with outside auditors or recent change of auditors
46. Restated or obscure financial reports; dependence on pro forma accounting
47. Excessively paid executives; unreasonable financial goals
48. Related party or subsidiary transactions, family ownership
49. Prolonged financial growth mismatches (e.g., revenue without cash, inventory without revenues, receivables without revenues, depreciation without investment, maintenance backlog without revenue, deferred payables)
50. CEO or CFO unexpectedly left "to pursue personal interests"

SCORE: 5 or less: It's time to wake up; *6 to 10:* You're headed for trouble; *11 to 15:* You're already in trouble; *16 to 19:* You're already in deep trouble; *20 or more:* Check your D&O insurance.

A MODEST PROPOSAL

I would like to put forward a modest proposal for the future of corporate governance involving the following five components:

Pricing Stock Options

The "strike price" of stock options would be escalated each year by the percentage realizable from an investment in Treasury bills. An investor does not need the management of corporate America to realize the (risk-free) return offered by Treasury bills. Thus, management should be rewarded only in relation to the amount by which their corporation's performance exceeds risk-free returns. Similarly, the vesting period should be considerably longer than is the current practice for most companies. In addition, senior executives exercising options should be paid in restricted shares not exercisable for three years.

Long-Term Capital Gains

To reduce the pressure on executives to chase short-term profits and—importantly—to permit American industry to take a sounder, longer-term perspective, the capital gains tax rate should be revised so as to be inversely proportional to the period in which the investment producing the gain is held. The actual tax rate schedule could, if desired, be made revenue-neutral, but a substantial tax would be imposed on very short-term gains and a minimal tax, if any, on very long-term gains.

Pension Funds

Corporate pension funds should no longer be permitted to hold shares of the "parent" company's securities. Although very plausible arguments can be made that holding stock in the company provides a significant incentive to employees, it also increases their vulnerability in times of business reversals to the loss of their jobs and their pensions simultaneously.

Banker Conflicts

Investment banking firms advising management on mergers and acquisitions should no longer be permitted to provide fairness opinions on transactions in which they are involved. Similarly, firms providing advice to boards on executive (and board!) compensation should either be precluded from doing work for management or a second consulting firm should be retained to provide an independent "check" on executive and board compensation.

Annual Meetings

Annual meetings should be recognized for what they are: an anachronism of corporate democracy. Typically, when an annual meeting is called to order, 80 percent of the votes have already been cast and are safely in the chairman's pocket. Furthermore, 99 percent of the discussion time is usurped by individuals holding less than 1 percent of the shares and the majority of topics raised are either outside the purview of the corporation (for example, U.S. policy regarding, say, South Africa) or are not germane to the forum in the first place (for example, consumers with complaints or union representatives seeking to negotiate collective bargaining agreements). Annual meetings are extremely costly in terms of both money and management time, are often nonsubstantive, and are rarely even attended by most shareholders, certainly not major shareholders.

Although there will be those who view these quasi-charades called annual meetings as the price of corporate democracy, there may be a better means to achieve sound governance still in a democratic fashion. An alternative would be for shareholders to submit to the corporation's outside auditor those questions to which the shareholders would like to have management provide a considered response. The outside auditor would then consolidate those questions, eliminate duplication and the frivolous, and submit the resulting questions to management, which in turn would provide formal written responses on the Internet, by snail mail, or both to all shareholders. Shareholder proposals would continue to be handled much as is the case today but would be provided in time to impact any questions shareholders may wish to submit. Such an approach would provide a more efficient, constructive, and informative manner to engage in corporate democracy than the current annual meetings.

THE BOTTOM LINE

While all the oversight, regulations, and best practices in the world can be helpful in ensuring sound corporate governance, in the end, one must have executives who are ethical, who possess a strong moral compass, and who understand that they have merely been entrusted on a temporary basis with the care of a firm that does not belong to them. Peter Drucker put it this way: "What executives do, what they believe in and value, what they reward and whom, are watched, seen, and minutely interpreted throughout the whole organization. And nothing is noticed more quickly—and considered more significant—than a discrepancy between what executives preach and what they expect their associates to practice."

NOTE

1. Norman Augustine, "The 20th Century Company Meets the 21st Century Board," *Directors and Boards,* Fall 1996.

CHAPTER 10

WHITHER GOVERNANCE

PROCESS OR PEOPLE?

WILLIAM W. GEORGE

WE LIVE in a post-Enron era of governance, characterized by Sarbanes-Oxley and a myriad of governance rules and regulations. The board of every publicly held company is working feverishly to ensure that it is in compliance with these new regulations and can escape the long arm of the Securities and Exchange Commission.

But will that solve the governance problems that became so evident in the wake of the corporate scandals of 2001–2003?

CHANGES IN GOVERNANCE PROCESSES: NECESSARY BUT NOT SUFFICIENT

My contention is that these process changes to board governance were a necessary but not sufficient condition to bring the governance of publicly held corporations to the level required to ensure their long-term viability and their capacity to create lasting value for all their stakeholders.

Long before the downfall of the House of Enron, it was evident that corporate boards were not fulfilling their responsibilities. They were ceding far too much power and authority to their elected chief executive officers (CEOs) and not providing even the minimum amount of oversight, supervision, and control. In a rising stock market, many boards became very lax in fulfilling their fiduciary responsibilities to shareholders. Often the directors were the last to know that their companies were getting in deep trouble. Regardless of whether they were technically independent, the actions of many boards strongly suggested that they viewed themselves more as subordinates or peers of their CEOs than as supervisors. Their role devolved in supporting strong-willed CEOs as long as the stock price was up. In the market boom of the 1990s it was pretty hard for it *not* to be up.

So we got what we deserved: a very detailed piece of legislation, hastily thrown together, that potentially criminalizes a myriad of board actions that used to fall into the realm of considered judgment. Actually, the tenets of Sarbanes–Oxley are quite sound, as the bill codifies the best practices of our best-performing boards. The problem, as it often is in federal legislation, is that the detailed rules required to put those tenets into place often result in cumbersome and highly bureaucratic procedures to ensure their proper implementation. Not infrequently, these rules produce unintended consequences that defeat the very purpose of the legislation in the first place.

Unfortunately, many boards today are behaving like box tickers, merely wanting to ensure that all the provisions of the law are covered so they can escape the long arm of the Securities and Exchange Commission and stay out of jail. Not only is this approach time-consuming and of questionable value, but it distracts them from the essence of good governance.

At the same time, board members are being influenced by a myriad of self-appointed governance gurus, who are just agitating for additional regulations, often in response to their own particular pet peeves. Several of these so-called gurus generate their income by first rating boards and then charging them consulting fees to get their ratings up. Most have never served on a board themselves, however, so they haven't observed how one behaves when it goes into executive session. For them, it is difficult—if not impossible—to tell an effective board from an ineffective one, because they are merely looking at ratings forms that tell little or nothing about their internal workings.

At this stage, further governance regulations will likely be counterproductive. Even the best boards will begin to see themselves as under siege from the outside. As a result, they will circle the wagons—by going through the motions of meeting external requirements, but not stepping up to their real responsibilities within the boardroom.

BUILDING AN EFFECTIVE BOARD

The primary difference between effective boards and ineffective ones is the attitude of the directors who sit on them and their relationship to the CEO. If we are ever to have strong corporate governance, we need a group of highly experienced, diverse, and wise independent directors governing the corporation on behalf of its long-term owners. They must fully accept the fact that it is they—not the CEOs—who are ultimately responsible for the preservation, governance, and direction of the corporation. Such an engaged group of directors recognizes the clear distinction between governance and management. When a powerful CEO amalgamates these roles into a single modus operandi, inevitably it is governance that suffers, with the board assuming a role that is subordinate to the CEO. No amount of processes, procedures, and laws can change this reality, as it is impossible to legislate integrity, stewardship, and good governance.

To ensure proper governance, these independent directors must elect a leader who can get them organized, focus them on the most crucial issues, and provide a power balance with the CEO. Executive sessions are critical, as they provide the opportunity for candid discussions with the CEO, ranging from the state of the business to honest assessments of key people in the organization. Executive sessions without the CEO are valuable, too, as they give directors the opportunity to raise issues that are too sensitive to discuss with the CEO, such as the length of his or her tenure and the adequacy of likely succession candidates.

Another crucial issue facing independent directors is the building of a diverse board, the evaluation of fellow board members, and the selection of new directors. Granted, the CEO should take part in this dialogue, but in the end the selection of new directors must be the board's decision, just as questions of CEO succession must be undertaken by the independent directors acting on their own.

It is also essential that boards have clear criteria for the departure of their members at a specified age or years of service. Without these criteria, boards tend to age and often become complicit with the CEO, as they lose their energy for challenging management about its performance. They also make it virtually impossible to bring the kind of new blood into the boardroom that will make both the board and the management more effective, in spite of their lack of experience.

THE TRAGIC CASE OF THE DISNEY BOARD

In recent years, the Disney board has come under increasing criticism for being poorly governed. There has been much focus on the independence of the directors themselves, as well as the selection and compensation of Michael Ovitz during his brief, ill-fated tenure as Disney's chief operating officer. To their credit, CEO Michael Eisner and the Disney board have undertaken a concerted effort to strengthen the board and improve its governance, appointing former U.S. Senator George Mitchell as board chair.

Unfortunately, the board has still not faced up to the essential issue—what some call the elephant on the table that no one likes to talk about—the fact that the Disney board has been unwilling to provide succession for the CEO. Eisner's first 15 years as CEO were outstanding, and shareholders were big beneficiaries of his leadership. Had he turned over the reins to a qualified successor back in 1999, he would have gone down in history as one of Disney's truly outstanding leaders. Now, after serving 20 years as CEO, Eisner still has no successor in sight, and an astounding 43 percent of shareholders withheld their votes from Eisner's reelection as CEO at the 2004 annual meeting.

Sadly, the last five years have erased many of Eisner's early gains, resulting in a rupture on the board, with directors Roy Disney and Stanley Gold resigning in protest. It appears that the Disney board committed the cardinal sin of placing its loyalty to the CEO above the interests of the institution itself. As a result, the company is highly vulnerable to the hostile takeover attempt by Comcast. It's sad to say, but Disney, that great American icon, may not survive as an independent organization.

Two other American icons—Boeing and the New York Stock Exchange—faced similar situations during 2003, with their boards supporting powerful CEOs through a series of mishaps. Fortunately, in both cases, committed board members stepped up to the plate and replaced their CEOs with outstanding leaders like Harry Stonecipher at Boeing and John Thain at the stock exchange.

CREATING BOARD CHEMISTRY

Effective boards are able to create chemistry among their directors and with the CEO that enables them to engage in honest discussions and have sharp disagreements between their members, without those differences becoming personal. They are comfortable in challenging their CEOs in a way that helps management do its job better. In turn, the CEO responds by actively involving them in important decisions and using them as valuable counselors in deciding the crucial issues facing the company. These kinds of healthy debates and disagreements not only prepare boards to cope with inevitable crises but also help them get through them successfully.

So how does an organization go about building this kind of chemistry? The first requirement is a group of independent directors that are committed to good governance and who accept their full responsibilities to the shareholders and other stakeholders. The second essential is a CEO who truly wants to use the board to its fullest in order to build lasting value in the corporation. While it is true that CEOs can do a great deal to facilitate the chemistry of the board, they also can make it nearly impossible to have an open dialogue among board members, except when the board meets in executive session without the CEO's presence.

I continue to be amazed at the number of CEOs who want their boards to be rubber-stamp supporters rather than honest advisors. What a waste of time and talent! Ironically, the loser in this kind of situation is the CEO himself or herself. Without sound advice, however, many CEOs pursue their own egos and interests, rather than operating in the best interests of the company. Or, worse yet, as they gain time in the CEO's chair, they start to think that *they* are the company. The result is decline and ultimate disaster for them, as well as their boards and shareholders.

TOWARD A NEW PROFESSIONAL CLASS: THE PROFESSIONAL DIRECTOR

In the wake of the corporate scandals—followed by new regulations, such as Sarbanes-Oxley—many people are predicting that no one will want to serve as a corporate director. Regardless of whether or not this is true, we need to redefine the role of the board member and then begin earnestly developing a new professional class—that of the professional director.

Over the past two decades, CEOs and boards of directors have been eager to fill their boards with sitting CEOs. Their rationale was that the more sitting CEOs you had on your board—preferably from the largest, most prestigious companies—the higher status your board had and the easier it would be to attract other CEOs to your board. Consequently, a number of CEOs served on half a dozen or more corporate boards during their time in office.

Many boards had a policy that when CEOs stepped down from their position, they were obliged to resign from the board. Not surprisingly, many CEOs—faced with losing both their jobs and their prestigious board seats— fought to hang on to their chief executive position well past their prime, often into their late sixties. These days, however, sitting CEOs realize they simply do not have the time to serve on more than one outside board. Some, like Jeff Immelt of GE and Lee Scott of Wal-Mart, have neither the time nor the inclination to serve on any boards other than their own. Do the math and you will quickly discover that it is virtually impossible for a majority of organizations to have several CEOs on their board.

The declining tenure of CEOs and the large number of senior executives taking early retirement means there are many outstanding former business executives fully qualified to serve on corporate boards. By distancing themselves from their full-time jobs, they will be able to offer a broader perspective, greater objectivity, and increased wisdom to both the CEO and their fellow board members.

I am *not* advocating adding a horde of retired executives to boards to round out their twilight years. The last thing boards need is a group of backward-looking retirees that are entrenched in the ways of the past. But the executives just described are hardly retired; they have just moved on to the next phase of their careers. The ones with whom I have served are vital, engaged executives who are completely committed to the companies on whose boards they serve and are fully up to speed on the latest thinking about new directions in business.

Add to this group a rapidly growing number of qualified board members from a diverse set of backgrounds—ranging from academics, nonprofit executives, and venture capitalists to former government officials—and you have the makings of a whole new class of professional directors. When a board has this kind of diversity, its perspectives typically are broader and more thoughtful and the board is able to anticipate future trends and problems. As a result, it is able to keep the corporation from going down the wrong path and avoid the many pitfalls we have seen from boards of similar backgrounds engaged in a fraternal collegiality that leads to groupthink.

DIRECTOR EDUCATION

The legal responsibilities of board members are changing regularly, and most directors do not fully understand their fiduciary duties, even when it comes to the basics, like the duty of care and the duty of loyalty. As an integral part of developing a professional class of directors, therefore, board members should be required to attend a certified director education course both at the time they join their first board and every three years thereafter. There is no official certification at present, but such a process would be highly beneficial in order to help directors distinguish between the superficial, 24-hour courses popping up all over and the more substantive ones. Of course, this kind of education takes time, but if directors are serious about their responsibilities, they should be eager to engage in the intellectual learning process, just as they would for any other profession.

If we are to develop and attract a new class of directors that are not dependent on their full-time jobs for compensation, travel, and perquisites, then professional directors should be well compensated for their time and efforts. They are the elected representatives of the shareholders, after all, and as such they are often responsible for many billions of dollars of market value. Reasonable compensation, rather than just a token amount, should make them take those responsibilities very seriously. Look at it this way: what would it have been worth to the shareholders of WorldCom to have a serious group of directors that was able to preserve the $160 billion value of that enterprise, rather than letting a runaway CEO lead it into bankruptcy? I seriously doubt that a group of professional directors would ever have approved a $400 million "loan" for the CEO to buy land in Canada.

This new class of professional directors will be dedicated to building the lasting value of the corporation on behalf of the shareholders, rather than being part of the managerial club dedicated to supporting the CEO. For their part, progressive CEOs will welcome a board of honest, thoughtful, committed advisors, as they will be of invaluable assistance in enabling them to be successful. Of course, the ultimate beneficiaries will be the long-term shareholders whom the board is elected to serve in the first place.

CHAPTER 11

ENRON AND EFFECTIVE CORPORATE GOVERNANCE

CHARLES M. ELSON

THE BANKRUPTCY of the famed Enron Corporation was a seminal business event, as rarely does such a large and well-positioned company fail. It's also proven a watershed event in American corporate law and governance, inspiring numerous reforms in the corporate legal and regulatory regimes. The seminal question, however—and the one critical to understanding the reforms—is why did the company collapse or, more directly, who is responsible for this failure and what could have been done to have avoided it?

A number of commentators have concentrated on the failure of the gatekeepers—those objective outside monitors, such as auditors, rating agencies, and investment analysts—who either acquiesced in, did little to prevent, or altogether missed the problematic activity of management that led to the collapse.[1] It's been suggested that reforming the conduct and structure of these gatekeepers is necessary not only to prevent a repeat of Enron, but also to restore public confidence in the financial markets.

Clearly, the outside monitors failed miserably in their responsibilities. They were either incredibly negligent or sufficiently co-opted by Enron management to have lost all objectivity and efficacy. While creating better outside monitors may be helpful, the real key to the prevention of Enron-type scandals rests in the hands of the inside monitors—the company's directors—for they are in the best position to observe management. The secret, however, lies in making them both objective and engaged. But how?

This is where an examination of classical corporate governance theory becomes relevant and helpful. Under traditional theory, the board acts as an active management monitor for shareholder benefit. It not only decides when to engage and when to terminate a management team, but also acts to provide supportive management oversight between these two points. The concepts of independence and equity are central to this active monitoring. To fulfill their oversight responsibilities effectively, directors must be holders of a personally meaningful equity stake in the enterprise and remain independent of management.

Independence—the absence of any economic ties to management or the company itself other than equity ownership—provides a director with the distance and objectivity necessary to examine management action in the most effective manner. Economic relationships with management, including consulting, service provision, or other indirect arrangements, may cloud judgment and make it more difficult to review management conduct objectively. A lack of independence leads to ineffective monitoring because it makes a director either too comfortable with management and its representations, or due to relational concerns, unable to effectively disengage to objectively review management conduct. A good distance from company management allows the kind of reflective review of management conduct that is expected by public shareholders and necessary to long-term corporate success.

Independence is not only important for its impact on director conduct, but for management activity as well. The watchwords are accountability and responsibility. All of us must need to feel accountable to someone. Responsibility to a watchful intermediary spurs thoughtful decision making and reflection on management's part. However, this cannot occur unless the intermediary is independent of the examined party. This is why the concept of the independent board is so critical to modern governance theory.

While independence promotes objectivity, the board also must have an incentive to exercise that objectivity effectively. Granting board members equity ownership in the corporation may help achieve this goal. Therefore, modern governance theory emphasizes the need for directors to hold an equity stake in the corporation. When directors have no stake in the enterprise other than their board seats, there is simply no personal pecuniary incentive to engage in the active monitoring of management. As they shirk their duty to monitor management actively, stockholder interests are left unprotected. The most effective way to incentivize directors to address their responsibilities from the perspective of the shareholders is to make them stockholders as well. Thus, they, too, assume a personal stake in the success or failure of the enterprise. As active equity participants, they have an incentive to monitor management's performance more effectively, since poor monitoring may have a direct negative impact upon their personal financial interests.

Of course, where stock ownership is insubstantial compared to the other private benefits associated with being a director, the motivational impact is bound to be minimal. In many large public corporations, for example, outside directors have a nominal equity stake in the company, but receive far more substantial compensation in the form of annual fees—which often exceed $90,000—in exchange for attendance at a few board meetings per annum. Such a compensation system, of course, is wholly inadequate to promote the kind of personal incentive necessary to create an active board.

To have any sort of favorable impact on director behavior, the amount of stock that each director holds must be substantial. Therefore, director fees should be paid primarily in restricted company stock to align director and shareholder interests and promote effective monitoring. It is important to note that while equity ownership provides the incentive to monitor, it alone does not provide the proper objectivity to foster effective oversight. Independence creates this objectivity and that is why modern governance theory demands both equity ownership and independence. Independent directors without equity ownership may be objective, but they have little incentive to engage in active oversight. Equity ownership provides the incentive to exercise objective oversight. On the other hand, equity-holding directors who are not independent may have the proper incentive, but lack the necessary objectivity. Independence and equity ownership, acting in tandem, are the keys to effective corporate governance.

But how does this emphasis on director independence and equity relate to the board failure at Enron? The answer is most straightforward. The

Enron directors lacked independence from management. They may have held company equity, but without the appropriate independence from Enron management, they lacked the necessary objectivity to perceive the numerous and significant warning signals that should have alerted them to the alleged management malfeasance that led to the company's ultimate meltdown and failure.

These signs included five specific concerns that should have induced greater board probing of management initiatives. The first involved the management's request that the board waive, on two specific occasions, the company's code of ethics that prohibited officer conflict of interest transactions. The now infamous waivers allowed the debt-shifting, off-balance-sheet transactions that were allegedly designed to hide the company's true precarious financial situation from investors. The second warning signal involved massive sales of company stock by numerous high-level insiders. Management stock sales are never viewed as a good sign of the company's future prospects and they should have alerted the board to potential problems.

The third, fourth, and fifth signals involved the company's auditors—Arthur Andersen. Initially, Andersen had been engaged as Enron's external auditor. Its role expanded dramatically, however. Operating in a climate dominated by numerous authorities, including the chairman of the Securities and Exchange Commission, calling for substantial reform of the auditor/company relationship—Enron's affiliation with Andersen was problematic in several respects. In addition to its role as Enron's auditor, Andersen was also providing substantial amounts of consulting to the company, in one year billing approximately $27,000,000 for such services. As this was occurring, substantial criticism was being directed at this sort of auditor consulting, as it was argued that this led to compromised audits.

In addition to providing external auditing services, Andersen was also functioning as the company's internal auditor. This kind of activity also faced great criticism, as it was argued that commingling these two oversight responsibilities—internal and external audit—would compromise the effectiveness of both. Finally, senior members of the Enron finance department had been hired directly from Arthur Andersen. This practice, too, had been critiqued on the grounds that it had the potential of creating unwelcome pressure on the external auditor because of the relationships that existed between former and present firm employees.

These five warning signals, obvious to an outsider, were all missed by the Enron board. Had the directors asked questions about these actions, perhaps they would have discovered and responded appropriately to the management misdeeds that hastened the company's collapse. So why did the board miss these signs? They were a highly respected, intelligent, and influential group. What went so wrong to have rendered them ineffective proximate monitors? Simply stated, they lacked the appropriate independence from management to have the objectivity to appreciate the severity of the warnings that they were receiving.

Despite the fact that they were technically outsiders, a large number of Enron directors had financial or quasi-financial relationships with the company and its management that compromised their independence and consequent objectivity. Several directors had consulting relationships with the company for which they were well compensated. Others were officers of charitable organizations that were the beneficiaries of significant donations from Enron or members of its management. Some had business dealings with the company. A few had been directors for so many years that their board seats appeared to have become company-sponsored sinecures. Under the existing Securities and Exchange Commission or New York Stock Exchange requirements, most of these directors still would have been classified as independent. In reality, however, they were not, at least not in the sense that corporate governance theorists would consider appropriate.

Independence requires that there be no significant financial relationships with the company or its management. The problem with these types of relationships is that they compromise one's objectivity. They create a bond with company management that makes it more difficult to review management's actions objectively and dispassionately. That is what happened to the Enron directors. Their relationships with company management created a comfort level that made it possible for them to simply explain away or miss completely the various warning signs before them. Their independence deficit did not necessarily make them bad actors, only much less sensitive ones and, as such, wholly ineffective.

The lesson of Enron is not that inside monitors can never be effective or that reliance on an outside monitor is more appropriate. The failure of their directors was not due to their position within the organization, but to their lack of both independence and substantial equity ownership. After all, independence allows for objectivity, and equity provides the incentive to exercise that objectivity and ultimately protect shareholders' value. Had Enron's directors heeded this lesson, the company's fate—and its shareholders' fortunes—could have been very different indeed.

NOTES

More comprehensive versions of this chapter have appeared in the WAKE FOREST LAW REVIEW, Volume 38, p. 855 (2003) and the CORNELL LAW REVIEW, Volume 89, p. 496 (2004).

1. See John C. Coffee, Jr., *What Caused Enron?: A Capsule Social and Economics History of the 1990s*, 89 CORNELL L. REV. 269 (2004) (describing the role of corporate gatekeepers during the 1990s), and Jonathan R. Macey, *Efficient Capital Markets, Corporate Disclosure, and Enron*, 89 CORNELL L. REV. 394 (2004) (describing the different types of objective monitors and their roles).

CHAPTER 12

"SOMEBODY'S GOTTA KEEP AN EYE ON THESE GENIUSES"

WHAT WE MUST DO TO RESTORE OWNERS' CAPITALISM

JOHN CLIFTON BOGLE

THE EARLY years of the twenty-first century have not been happy ones for capitalism. Beginning with Enron in October 2001, scandals involving some of America's largest corporations have come to light. By September of 2003, they had spread to the mutual fund industry. But while these scandals are of relatively recent vintage, the underlying forces that led to them go back a decade or more. Indeed, since at least 1990 I've been challenging mutual fund America to improve its principles and practices, and, later on, challenging corporate America to return to its proud traditional roots. In one sense, it's easy for an insider with long experience in both areas to throw down the gauntlet, but in another sense, it's not so easy. Challenging the values and practices of longtime, well-respected colleagues is not the best way to win friends and influence people. And when the voice is lonely, it is easy to wonder whether it is ringing true. But now that so much that was hidden is out in the open, the facts speak for themselves.

CORPORATE GOVERNANCE— THE HEART OF THE ISSUE

Corporate governance is at the heart of the issues facing both corporate America and mutual fund America. As James Madison said about our Constitution, "If men were angels, no government would be necessary." Similarly, if business executives were angels, no corporate governance would be necessary. Even as our nation is not a *democracy,* controlled directly by its citizens, neither is the American corporation. Even approvals of corporate resolutions by shareholders are nonbinding, after all. Rather, like our nation, the corporation is a *republic.* While supreme power resides with its shareholders, they exercise their power through directors, whom they have elected to represent their ownership interests.

During the 1990s, our system of corporate governance broke down. Too many boards failed to adequately exercise their responsibilities to oversee management, and rare was the institutional investor that exercised its responsibilities of corporate citizenship and demanded that oversight. When the owners of corporate America don't care about governance, who on earth *should* care?

So what's to be done? Writing in *The New Yorker* a few months ago, business columnist James Surowiecki gave us an amusing but perceptive answer. He used the example of the 1956 comedy *The Solid Gold Cadillac,* in which Judy Holliday played Laura Partridge, a small investor whose continual harassment of the board finally gets the company to put her on the payroll as its first director of investor relations. She quickly uses the position to organize a shareholder revolt that topples the corrupt chief executive officer (CEO). As Surowiecki concludes, "American companies are the most productive and inventive in the world, but a little adult supervision (by the owners) wouldn't hurt. Laura Partridge had it right a half a century ago: 'Somebody's gotta keep an eye on these geniuses.'"

Under our governance system, the board of directors is the first "somebody" to hold management responsible for representing the interests of shareholders. And when the directors don't fulfill that responsibility, the second "somebody"—the shareholders themselves—must hold them accountable. Shareholder involvement in corporate governance can provide the "adult supervision" required to move us away from the existing system of Managers' Capitalism that we never should have allowed to come into existence in the first place. Thus, we can return to Owners' Capitalism, a system in which trusting and being trusted created a virtuous circle of progress.

What Went Wrong in Corporate America?

The fact of the matter is that something has gone profoundly wrong with the very system that we have come to know as American capitalism. The root causes of the disease are deep, and the remedies that are required to cure it will not be easy to come by. From what we have witnessed, the failure of corporate governance in America has been, in the words of journalist William Pfaff, "a pathological mutation in capitalism." He was right on the mark. The classic system—Owners' Capitalism—had been based on a dedication to serving the interests of the corporation's owners, maximizing the return on their capital investment. But a new system developed—Managers' Capitalism—in which "the corporation came to be run to profit its managers, in complicity if not conspiracy with accountants and the managers of other corporations." Why did it happen? "Because," says Mr. Pfaff, "the markets had so diffused corporate ownership that no responsible owner exists. This is morally unacceptable, but also a corruption of capitalism itself."

That transmogrification—that grotesque transformation—of a system of Owners' Capitalism into a system of Managers' Capitalism required only two ingredients: (1) the diffusion of corporate ownership among a large number of investors, none holding a controlling share of the voting power; and (2) the unwillingness of the agents of the owners—the boards of directors—to honor their responsibility to serve, above all else, the interests of their principals—the share owners themselves.

When most owners either don't, won't, or can't stand up for their rights, and when directors lose sight of whom they represent, the resulting power vacuum quickly gets filled by corporate managers. This is living proof that Spinoza was right when he told us, "Nature abhors a vacuum." Little good is likely to result when the CEO becomes not only the boss of the business but also the boss of the board, erasing the bright line that common sense tells us ought to exist between management and governance. Put more harshly, "When we have strong managers, weak directors, and passive owners, don't be surprised when the looting begins."

Adam Smith, that patron saint of capitalism, would not have been surprised by this outcome. More than two centuries ago, he wrote: "It cannot be well expected that the directors of companies, being the managers rather of other people's money than of their own, should watch over it with the same anxious vigilance with which partners in a private copartnery frequently watch over their own. Like the stewards of a rich man, they . . . very easily give themselves a dispensation. Negligence and profusion must always prevail."

THE PRESCIENCE OF ADAM SMITH

Adam Smith's words presciently describe corporate America in the recent era. While the actual known looting has been limited, negligence and profusion have indeed prevailed, and the managers have given themselves "dispensations" that would have appalled the thrifty Scot. We've all heard that the malfeasance in our capitalistic system has been confined to just "a few bad apples." In the context of our tens of thousands of corporate executives and Wall Street leaders, that's doubtless true. But the fact is that the very barrel that holds all of those apples, good and bad alike, has itself developed some considerable faults and is in need of major rehabilitation.

Ironically, it is the scandals exposed by the malfunction of American capitalism—the acknowledged bad apples—that have exposed the weaknesses in the system—the barrel. Consider the staggering levels of compensation that we pay our chief executives. The compensation of the average CEO has risen from 42 times that of the average worker in 1980 to an astonishing 420 times in 2001, an extraordinary increase in the portion of corporate earnings that corporate managers have arrogated to themselves.

From 1988 to 2001, the annual compensation of the average CEO rose 443 percent, from $2,025,000 to $11,000,000, while the compensation of the average worker rose 60 percent from $16,700 to $26,700—in real terms, virtually no increase at all. It would be one thing if this quantum increase in executive compensation were justified by corporate achievement, but that's simply not the case. During this period, executives promised investors earnings growth averaging 12 percent per year. However, they delivered growth of only 3.5 percent (0.5 percent in real terms)—even less than the 5.5 percent nominal annual growth in our nation's gross domestic product for that period. It's difficult to see any evidence in these figures that could possibly justify the outrageous riches that have been bestowed on our corporate leaders.

Much of that compensation increase was fueled by executive stock options. While options are almost universally described as linking the interests of management to the interests of shareholders, the fact is that they do no such thing. They are a lottery-like giveaway that focuses on easily manipulated stock price, not hard-to-come-by corporate value. They ignore dividends and reflect no cost of capital. Rather than holding onto their shares, executives typically sold them at the earliest moment, often without putting up a penny (cashless exercise). The very structure of the fixed-price stock option was fatally flawed, used to the exclusion of more rational option forms because these options did not appear as a cost in the company's income statement. Indeed, some consultants describe such options as "free."

The Beauty of Scandal— Bad Apples Illuminate Bad Barrels

Striking as they do at the heart of our capitalistic system, the corporate scandals of the recent era are unpleasant to witness. But even as it's an ill wind that blows no good, the bright spotlight of public attention that shines on a major scandal also illuminates all the nibbling around the edges of ethical practice that, were it not for the scandal, would persist indefinitely. The fact is that we owe a certain perverse kind of debt to the fallen idols of capitalism—the bad apples who illuminate the weakened barrel—as these examples suggest:

- *Kenneth Lay, Jeffrey Skilling, and Andrew Fastow* presided over the collapse of Enron, revealing a whole panoply of financial engineering that quickly turned to fraud. But Enron's bankruptcy also turned the spotlight on the profound failings of a blue-chip board ("America's Third Best Board," according to *Chief Executive* magazine), the co-option of its accounting and consulting firm, and the active participation of its bankers in deals of dubious validity.
- *Bernard Ebbers,* CEO of the now-bankrupt WorldCom, gained his fame when the firm cooked the books with an $11 billion accounting scandal. His demise also revealed that he had borrowed a stunning $408 million from WorldCom so as to avoid selling his shares to meet margin calls. Fortunately, the Sarbanes-Oxley Act now bans corporate loans to executives.

- *William Esrey and Ronald LeMay* of Sprint gained the spotlight with their $290 million in option compensation, paid to reward them for a merger that was never even consummated. Their subsequent attempt to dodge taxes through an allegedly illegal tax shelter also raised the issue of collusion by the independent auditor in executive compensation.

- *Dennis Kozlowski,* the CEO of Tyco, gained his first unwelcome attention for a clumsy attempt to illegally evade state sales taxes on $13 million of art purchases. That controversy was quickly followed by disclosure of the $2 million Roman-themed party given in Sardinia for his wife's birthday, which included the now-famous ice statue of Michelangelo's David exuding vodka. But the spotlight on those events quickly illuminated a classic case of a manager confusing the shareholders' money with his own, as he allegedly looted Tyco and its shareholders of $600 million.

- *Jack Welch* of General Electric (GE) gained an equally unwelcome spotlight for his extramarital peccadilloes. His divorce proceedings illuminated the largely undisclosed stealth compensation typically awarded to retired chief executives but rarely disclosed. While his total compensation as GE's CEO seems to have exceeded $1 billion, his lavish retirement benefits included a New York apartment with daily flower deliveries and wine, unlimited use of the company jet, and a nice retirement stipend of $734,000 . . . *per month.*

- *Richard Grasso,* chairman of the New York Stock Exchange, made news with the staggeringly large compensation package ($187.5 million) bestowed on him by those he regulated. But the spotlight also illuminated the salutary, if not explosive, effects of disclosure, as well as the Big Board's flawed system of governance and the near-monopoly it maintains for its specialists and member firms.

While there are lots of other bad apples in corporate America, these six examples should be enough to make the point that the scandals of the past two years have brought into sharp relief the painfully broad and baneful impact of Managers' Capitalism and the financial shenanigans that it fomented.

What Did the Directors Know?

When executives are paid based on the appreciation in the momentary price of a stock (*perception*) rather than the enhancement of the intrinsic value of a corporation (*reality*), the temptation for management to hype stock prices is apparently overwhelming. So we quickly developed concepts such as earnings guidance and meeting (or *failing* to meet) expectations. Never has there been a clearer example of the ultimate consequences of the management consultant's familiar bromide, "If you can measure it, you can manage it."

Pro forma earnings ignored managements' earlier mistakes, and the availability of cookie-jar reserves, so easily created by mergers, gave us paper companies that acquired rock companies for accounting reasons rather than with any strategic or financial rationale. (Remember the children's game Rock, Paper, and Scissors?) Accountants, with their consulting contracts ever more valuable, were co-opted, and generally accepted accounting principles (GAAP) became an oxymoron. As Wall Street sell-side analysts pushed the companies that looked good on, well, paper, buy-side institutional managers jumped uncritically on the bandwagon. Investors love rising stock prices, and everyone joined in the happy conspiracy to drive them even higher.

It all went on right under the noses of those who were elected to make sure that corporate managements were operating in the interests of the stockholders they represented (i.e., those who were there to keep an eye on the managers). Yet the mania went on, stock prices became completely unlinked from corporate value, and the inevitable day of reckoning came for the stock market and for our society. It is simply impossible to believe that directors were unaware of what was going on. Surely it is fair to say that our corporate directors should bear the ultimate responsibility for what went wrong with capitalism in corporate America.

From Directors to Owners

Or should they? Think about it for a moment. Why should the board bear the ultimate responsibility when it doesn't even have the ultimate control? Yes, directors have a lot to answer for, but it is the stockholders—the owners themselves—who bear the ultimate responsibility for corporate governance. When the directors can't or won't or don't demand that managers place the interests of owners first, it would seem to follow that the owners would step in and do the job themselves. And in corporate America today, owners have the power—the real power, not merely the theoretical power—to do just that. Once dispersed among a diffuse and inchoate group of individual investors, each one with relatively modest holdings, the ownership of stocks is now concentrated, for better or worse, among a remarkably small group of institutions whose potential power is truly awesome. The 100 largest managers of pension funds and mutual funds now represent the ownership of fully 56 percent of all U.S. equities: absolute control over corporate America. Together, these 100 large institutional investors constitute the great 800-pound gorilla who can sit wherever he wants at the board table.

But the gorilla doesn't even come to the meetings. With all that power has come little interest in corporate governance. There is an amazing disconnection between the potential and the reality—the awesome power, yet the rare exercise of it. As the stock market bubble inflated, however, institutional managers could hardly have been ignorant of what was going on in corporate America. They seemed blissfully unaware of what was going on in the financial statements of the companies into which they were pouring literally hundreds of billions of dollars of their clients' assets. Somehow, our professional investors either didn't understand or simply ignored the obvious danger signs.

Astonishingly, even after the bear market that has devastated the value of the equity holdings of fund shareholders, the only response we've heard from the mutual fund industry is the sound of silence. Why? Because the overwhelming majority of mutual funds continues to engage, not in the process of long-term investing on the basis of intrinsic corporate values, but in the process of short-term speculation based on momentary stock prices.

The typical fund manager has lots of interest in a company's price momentum—its quarterly earnings and whether they are meeting the guidance given to Wall Street. But when it comes to what a company is actually worth—its fundamental earning power, its balance sheet, its long-term strategy, its intrinsic value—there seems to be far less interest. Yet focusing on the price of a stock (a perception) rather than on the value of a corporation (the reality) can hardly be a winning strategy over the long run. When Oscar Wilde described the cynic as "a man who knows the price of everything, but the value of nothing," he could as easily have been talking about the typical fund manager.

The Mutual Fund Barrel

Without a doubt, the mutual fund industry was one of the participants in the happy conspiracy, reveling in its burgeoning asset growth as the great stock market bubble expanded to the bursting point. When the bull market virus reaches epidemic proportions, there are few investors who aren't infected by it. But I would argue that much of the fund industry's failure to be concerned about its responsibilities of corporate citizenship grew directly from its own governance system. The mutual fund governance barrel, if you will, is also deeply flawed.

For just as Owners' Capitalism turned to Managers' Capitalism in corporate America, so, too, did Owners' Capitalism turn to Managers' Capitalism in mutual fund America. Despite the express language of the Investment Company Act stating that funds must be organized, operated, and managed in the interests of their shareholders rather than the interests of their investment advisers and underwriters, it is the interests of the managers that usually prevail.

It wasn't always that way. While true Owners' Capitalism has never been possible in the fund industry, whose millions of owners are largely individual investors of relatively modest means, for years we enjoyed Owners' Capitalism by proxy. From the industry's inception in 1924 through the mid-1960s, most fund managers operated as prudent trustees of the assets that investors entrusted to them. The managers of yore—relatively small, privately owned professional firms that saw themselves largely as fiduciaries of other people's money—put their investors' interests first, faithfully honoring the interests of the actual owners.

Over the years, however, funds became big business. Managers sold their shares to the public, and many became part of giant financial conglomerates. Amassing assets under management became the fund industry's primary goal, and our focus gradually shifted from stewardship to salesmanship. The principle of long-term investing in highly diversified equity funds morphed into short-term speculation in ever-more-aggressive specialized funds. Portfolio turnover for the average fund went right through the roof, soaring from the 15 percent range in the 1950s—a six-year holding period for the average stock—to 110 percent last year, an average holding period of just 11 months. We were no longer an own-a-stock industry. We were a rent-a-stock industry, a world away from Warren Buffett's favorite holding period: forever.

CONFLICTS OF INTEREST PREVAIL

Just as the scandals that unfolded in corporate America illuminate a whole variety of serious problems, so the recent scandal in mutual fund America illuminated this industry's profound conflict of interest between managers and fund owners. As the scandal spread, the managers of the Bank of America, Janus, Strong, BancOne, Alliance, Alger, Federated, Massachusetts Financial Services, Putnam, and Pilgrim Baxter funds (among others) were implicated. They stand accused of aiding and abetting or passively permitting selected shareholders to buy and sell fund shares at prices established earlier, thereby gaining returns at the expense of their fellow shareholders, and benefiting the managers by building the asset base on which they earn fees.

Remember what happens when we have "strong managers, weak directors, and passive owners"? Fund shareholder accounts were effectively looted, albeit in what so far appear to be relatively small amounts, and their managers happily profited. But the bright side of this scandal is that it, at long last, shone the spotlight on the profound conflict of interest that exists in our industry—the trade-off between what's best for the manager and what's best for the fund shareholder.

Fund managers have been rewarded at the expense of fund shareholders for a long time. When the fund's chairman is the management company's chairman; when the fund's officers and employees are supplied by that company; and when the board is populated by even a minority of that company's executives, how could it have been otherwise? If these perverse interrelationships are not incestuous, how would one describe them?

The first level of conflict is the fund's fee structure. The higher the fee, the lower the return to the fund investor, and vice versa—dollar for dollar in commodity-like money market and passively managed index funds. But even in actively managed equity funds, the relationship is clear: over time, the lowest-cost quartile of funds in the aggregate—and in each category or style—typically outpaces the highest-cost quartile by two to three percentage points per year.

But the conflict doesn't end there. It is hardly unusual for managers to let funds grow to muscle-bound asset sizes, far beyond their ability to implement their earlier strategies, so that fees can swell accordingly. And it is common practice for managers to bring out new, untried, and often speculative funds to capitalize on the fads and fashions of the markets. Fund investors rarely make money on such funds, but managers always do. If the recent scandals help this industry return to its proud past in which stewardship, not salesmanship, called the tune, they will have performed a noble service.

Part of our stewardship must focus on behaving as responsible corporate citizens, with appropriate involvement in governance. Way back in 1949, *Fortune* wrote that mutual funds were "the ideal champion of . . . the small stockholder in conversations with corporate management, needling corporations on dividend policies, blocking mergers, and pitching in on proxy fights." This treatise appeared even as the Securities and Exchange Commission (SEC) was calling on mutual funds to serve "the useful role of representatives of the great number of inarticulate and ineffective individual investors in corporations in which funds are interested." Back then the industry owned less than 2 percent of all stocks. Yet even though our ownership has soared to 23 percent, it was not to be.

THE GOVERNANCE FAILURE OF MUTUAL FUNDS

The majority of large fund managers go through the motions of proxy voting, endorsing the board slate and most management proposals, though sometimes voting against excessive stock option awards. With rare exception, managers assiduously refrain from any form of corporate activism. In part, this is because we face a profound conflict of interest when we come to vote the shares of the corporations whose pension and 401(k) assets we manage. In addition, our industry's own weak governance system—where separately owned management companies essentially control the boards and operations of the funds they manage—places us in the role of people who live in glass houses: we've implicitly decided that it doesn't seem like a good idea to cast stones at the governance of corporate America.

Nowhere was that fact made more obvious than in the fund industry's almost unanimous opposition to the SEC's proposal that we disclose to our own shareholders how we vote the proxies of the companies that they own in our fund portfolios. While it would seem utterly obvious that a fund manager (the agent) would be expected to report his actions to the fund owners (the principals), the industry fought the proposal tooth and nail. In this opening skirmish in the battle to return this industry to the role it must play in restoring Owners' Capitalism in corporate America, the industry lost. But our shareholders won.

Returning the mutual fund industry—and institutional investing in general—to its traditional focus on long-term investing and good corporate citizenship will be no mean task. It is a curious paradox that the increasing problems created by Managers' Capitalism in mutual funds has—by making funds reluctant to assume their responsibilities of corporate citizenship—been a major force in the rise of Managers' Capitalism in corporate America. So the point is worth repeating: *when no responsible owner exists, capitalism itself is corrupted.*

CORPORATE DEMOCRACY

The problem with corporate America and mutual fund America lies in the fact that far too many corporate executives and directors have been placed in positions of great power and authority without an adequate understanding of their fiduciary duties. However, far too many institutional intermediaries have failed to take them to task and insist that the interests of shareowners be served. I see no other way to solve that problem than by enabling both groups to assert their obvious authority, indeed, demanding that they do. It seems utterly logical to believe that the owners should be in a position to have the primacy of their interest honored. The corporation, after all, is their property. In other words, I urge a return to corporate democracy.

Not everyone agrees! Logical or not, the reverse has been authoritatively argued. Top securities attorney Martin Lipton argues that enhancing shareholder ownership rights to nominate directors and make proxy proposals could "disrupt the proper functioning of the board and limit the ability of the directors to fulfill their fiduciary duties." And in a 2002 op-ed in *The Wall Street Journal,* Henry G. Manne, Dean Emeritus of the George Mason University School of Law, argues that "the theory of corporate democracy . . . has long been a standing joke among sophisticated finance econo-mists. . . . A corporation is not a small republic . . . and the board is not a legislature. . . . [A] vote attached to a share is totally different from a politi-cal vote. . . . [T]he essence of individual shareholder participation is 'exit,' not 'voice' . . . and they can exit their corporate 'citizenship' for the cost of a stockbroker's commission." In other words, if you don't like the way your company is being run, just get out—sell to the first bidder, whether or not the price reflects the corporation's intrinsic value. "Like it or lump it," how-ever, doesn't seem a particularly enlightened policy.

Dean Manne's objections seem to assume that those who are interested in embracing ownership rights are "special pleaders with no real stake, activists [whose] primary interest . . . is to facilitate publicity for their own special-interest programs . . . and to interfere with the property and contractual rights of others in order to achieve their own ends," describing corporate democracy as a "form of corporate fraud." Though I'm confident that at least some corporate activists have agendas that might not comport with the pub-lic weal, I confess that I don't know quite what to make of such a diatribe.

But what about those who have no such agenda, only the simple convic-tion that owners should be allowed to behave as owners? If ownership rights are not placed front and center, where should they be placed? Who would dare to suggest that barriers should be placed in the way of the right of share-holders to elect as a director anyone they wish to serve as their agent? To compel management to function in the way the shareholders wish? To re-linquish responsibility for how the executives of their company are com-pensated? Aren't these the essential rights of ownership?

Clearly, they are the rights of the 100 percent owner, who brooks no in-terference with his will. And any manager who flatly refused to consider the views of a 50 percent owner or even a 20 percent owner would soon be looking for another line of work. What about a dozen institutions, each holding a 3 percent interest and sharing a particular viewpoint or wishing to nominate a director? Where does the proverbial shovel break? And does the argument that it might break when no single shareholder owns more than, say, 0.10 percent of the shares justify depriving these shareholders of the same rights? Not for me it doesn't. For I believe, after Churchill, that corporate democracy "is the worst form of government . . . except for all those others that have been tried from time to time."

The legendary Benjamin Graham long ago put his finger on the problem.

In the early editions of *The Intelligent Investor,* he had some important things to say about stockholder-management relationships. In "legal rights and machinery, the stockholders as a class are king. . . . [T]hey can hire and fire managements and bend them completely to their will." He was—and is—right. But he also was—and is—right when he added that "the assertion of rights by stockholders in practice is almost a complete washout. Unless prodded violently into action, they show neither intelligence nor alertness. They vote in sheep-like fashion for whatever management recommends and no matter how poor the record of accomplishment may be. . . . This attitude of the financial world toward good and bad management is utterly childish." He noted, "The leading investment funds could contribute mightily to the improvement of corporate managements . . . but have shied away . . . missing a great opportunity for rendering service to the investing public." And so it remains today.

RESTORING OWNERS' CAPITALISM

Yet the cause is not lost. Even after all these years, perhaps Benjamin Graham's words can awaken us and force us to consider ways that institutional stock owners, working in concert with corporate directors, can root out the problems that plague our system. Here are eight steps we might take in the quest to restore Owners' Capitalism.

1. *Encourage corporate citizenship.* The only way that investors—and particularly institutional investors—will become better owners is if we return to behaving as responsible corporate citizens, voting our proxies thoughtfully and communicating our views to corporate management. The SEC's decision to require mutual funds to disclose to our owners how we vote their proxies is a long- overdue first step in increasing our motivation to participate in governance matters.

But investors also need the ability to act—in the form of access to corporate proxy statements—so that we can place both nominations for directors and proposals for compensation policy and business conduct directly in the proxies. I am heartened by the possibility that the SEC will act favorably on this issue, and I hope they will include restraints that keep the process from becoming a circus—for example, extending such rights only to investors who have held their shares for, say, two years, and whose aggregate holdings exceed 5 percent of the corporation's voting shares.

2. *Clearly separate ownership from management.* We need to recognize the bright line between *directing*—the responsibility of the governing body of an institution—and *managing*—the responsibility of the executives who run the business. It's called *separation of powers.* While the CEO should be boss of the business, an independent chairman should be the boss of the board. We need higher standards of director independence; and directors should rely on outside advisors, or even a small staff, to provide them with independent information that is bereft of management bias, not only on compensation and accounting matters but on everything else as well. These steps will begin the process of reforming board governance and clarifying the role of directors as stewards of the property of the owners.

3. *Return to a long-term focus.* Owners and managers must unite in the task of returning the focus of corporate information to long-term financial goals, cash flows, intrinsic values, and strategic direction. Quarterly earnings guidance, pernicious yet still omnipresent, should be eliminated. So should efforts to meet financial targets through creative accounting techniques.

It must be obvious that the sharp decline in trading costs that has come with electronic communication networks has enabled, and doubtless encouraged, managers to trade with carefree abandon. In fact, trading activity has risen even faster than unit trading costs have declined, so that aggregate trading costs have risen, to the detriment of investors. The iron law of investing has not been repealed: "Gross return of the stock market, less the costs of financial intermediation, equals the net return earned by investors."

Sterner measures to enhance a long-term focus may be required, and we ought to keep an open mind about them. Warren Buffett once suggested (supposedly with tongue in cheek) that the federal government impose a 100 percent tax on capital gains realized on stocks held for less than six months, to be paid even by nontaxable institutions. But we ought not dismiss out-of-hand variations on this tax theme. And while we're about it, why not consider the creation of a special class of stock, which rewards investors with a premium dividend on the shares they have held for longer than, say, one year? If we have the will to foster a long-term focus by investors, we can find the way.

4. *Fix the stock option mess.* At the end of the tedious process followed by the Financial Accounting Standards Board, I expect that GAAP will require

that the cost of fixed-price stock options be expensed, putting them on an equal footing with other stock-based compensation. But directors and owners should not be fooled into awarding such options, as they are fundamentally flawed. Options are indifferent to dividends; their prices are not adjusted for the cost of capital; they don't relate rewards to the performance either of peers or of the stock market itself; they pay off for raising momentary stock prices rather than building enduring corporate values and cash flow; and they rarely require that optionees hold their stock, once purchased, for the long term. Any option plan that fails to correct these shortcomings fails to represent the interests of the long-term shareholders of the corporation. Restricted stock surmounts most of these obstacles; tomorrow's options should do so as well.

5. *Let the sunlight shine on accounting.* Given the enormous latitude accorded by GAAP, owners must demand—and managers must provide—full disclosure of the impact of significant accounting policy decisions. Indeed, maybe we ought to require that corporations report earnings not only on a most aggressive basis but on a most conservative basis as well.

While that harsh policy may be too much to expect, serious work has already begun to improve the reporting of financial results and increase their relevance. A fine new book, *It's Earnings That Count,*[1] presents two supplemental income statements that the author dubs "enterprising" (showing the company's return relative to its total capital base) and "defensive" (showing the extent to which a company depends on outside sources of capital). Do we really need three earnings reports, including the present weak GAAP statement? Why not? For anyone who recalls the ancient rule of the carpenter, "measure twice, cut once," measuring thrice can hardly be harmful.

6. *Bring back dividends!* Earnings are easily subjected to manipulation and interpretation, but dividends speak for themselves. Benjamin Graham reminded us of something that we've long forgotten: "There is no truth more fundamental in investment than that dividends and market value are the only concrete returns a public stockholder ever gets on his investment. Earnings, financial strength, and increased asset values are of vital importance only because they will ultimately affect his dividend and market price." Again, he was—and is—right.

History tells us that higher dividend payouts are actually associated with higher future returns on stocks. Yet despite the evidence that earnings retention leads to counterproductive capital allocations, the dividend payout rate has been declining for years. To state the obvious, investing for income is a long-term strategy and investing for capital gains is a short-term strategy. (The turnover of dividend-paying stocks is one-half the turnover of non-dividend paying stocks.) It is high time that owners and managers unite to bring a new focus on the issue of dividends.

7. *Reform the fund industry.* It will take a mutual fund industry focused on stewardship and long-term investing to assume its proper role as a responsible corporate citizen. Unlike corporate America, however, ownership of mutual funds is so diffused that there is no natural bloc of giant owners to lead the way. So we must build a shareholder-oriented board structure, dismantling today's structure that permits such incestuous conflicts between managers and shareholders. We must amend the Investment Company Act of 1940 to require an independent board chairman, limit the manager to no more than a single board seat, and enable the board to retain its own staff to provide information that is independent and objective. We also must establish a federal standard of fiduciary duty that requires fund directors to place the interest of the fund's shareholders ahead of the interests of fund officers, advisers, and distributors, just as the existing preamble of the 1940 Act suggests. We also need full disclosure of the often staggering compensation paid to management company executives, including their share of the company's profits. As the disclosure of the compensation paid to the deposed chairman of the New York Stock Exchange drove home, sunlight is a powerful disinfectant.

8. *"Institutions of the world, unite!"* Since at least 1998—long before the recent spate of corporate and mutual fund scandals—I've been calling for mutual funds and other private institutional investors to make their will known by taking an active, even collective, role in governance. While many of these institutions are focusing on short-term speculation, there remains a strong cadre of others; hence the working designation I suggested for the group, "The Federation of Long-Term Investors." Index funds—the consummate long-term investors, who simply buy and hold the stocks in their benchmark portfolios—now represent 12 percent of mutual fund assets and an estimated 25 percent of pension fund assets. Such funds would constitute the core of such a federation, joined by the active managers who eschew a short-term focus. While most managers are publicity-shy—neither notoriety nor controversy is good for the marketing side of the house—this embryonic effort seems destined to become an important reality.

Taken together, these eight changes would forcefully continue the present wave of reform in corporate governance and help turn America's capital development process away from speculation and toward enterprise. But there's even more at stake than improving the *practices* of governance and investing. We must also establish a higher set of *principles*. This nation's founding fathers believed in high moral standards, in a just society, and in the virtuous conduct of our affairs. Those beliefs shaped the very character of our nation. If character counts—and I have absolutely no doubt that character *does* count—the ethical failings of today's business and financial model; the manipulation of financial statements; the willingness of those of us in the field of investment management to accept practices that we know are wrong; the conformity that keeps us silent; the selfishness that lets our greed overwhelm our reason—all have eroded the character of capitalism. Yet character is what we'll need most in the years ahead, more than ever in the wake of a great bear market and the investor disenchantment it reflects; more than ever in these days when economies around the globe are struggling to find their bearings; more than ever in the strife-ridden world around us, where America's strength lies more than ever in her values, her ideals, her goodness.

The motivations of those who seek the rewards earned by engaging in commerce and finance struck the imagination of no less a man than Adam Smith as "something grand and beautiful and noble, well worth the toil and anxiety." But few observers of the scandalous events of the past few years would use those words to describe what capitalism has been about in the recent era. The sooner we can again apply those words to our business and investment leaders—and *mean* them—the better. All responsible corporate leaders and institutional managers must be part of this vital mission.

What is that mission? It is restoring Owners' Capitalism by taking it back to its roots: "trusting and being trusted," no more than what St. Paul told us in Corinthians I: "It is required of stewards that they be found trustworthy." The bad apples that I listed earlier—too often arrogant, greedy, and vainglorious, convinced that "we did it all by ourselves," bereft of doubt that they deserve every penny they've been paid, and imperial by nature—have illuminated a whole host of weaknesses in the troubled barrel of capitalism. They've given us the opportunity to fix the system. It's high time that we capitalize on it.

Yes, "somebody's gotta keep an eye on these geniuses" who manage our corporations and our mutual funds. If the directors aren't willing to do it, the owners must. It *is* as simple as that.

NOTE

1. Hewitt Heiserman, *It's Earnings That Count* (New York: McGraw-Hill, 2003).

PART IV

TOWARD REFORM

Since the dawn of the new millennium, public perception of CEOs has plummeted. Seemingly overnight, they went from being viewed as rock star–like figures of glamour and magic to being looked upon as wicked, despicable, greedy troll-like creatures, seeking only to make a buck without any regard for the welfare of others. Indeed, the recent rash of corporate scandals has revealed a severe lack of integrity in the C-suites of many organizations. The unprincipled behavior among those at the top has not only been unsettling, it has also cost investors hundreds of billions of dollars and sent thousands of employees out on the streets looking for work, while senior management continued to line their pockets.

Courts and shareholders alike have responded to the recent spate of scandals by taking a closer look at whether corporate managers are taking appropriate actions to deter and respond to criminal behavior within firms. In this final section, the authors make the case for reforming the current corporate governance structure, both in America and Europe, beginning with a new type of business culture and daily practice of management. Recognizing that executive compensation gone awry is a key contributor to abuse in the current system, they examine the relationship between compensation and promotion structures and employee and managerial wrongdoing and then lay out characteristics of executive compensation that stands the test of time. In addition, they make the case for transparency in executive remuneration reporting as well as the need to reexamine the aspects of financial reporting and auditing.

CHAPTER 13

SHEDDING THE IMAGES
AND GETTING REAL ABOUT
BUSINESS RESPONSIBILITY

BARBARA LEY TOFFLER

"YOU'VE SPENT a quarter of a century working in business ethics. When you look at corporate America now, do you think your life's work has made a difference?" That was the painful question an old colleague asked me about a year ago. I could only answer that I believed I had helped some individual companies and people but that, over the years, my colleagues and I had not achieved what our salad days had promised.

The year was 1978—the closing stages of an emotional and often ugly decade that saw the end of the Vietnam War, the fall of Richard Nixon, and the attendant ravages of Watergate. The unruly decade wasn't all bad, as it also brought forth an awakening of interest in professional ethics—and business ethics, in particular. Among other things, this resulted in the U.S. Foreign Corrupt Practices Act of 1977 and the first corporate ethics programs at Allied Chemical and Cummins Engine Company.

In the spring of 1978, the Yale School of Organization and Management (SOM), graduating its first class, and the Society for Values in Higher Education (SVHE)—a then New Haven–based nonprofit loosely affiliated with Yale—organized and hosted the first session of a two-summer program called "The Institute for the Teaching of Ethics in Public and Private Sector Management." To many of the 60 corporate executives, government administrators, and professors in attendance, that program was the seminal event in the launch of the modern business ethics movement—a movement that held bright promise.

While the institute had an academic core, it was particularly noteworthy for a critical aspect of its approach: reality. "What," it was asked, "is the reality about individuals and the organizations in which they work that results in either profitable, responsible contributors to a successful economy or the opposite?" None who were present will forget the impassioned statement of a longtime senior executive from a still-prominent Fortune 500 company, who slapped down his hand on the conference table and bellowed, "You want to know what business ethics is? Business ethics is when the boss at the top says move it—just meet that deadline; show those numbers; get the product out the door. Don't tell me you need more money, time, or people. If you can't get it done, we'll find someone who can! And down the line it goes," he said, "Move it, move it, move it."

Poor ethical performance may be somewhat more complicated, but that statement was a rallying cry to address the real problems that led to unethical corporate behavior. What fruit we thought it would bear! And how horrifying the present reality.

At the annual Ethics Officer Association (EOA) meeting in October 2003, I was invited to participate on a panel titled "Are Ethics Officers Doing the Job? Some Feedback and Constructive Criticism." I began my presentation with a request to the audience: "Think for a minute about the wrongdoing that has become apparent in the corporations of our country over the past year or two. How many of you believe that your company's ethics program could have prevented such incidents?" Not one person raised a hand. "But," I said, "isn't the goal of your program to prevent illegal and unethical behavior?" Heads nodded in agreement. "So," I continued, "what's the problem? Why isn't it working?" Dead silence.

Those ethics officers may have truly been bewildered or unaware of the problem. Maybe they were too embarrassed to raise a voice of explanation. I believe there's another reason why the ubiquitous corporate ethics programs have had little or no effect on the behavior of executives and other employees—and let's be very clear that we are not talking about just the people who have made it onto the front business pages of our national newspapers. The reality is that *hundreds of thousands of people* either did wrong, covered up wrongdoing, or saw wrongdoing and did nothing.

Why are our corporate ethics programs not doing the job? Very simply—

because they are not designed to prevent wrongdoing. Their primary purpose is to provide legal protection should the organization—by virtue of the
behavior of individual members—break one or more federal laws. Today's
corporate ethics programs respond to the Federal Sentencing Guidelines for
Organization (FSGO),which require an ethics officer, a code of ethics, an
ethics program (usually computer-based and administered at least once a
year), and a reporting mechanism, such as a telephone hotline, often connected to an outside service. There is nothing that requires examination of
an institution's culture, the skill and decency of its leadership, the incentive
systems that drive people's behavior, or the changing of any dysfunctional aspect of an organization. As long as the mechanisms are in place, a company
is deemed ethical. In 1999, Arthur Andersen put forth its values statement:
"To be successful in the future we must hold fast to our core values: Integrity,
Respect, Passion for Excellence, One Firm, Stewardship, Personal Growth."
Surprised that Andersen had a values statement? Even Enron had a code of
ethics.

To make matters worse, the core of ethics in corporate America today is
that hotline and the willingness of employees to report on the misbehavior
of their bosses, peers, and subordinates. In other words, ethics in business depends on the willingness of individuals to be whistle-blowers.

I asked a second question of the EOA audience, all of whom, as ethics
officers, administered their companies' hotlines: "Who here has ever been a
whistle-blower?" Only two people raised their hands. "How did it feel?"
The answer: "Not very good." I continued: "Didn't your company celebrate
your act of responsibility?" That question generated rueful laughter among
the audience members.

The reality, of course, is that no one likes a whistle-blower. In fact, the
revered advice columnist Ann Landers expressed a deeply held American
belief when she wrote, "When we were in school, they called kids who
snitched 'stool pigeons.' They were not respected. In fact they were disliked."
Over the past three decades, history has shown that whistle-blowers, despite
prominently touted nonretaliation policies, have tended to be treated shab-
bily by the organizations they were attempting to save. From B.F. Goodrich's
Kermit Vandivere in 1969 through the Morton Thiokol's Roger Boisjoly,
who warned of the danger of cold temperatures to the Challenger's O-rings
in 1976, to the three *Time* magazine Persons of the Year 2002, not one
was celebrated or rewarded by his or her organization. One of the best

corporate ethics officers I know was completely honest: "Of course, we have a nonretaliation policy. But before I let anyone blow the whistle, I always say, 'I will do what I can to protect you. But you must understand that if you are fired two years from now, I probably won't be able to do anything about it.'"

So here we are in 2004, after massive corporate debacles have wrought havoc with the public trust of financial and business institutions, relying for good corporate behavior on the willingness of individuals to risk their jobs and careers, their reputations, and even their friendships by informing on others. Even if those reported are ultimately found guilty and removed from their positions (and the issue of false allegations under this system is yet another frightening aspect of it), the culture of their organizations—which in all likelihood contributed significantly to their misbehavior—will remain unchanged.

Almost nowhere is there a demand that leaders spearhead an examination of their own leadership and their institution's policies, systems, and business practices. Almost nowhere is there an investigation into why people do wrong. Almost nowhere are there voices challenging business as usual.

Therefore, despite high-minded talk about business ethics, little has actually been done to change behavior and prevent illegal or unethical activity. We target the supposed bad guys, get rid of them, maybe write a new regulation or two, add more outside members to the board, and continue on. This approach will *never* bring about the radical change that we need. Indeed, change will come only when people with power and authority want it and act aggressively to achieve it. And change will not be easy. Commissions and oversight boards, increased laws and regulations, and new corporate governance structures will provide only the framework for change. Creating a culture in which people are committed to abiding by those new guidelines is the challenge. The trustworthiness that so many of our economic institutions have squandered will be restored only when that goal is achieved.

A MODEST PROPOSAL[1]

A change of the magnitude required to create truly responsible companies, leaders, and employees will take a long time. Indeed, the greatest challenge lies in getting leaders to change the way they think. To get the ball rolling, therefore, let me propose some important first steps for rebuilding trust in our corporations and business leaders:

1. *Drop the word* ethics. *Ethics* is such a loaded word that it has lost its meaning. Whenever you are tempted to use it, substitute either *responsibility* or *decency.* Instead of asking, "Is it the ethical thing to do?" ask, "Is it the responsible or decent thing to do?" Note the way you feel when you change that one little word. Makes it much clearer, doesn't it? Now, act accordingly.

2. *Take the values statement challenge.* Like practically every company on the planet, your values statement probably includes words like *honesty, respect, integrity, teamwork, and commitment.* Take the time to write a short essay defining each value with specific, real-life examples from inside your company. Next, identify examples of practices within the company that contradict those values. Take honesty, for example. During your annual budgeting, do people use up remaining dollars from this year's budget so they won't be cut next year or inflate next year's request? Is that honest? If you can come up with even one example of a practice that compromises a stated value, rest assured that your employees will have plenty more of them and will choose their reality over your elegant values statement.

3. *Evaluate your internal values.* Make a list of all the *external* values hailed by your company. Those are the standards that represent all the good things you publicly claim to value (e.g., serving the needs of customers and clients, providing growth for employees, respecting the environment, being a good neighbor to the community, earning a respectable profit, etc.). Now, no holds barred, make a list of the *internal* values driving your company (e.g., survival, beating competitors at all costs, keeping labor costs down). Would you feel comfortable printing the internal values in your annual report and posting them on your Web site? If the answer is no, decide what you are going to do to change them.

4. *Know what you know.* Deep down in your gut, what bothers you that you just haven't wanted to recognize? Are you feeling uneasy about those new financial products you're selling? Did that environmental impact statement for the new facility belong on the fiction pages of the book review section? Are your hiring practices a discrimination

lawsuit waiting to happen? What do you really know that you don't want to know? Cough it up and face those gut feelings head on! Your new mantra, starting today, is *There is nothing I don't want to know.* Your director of public relations is a great source of information. After all, he's the one who takes all the nasty issues and pretties them up. Convince him that you want the clear, unadulterated truth from this day forward.

5. *Slash your pay.* Are you earning more than $1 million, while many of your employees are losing their jobs or taking pay cuts? If so, you should negotiate a lower compensation package and then publicize what you've done. In an environment of mistrust, sacrifice on the part of top executives goes a long way toward creating a culture of trust, mutual respect, responsible behavior, and decency.

A modest proposal—but some important first steps to rebuilding trust in our corporations and our business leaders.

NOTE

1. This section appeared in slightly different form in *Fast Company* magazine, October 2003.

CHAPTER 14

GETTING WHAT YOU PAY FOR

INSTITUTIONAL INVESTORS TAKE ON EXECUTIVE PAY

NELL MINOW

A 2002 cartoon by Mark Magee showed a mother trying to break up a fight between two children. "Mommy!" one of them said, in tears. "Billy just called me a CEO!"

A year earlier, chief executive officers (CEOs) were up there with rock stars as figures of glamour and magic. For decades, *Time* magazine's men of the year were figures from politics and international affairs. In the 1990s, however, three were from business: CNN's Ted Turner, Intel's Andy Grove, and Amazon.com's Jeff Bezos. When longtime General Electric CEO Jack Welch retired, he was lauded as the greatest business leader of the twentieth century.

By the end of 2002, however, the CEOs that were household names were the ones refusing to testify before Congress. And Welch was making new headlines for his messy divorce and postretirement goodies. CEOs like to think of themselves as leaders who communicate and inspire. But the business community has shown little leadership when it comes to speaking out on the failures at Tyco, WorldCom, Enron, Qwest, Adelphia, HealthSouth, Global Crossing, and Parmalat. Mismanagement at those companies cost investors hundreds of billions of dollars and thousands of employees their jobs. Business leaders blamed the victims by describing the declining market as a crisis of investor confidence when it is more accurately a crisis of management credibility.

It is not coincidental that the 1990s saw one of the greatest wealth transfers in history, as CEO pay skyrocketed both in absolute terms and as a multiple of what the average worker took home. The average CEO makes 411 times more than the average worker. (If the minimum wage had risen at the same rate as executive pay since 1990, it would be $21.41 an hour as opposed to $5.15.) CEOs reaped windfall profits from mega-grants of stock options, made possible in part by accounting quirks that did not require the value of the options to be subtracted from the balance sheet at the time of the award. CEOs also overdid the perks. Investors and employees believe that executives who are paid tens of millions of dollars should pay for their own cars and plane tickets. As John Kenneth Galbraith said, "The salary of the chief executive of the large corporation is not a market award for achievement. It is frequently in the nature of a warm personal gesture by the individual to himself."

In the 1990s, the cult of the CEO was based on the idea that vision and the ability to inspire were what made them worth the hundreds of millions of dollars they were paid. But a book by Harvard Business School professor Rakesh Khurana, *Searching for a Corporate Savior: The Irrational Quest for Charismatic CEOs,* makes a compelling case that corporate boards err seriously when they pick chief executives based on leadership and vision. Bringing in a CEO with a great record at another company may give the stock price a short-term boost, but considering such high-profile transplants as Al Dunlap at Sunbeam (now in bankruptcy) and Gary Wendt at Conseco (also in bankruptcy), CEOs should have to make the same disclaimers that money managers do: "Past performance is no guarantee of future performance."

Corporate board meetings have more often been like pep rallies than meaningful exchanges. In nearly all companies, the CEO also acts as chairman, setting the agenda and determining the quantity, quality, and timing of the information. There have been encouraging reports that boards are asking more questions and insisting on meeting without management present. But there have also been discouraging reports that CEOs are responding by drowning board members in the minutiae of the financial reports, and of the forest of corporate governance as risk management getting lost in the trees of compliance checklists. The board is supposed to pay attention to the big picture. Many reformers believe it is time to adopt the British approach and have an independent outside director serve as the chairman in order to keep the board focused on the forest, rather than the bark.

CEOs also have not set a good example of responsible share ownership. The largest investors in the world are America's corporate pension plans. The trustees of those plans are the very CEOs who run public companies. CEOs entrust their employees' retirement money to fund managers who have too often neglected early signs of problems at companies, such as Global Crossing and Enron, because they were dazzled by short-term returns. Before fund managers invest employee retirement money in the stock of a company, CEOs should have made sure that the managers look carefully at its corporate governance practices. While they hold the stock, CEOs should insist that fund managers continue to monitor the boards of the companies they invest in on behalf of America's working families.

Astonishingly, in its response to the Securities and Exchange Commission's proposal to give shareholders limited rights to nominate director candidates using the company's proxy card, the Business Roundtable argued that shareholders vote proxies by rote, in effect indicting themselves for failure to act as fiduciaries for past and present employees. They often complain, too, about churn. This recalls Pogo's famous statement: "We have met the enemy and he is us." Corporate America should be providing the key infrastructure of the country's capital markets by ensuring that pension funds subject to the Employee Retirement Income Security Act (ERISA) are patient in making a long-term commitment to their holdings but vigilant in terms of making sure that those portfolio companies are always responsive to shareholder concerns.

The CEOs of the early twenty-first century may resemble the Pharonic model in some respect, particularly in the level of pay. Long before Enron, however, a 1998 report by Spencer Stuart's Tom Neff and Dayton Ogden identified "several trends that make the job of today's CEO more like 'The Perils of Pauline' than the 'Triumph of Succession.' The principal pressure comes from a demand for performance and board control of succession. Independent directors have made a CEO's seat much less secure and open to external benchmarking—not just within the industry where a company competes, but across industries." In addition, they noted the impact of mergers and acquisitions, pressure to perform, and another kind of pressure—from potential successors—as factors in reducing tenure. They found that 60 percent of the CEOs in the Fortune 200 served only five years or less.

Still, the idea of the CEO as benevolent dictator has some support. In a 2002 speech at the Stern School of Business, Federal Reserve Chairman

Alan Greenspan said that "it has increasingly fallen to corporate officers, especially the chief executive officer, to guide the business, hopefully in what he or she perceives to be in the best interest of shareholders." He admits that there is no such thing as an independent director, as long as management decides who gets to be on the board. But what if the CEO doesn't pay enough attention to shareholder value? Greenspan is sanguine. "When companies do run into trouble, the carte blanche granted CEOs by shareholders is withdrawn." He is content to rely on "existing shareholders or successful hostile bidders." But there is an inconsistency in his position because he then says that only a handful of investors have the capacity to make these judgments.

In his book, Khurana documents the mistakes made by boards of directors in selecting superstar CEOs who can dazzle the analysts and investors but who may not have what it takes to run a company. He makes it clear that the top priority should be managerial skills, not so-called leadership. Indeed, the kind of showboating that leads to magazine covers and paying for sports stadiums should be a sell signal or even an indicator to go short.

The one certainty in business, as in life, is change. If it were possible, we all—investors, lenders, communities, employees, and customers—would want a CEO who could predict the future and guide the company accordingly. Since that is impossible, what we want is a CEO who is able, by virtue of ability, expertise, resources, motivation, and authority, to keep the company not just ready for change but ready to benefit from changes, ideally to lead them. The CEO must be powerful enough to do the job but accountable enough to make sure it is done correctly. The challenge for all of the participants in corporate governance is to make sure that there is enough of a balance between the two so that, overall, the decisions made by the CEO are in the long-term interests of the shareholders (and thus, by definition, all other constituencies), rather than in his own interests.

One of the key areas for achieving and evaluating this balance is executive compensation. The essential conflict between the goals of shareholders and management is not over the amount of pay but over its variability and risk. Shareholders want a compensation plan with maximum variability based on corporate performance, while management's natural tendency is to want a compensation plan with maximum security.

All methods of evaluating a company's value and performance are useful for evaluating the CEO. But perhaps one of the clearest indications of CEO quality is the structure of the organization itself. In general, the more diversified and conglomerated the company, the more likely it is to reflect the CEO's empire-building and the less likely that it demonstrates focus and commitment to shareholder value. As one management consultant put it, "The design trick is to be small where small is beautiful and then be big where big is beautiful."[1]

Unquestionably, the biggest challenge a company faces is not failure but success. If we look at the most spectacular swan dives and meltdowns of the last thirty years, most were at one time spectacular successes. The giants of the 1960s—Xerox, Kodak, Sears, Waste Management, General Motors, and others—became the problems of the 1980s and 1990s. Likewise, Enron, Tyco, Global Crossing, Qwest, Adelphia, and WorldCom—and others that set earnings records in the 1990s—saw their names become synonyms for corruption and mismanagement in the early years of the twenty-first century. When a company is failing, it will try almost anything. But when a company is successful, it generally does not know why it is successful, and so, like an athlete on a lucky streak who won't change his socks, it will fall into an almost superstitious pattern of not changing anything.

It took the abuses of the takeover era to wake up the institutional investors. Almost before they got started, however, the takeover era ended. But by that time, there was a new issue to provoke outrage: excessive CEO compensation. In some ways, this was an ideal corporate governance issue for the new activists. Complaints about compensation could be made in a sound bite, with political and economic appeal, to say nothing of the gossip value. This was the first corporate governance issue to go from the financial pages to the front pages to the editorial pages to the comic pages—even "Doonesbury" got in a few digs. And this was not just some Capra-esque populist movement. No one complained about the money Bill Gates made at Microsoft. But when pay was not related to performance, the business press was just as outraged as the shareholders. Even Forbes's cover story on executive pay bore a banner headline: "It doesn't make sense."[2]

It was also an issue uniquely suited to being addressed by shareholders. Compensation for performance is the perfect issue, as no shareholder initiative could have a more direct impact on shareholder value. If compensation is connected to performance, all other shareholder initiatives become secondary. If compensation is unrelated to performance, however, all the shareholder resolutions in the world won't make a difference.

The role of the shareholders with regard to compensation starts with one simple point: compensation presents an investment opportunity. The compensation plan is a clear indicator of the company's value as an investment. It reveals what the CEO's incentives are. If home owners are deciding between two realtors who want to sell their house—one who charges a flat fee and one who charges a percentage of the sale price—they know they are likely to do better with the one whose compensation is tied to the money they themselves will eventually receive. Similarly, a shareholder should want to invest in a CEO whose compensation depends on the money the shareholder will receive. Compensation plans also reveal the company's goals and how confident the CEO and board are of the company's future.

In his book on executive compensation, *In Search of Excess,*[3] Graef Crystal discussed the impact that compensation plans should have on stock picking by sophisticated investors. His conclusion—that restricted stock grants are made by boards who do not think the stock will go up—is supported by his data on companies that have made these awards. If his analysis is correct, selling short on companies that make restricted stock grants should be a highly profitable investment strategy.

Furthermore, compensation issues present shareholders with some of their most cost-effective (highly leveraged) opportunities for investing in shareholder initiatives. A shareholder can submit a proposal about executive compensation for little more than the cost of a stamp. For little more than the cost of a couple of dozen letters or phone calls, they can distribute information about their views to other shareholders under the enormously simplified revised proxy rules. With a high likelihood of improving returns through this visible focus, and negligible, if any, downside risk, this is an investment that shareholders, especially fiduciary shareholders, will find increasingly appealing.

Shareholder initiatives on compensation have special appeal. CEOs get paid a lot for one reason—they take risks. Their compensation should provide the appropriate incentives for those risks. To the extent that a shareholder initiative can better align these incentives, it is an investment with substantial returns.

The question, then, is not whether there will be increased activism by shareholders on the subject of compensation; the question is what form it will take. With the exception of a few extremists, shareholders have not objected to chief executives' earning a lot of money, as long as they created a lot of value for shareholders first. The late Roberto Goizueta's $81 million stock grant got four standing ovations from the Coca-Cola shareholders, who were delighted with the 38.2 percent annual returns during his tenure. What shareholders have objected to is chief executives' being paid a lot of money without earning it. Rather, their focus has been on strengthening the link between pay and performance.

It is a very small group at the top of the compensation scale: rock stars, movie stars, athletes, investment bankers, and CEOs. All but CEOs are compensated for performance. And it is not coincidental that CEOs are the only ones who pick the people who set their compensation. In all of the other categories, pay and performance are closely linked. And that means financial performance. Meryl Streep can get a record number of Oscar nominations, but she doesn't sell a lot of tickets. Therefore, she receives an average of $7 to $9 million for a movie, while unlikely-to-get-anywhere-near-an-Oscar Arnold Schwarzenegger gets a record $30 million for making Terminator 3. (That's a good deal more than he is now making as governor of California, by the way, but no one ever suggested that public service was pay-for-performance.) But statistics showed that CEOs do well regardless of performance, and the publicity for those numbers provided much of the momentum for the reforms on compensation disclosure.[4]

The extreme cases point out the failure of the system as a whole. If shareholders, as the consumers of executive compensation, cannot act when it is out of control, the system simply isn't working. Executive compensation unrelated to performance is just one symptom of a corporate governance system that fails to ensure management accountability.

Shareholders want compensation to vary with performance as much as possible, while managers understandably want as much certainty as possible. Even those who want a lot of variability on the upside are less willing to allow it on the downside.

The issue is not only matching compensation to performance. It is also defining what performance means. There is almost always some standard that can be used to support a bonus, and compensation consultants are good at providing a mix of performance plans that ensure that at least one of them will pay off. The issue shareholders should focus on is not just tying compensation to performance, but really *improving* performance.

In 1999, Graef Crystal named Linda Wachner of Warnaco his "pay antihero," based on the following excerpt from the Crystal Report (April 19):

- Base salary of $2.7 million—299% above the market. And that doesn't count further salary of $1.1 million she received for running a smaller public company, Authentic Fitness. [Given the company's performance, it is particularly striking that her board allowed her to have another full-time job. Perhaps this is why they voted to buy Authentic Fitness from her in 1999, a deal in which she and several of her directors were on both sides of the table.]
- Total Current Compensation of $8.7 million—638% above the market.
- Total Direct Compensation of $73.8 million—1,818% above the market.
- That 1,818% market overage was higher than that for any of the 857 CEOs in our 1998 pay study. The next overage was a mere [sic!] 893%.
- The options granted in 1998 had an estimated present value of $58.2 million.
- In addition, she exercised options in 1998 for a gain of $75.6 million.

Crystal noted, "Her board is also excessively paid—large fees and extra-large option grants."

In June of 2001, Warnaco filed for bankruptcy, its stock trading at 39 cents a share, down from $44 dollars a share in 1998. The press release about the bankruptcy blamed a soft retail market and insufficient support of the retailers. The fault was entirely the board's, once described by Fortune as "notoriously ineffectual," for not just enabling but rewarding a CEO whose self-dealing and bad decisions all but destroyed the company.

Wachner took over Warnaco in 1986 in a hostile takeover and built the apparel maker into a $1.4 billion company, responsible for manufacturing and distributing more than a third of all the bras sold in the United States.

Wachner was fired shortly after the bankruptcy filing. It should be noted that Wachner submitted notice to the bankruptcy court that since she had been terminated without cause, she was entitled to have her $25 million severance payment classified as an administrative expense and thus given top priority among the creditors. This could serve as the dictionary definition of chutzpah. Wachner later settled for $452,000, promising to donate $200,000 of that to charity. And Warnaco emerged from bankruptcy in February of 2003.

It is all very well to talk about incentive plans, but all the incentives in the world cannot work if there are other impediments to getting the job done. Some so-called incentive plans can be manipulated. Targets can be hit by divesting a subsidiary instead of increasing product sales. More important, there is no incentive plan that can make a weekend athlete into an Olympic gold medalist. And no incentive plan will make a CEO who is in over his head suddenly able to turn the company around.

When companies are doing well, the capacity for outrage dissipates. As long as everyone is making money, no one minds that some people are making too much. But when the economy slows down, and especially when there are layoffs, compensation becomes a flashpoint. This happened in the early 1990s, when executive compensation became the subject of magazine cover stories, *Nightline* and *Crossfire* debates on television, and hearings before the U.S. Congress. In 1991, CalPERS called for share holders to withhold their votes from the board of directors of ITT, where CEO Rand Aroskog's compensation more than doubled as the stock sank. The 1 percent of "withhold" votes cast led to a massive overhaul of the company's compensation plan. At Fairchild, an overpaying company that merited an entire chapter in Crystal's book, the board approved substantial revisions to the company's compensation plan, including a $250,000 cut in CEO Jeffrey Steiner's cash compensation, cancellation of 50,000 options, and agreement to no new options until 1993 and no raises until 1996. This was in settlement of a shareholder lawsuit, worth noting because courts are very reluctant to permit challenges to executive compensation.

General Dynamics reacted to the sobriquet "Generous Dynamics," accorded it by *Business Week* for a compensation package that gave its executives double their salary for a 10-day rise in stock prices. The company called a special meeting to get shareholder approval for substantial changes after pressure from shareholders—and a visit from *60 Minutes.* United Airlines executives agreed to increased disclosure of their compensation in the proxy statement, after negotiations with the United Shareholders Association. Many companies announced cuts; at USAir, the directors took a 20 percent compensation cut, to mirror the cuts they were asking of employees.

In 1992, the focus on compensation continued, as the Securities and Exchange Commission (SEC) reversed its longtime policy and allowed advisory (nonbinding) shareholder resolutions on compensation. Later, they reversed another policy to allow votes on proposals that would require companies to obtain shareholder approval before repricing stock options.

The media and the politicians emphasized the size of certain executive compensation packages. Shareholders focused, as Michael Jensen and Kevin Murphy put it, not on "how much" but on "how."[5] Two crucial elements of the "how" are stock options and restricted stock grants, and shareholders began to make some important distinctions.

Consultants at Hewitt Associates found that the average face value of stock options to CEOs from the mid-1980s to 2003 have grown sixfold, and nearly all U.S. publicly traded companies offer stock options as part of the compensation package. According to one study, 53.92 percent of firms included stock options as a part of a compensation package in 1992. By 1997, the figure had risen to 71.85 percent.

In the late 1990s, a "how you gonna keep 'em down on the farm" attitude caused the CEOs of established companies to insist on pay to match that of the new economy high-tech entrepreneurs. Most of their boards complied, even in the absence of any evidence that there was any risk they might accept—or even get—a competing offer. The new economy executives received superstar pay for lackluster performance. AOL's Steve Case grossed $303.3 million from 1996 to 1999, while average return on equity was 119 percent. The old economy executives did the same. Disney's Michael Eisner, once the poster boy for good pay due to his premium-priced options, came in last in the annual *Business Week* pay-performance survey, with three-year pay of $636.9 million for a three-year performance of 28 percent. Metro-Goldwyn-Mayer repriced the options of a retired CEO from $24 to $14.90 per share. Phillip Morris decided to pay dividends on stock options, so that even if the options were underwater the executives would still get an income stream. Reacting to the news that its employees did not meet the performance goals that would have triggered bonuses, Sears, Roebuck extended the deadline, subverting the pay-performance link. The sheer number of options granted became staggering. In addition to 1.25 million unrestricted shares, George Sheehan of Webvan received 15 million options. When the company later went into bankruptcy, his guaranteed lifetime annuity made him one of the company's biggest creditors.

As the bull market roared and people just out of their teens became dot-com zillionaires, the objections to CEO pay carried less force. But corporate scandals and a weakening economy put the focus back on pay as a symbol of everything that was wrong.

In 2002, the International Corporate Governance Network adopted a statement on executive compensation. These excerpts give some sense of its take on the issues:

> The fundamental requirement for executive remuneration reporting is TRANSPARENCY. The base salary, short-term and long-term incentives, as well as other payments and benefits for all main-board directors, should be published. Remuneration committees should publish statements on the expected OUTCOMES of the remuneration structures, in terms of ratios between base salaries, short-term bonuses and long-term rewards, making both "high" and "low" assumptions as well as the "central" case. . . .
>
> The Committee recommends that a remuneration report be presented as a separate voting item at every annual meeting. . . .

Stock options, of course, are supposed to be the ultimate example of compensation for performance. The company gives the option recipient the right to purchase a block of the company's stock at some specified point in the future at a "strike price" set at the time of award, often the current trading price. So if the stock rises between the time of award and the time the option is exercised, the executive will get the benefit of the gain, without having had to make the capital expenditure to buy the stock.

Theoretically, at least, the person granted the options will not make any money unless the stock goes up. A typical description of a stock option plan notes, "The company's stock option program is designed to focus attention on stock values, develop Company ownership, promote employee loyalty, reward long-term business success and develop a parallel interest between key employees and shareholders." But as one compensation consultant argues, market and industry factors (over which company management have no control) account for about two-thirds of the stock price's movement.[6] Warren Buffett noted in one of his annual reports that stock options do not tie individual performance to individual compensation:

> Of course, stock options often go to talented, value-adding managers and sometimes deliver them rewards that are perfectly appropriate. (Indeed, managers who are really exceptional almost always get far less than they should.) But when the result is equitable, it is accidental. Once granted, the option is blind to individual performance. Because it is irrevocable and unconditional (as long as a manager stays in the company), the sluggard receives rewards from his options precisely as

does the star. A managerial Rip Van Winkle, ready to doze for 10 years, could not wish for a better incentive system.

Ironically, the rhetoric about options frequently describes them as desirable because they put owners and managers in the same financial boat. In reality, the boats are far different. No owner has ever escaped the burden of capital costs, whereas a holder of a fixed-price option bears no capital costs at all. An owner must weigh upside potential against downside risk; an option holder has no downside. In fact, the business project in which you would wish to have an option frequently is a project in which you would reject ownership. (I'll be happy to accept a lottery ticket as a gift—but I'll never buy one.)[7]

Fans of options say that they are effective in motivating long-term performance. But Philip Morris gave CEO Hamish Maxwell options on 500,000 shares at his retirement, when motivation and performance were scarcely relevant.

One troubling aspect of stock option awards is repricing, reissuing stock options when the stock price is below the option price. Companies that have repriced executive options included Apple Computers, Salomon Brothers, and Occidental Petroleum.[8] This removes all the management risks (and all the shareholder benefits) of a stock option grant. For the purpose of incentives, it is just like giving the managers cash. One of the most beneficial aspects of shareholder involvement is that repricing of stock options has been widely discredited.

At the same time, another kind of option award with almost no relation to performance is gaining in popularity. That is the awarding of huge option grants, so that even an increase of one dollar a share will lead to a million-dollar payoff, regardless of whether the gain is at or less than the rest of the market. Like repricing, enormous option grants remove any downside from the compensation plan. Leon Hirsch, CEO of U.S. Surgical, was awarded so many options that his compensation risk was all but removed. Four years' worth of grants gave him nearly six million shares on option. If the stock climbed by as little as one dollar, he would make $5.9 million. As then SEC chairman Richard Breeden noted, "Mega-grants of options are an increasing and quite disturbing trend. Some mega options make mini sense for shareholders. . . . [S]hareholders are entitled to expect the directors who make those awards to have an affirmative reason for every award and its pricing."[9]

Chairman of the Federal Reserve Alan Greenspan made some thoughtful comments on stock options in a speech delivered at the 2002 Financial Markets Conference of the Federal Reserve Bank of Atlanta:

> The seemingly narrow accounting matter of option expensing is, in fact, critically important for the accurate representation of corporate performance. And accurate accounting, in turn, is central to the functioning of free-market capitalism—the system that has brought such a high level of prosperity to our country. . . . I fear that the failure to expense stock option grants has introduced a significant distortion in reported earnings—and one that has grown with the increasing prevalence of this form of compensation.

Regrettably, some current issuance practices have not created the alignment of incentives that encourages desired corporate behavior. One problem is that stock options, as currently structured, often provide only a loose link between compensation and successful management. A company's share price, and hence the value of related options, is heavily influenced by economy-wide forces—that is, by changes in interest rates, inflation, and myriad other forces wholly unrelated to the success or failure of a particular corporate strategy.

There have been more than a few dismaying examples of CEOs who nearly drove their companies to the wall and presided over a significant fall in the price of the companies' stock relative to that of their competitors and the stock market overall. Nonetheless, they reaped large rewards because the strong performance of the stock market as a whole dragged the prices of the forlorn companies' stocks along with it.

To assume that option grants are not an expense is to assume that the real resources that contributed to the creation of the value of the output were free. Surely the existing shareholders who granted options to employees do not consider the potential dilution of their share in the market capitalization of their corporation as having no cost to them.

What shareholders look for in options is some way to make sure that they tie returns to the particular company's performance rather than to the performance of the market as a whole. One way to do this is to index the options, so that the strike price rises with the stock market. That way, the compensation reflects the performance of the particular company's stock. Another option is to grant the options at a price greater than the current stock price. Hay Group compensation consultant Ira Kay says that commit-tees should build downside risk into their plans by selling jumbo stock op-tion grants, paying bonuses for executives who retain option shares, and granting premium options. Shareholders are becoming more sophisticated about compensation. According to the Investor Responsibility Research Center, the percentage of shareholders voting against option plans was 3.5 percent in 1988 and 12 percent in 1991. In 1998, 15 proposals were defeated by shareholders, while 270 had at least 30 percent opposition.

Instead of stock options, some companies make restricted stock grants, awarding stock with limits on its transferability for a set time (usually two or three years, but sometimes for the executive's tenure with the company). Some restricted stock grants have performance requirements as well, such as at FleetBoston, where the stock will vest only if executives meet aggressive financial targets. Restricted stock becomes more appealing in a down mar-ket (or when executives think the stock is not going to increase in value) be-cause, unlike an option, restricted stock has value unless the stock goes down to zero. Crystal is leery of restricted stock grants, arguing that they should be a signal to the market that even management does not think that the stock price will go up. They are low in risk. Unless there are performance triggers, an executive granted restricted stock will always make money, unless the stock goes down to zero.

In 2002, the board of Bank of America Corporation granted Chief Exec-utive Kenneth Lewis an $11.3 million restricted stock award, in addition to 750,000 stock options. Awards of restricted stock instead of, or in addition to, stock options are increasingly appealing as market pressure or changes in accounting rules force options grants to be expensed, thus removing the bal-ance sheet advantage of options over stock, and as CEOs hedge their bets in an uncertain market.

In the early twenty-first century, executive contracts provided for so much money before starting work and after leaving that the amount to be paid for the time on the job became all but irrelevant.

Sometimes called joining bonuses, compensation for income opportuni-ties forgone or reimbursement for benefits forfeited from a former employer, these so-called golden hellos are now almost ubiquitous in executive re-cruitment. The range of terms used to describe golden hellos is only ex-ceeded by the range in the size of such payments, from a high of $45,000,000 paid to Gary Wendt by Conseco to a low of $150,000 for Steve Odland of

AutoZone. In one case that attracted a lot of attention, Ron LeMay was re-cruited from Sprint to be the CEO of waste management. His pay package included Sprint options, on the theory that waste management shareholders should make sure he was able to benefit (apparently without having to buy any stock) from the work he had done at Sprint. Those who thought this continuing interest in Sprint was a bad sign about his commitment to waste management were proven right when he returned to Sprint after less than five months. LeMay and his boss, CEO William Esrey, were removed from their positions at Sprint in 2003 after disclosure of a tax avoidance scheme that allowed them to shelter $288 million in stock option profits.

The golden parachutes for Sprint executives were triggered not by com-pletion of a merger with MCI but by a vote in favor of the merger by the board. Thus, when the merger was not approved by federal regulators, the shareholders got the worst of both worlds—a failed deal for which they had to pay out bonuses to the executives. Some CEOs also get transaction bo-nuses for acquisitions, regardless of subsequent performance by any measure. To give a bonus for a transaction is to create a perverse incentive, especially if the executive can get another transaction bonus for selling or spinning off the acquisition when it does not work out.

Postemployment compensation for CEOs is not subject to the same rig-orous disclosure standards as pay while the CEO is still in his job. It took an ugly divorce proceeding to make public the lavish benefits given to former GE CEO Jack Welch. The public filing simply said that he would have "con-tinued lifetime access" to company facilities. Companies that make a clear statement about what is—and is not—covered after retirement will benefit from enhanced credibility as shareholders learn to be more skeptical and more inquisitive about this category of compensation.

Other popular places to pad executive pay are described in the following sections.

Gross-Ups

Just about all CEOs of major corporations end up owing some extra income taxes—in particular, a special excise tax. Most of the contracts have a provi-sion requiring the company to pay it. There may have been some justifica-tion for these payments to prevent unequal treatment during a transition period just after the excise tax rules were adopted, but it is harder and harder to justify as time goes on. This is the Leona Helmsley "only little people pay taxes" approach. These people are getting paid a lot. They should be able to pay their own taxes, just like the rest of us.

DEEMED YEARS OF SERVICE

When the CSX Corporation calculates pension benefits for its chief executive, John W. Snow, later treasury secretary in the second Bush administration, it includes credit for 44 years of service to the company, although he worked there just 20 years. Moreover, Snow's benefits will be based not just on his salary, or even his salary and bonus, but also on the value of 250,000 shares of stock the CSX board gave him. This is a recent trend in compensation, basing pension benefits on imputed (basically, made-up) years of service.

CAUSE

CEOs who are terminated for cause do not receive the full package of termination benefits that they would if they were terminated without cause. This makes sense. Anyone terminated without cause should be entitled to some financial arrangement as compensation.

The problem is that in the world of CEO employment contracts, terms like *cause* are redefined. The contracts whittle away at the definition to make it impossible to terminate employment based on poor performance without substantial expense. Cause is most often defined as felony, fraud, embezzlement, gross negligence, or moral turpitude. At Toys R Us, the contract for former CEO Michael Goldstein provided that he could not be fired for cause without a felony involving moral turpitude. Newmont Mining's Ronald C. Cambre has a contract that requires three-quarters of the board to find that he acted in bad faith in order to support termination for cause. Richard J. Kogan's contract at Schering-Plough provides that if he challenges a for-cause termination, his own determination of good faith prevails unless there is a final and nonappealable judgment to the contrary by a court. The most outrageous of these provisions was surely the now-notorious contract for Dennis Kozlowski of Tyco, which provided that conviction of a felony was not grounds for termination unless it was directly injurious to the company. He had no contract for the first four years he served as CEO, so it now seems clear that he only asked for it after he knew he was under investigation for sales tax evasion. Apparently, his board did not consider the timing or language to be of concern.

Very few contracts even mention poor performance as the basis for termination for cause, although some contracts do include willful refusal to follow the direction of the board. Some of those that do refer to performance require a showing of bad faith to make it clear that failure to perform alone is not sufficient for cause.

The recent push to make termination-without-cause payments equal those for termination in connection with a change in control is particularly troubling. Change-of-control payments are intended to align the interests of the CEO with the shareholders in evaluating a business combination. Payments for termination without cause are intended to ease a nonperforming CEO out the door. They can also provide an incentive for a bored CEO to trigger his own parachute with a buy-out deal that may be contrary to the long-term interests of the shareholders.

The cost of these provisions may be small in comparison to the peace of mind that comes from being able to fire an unsatisfactory CEO without worrying about litigation. But we think that boards can do better than this. One of the justifications often claimed for the astronomical amounts of CEO pay is the element of risk. But provisions like this can make the position risk free or even provide an incentive to leave, as departures from CEOs at ATT, Mattel, Disney, and Global Crossing demonstrate.

CHANGE OF CONTROL

As with cause, there is a through-the-looking-glass quality to the definition of *change of control*. Summit Bank is one company that requires acquisition of 51 percent of the stock. But other boards do not make any effort to require a CEO to work with substantial block holders of stock, even though studies show that block holders can be effective monitors of shareholder value, especially when they have representation on the board. Many contracts define change of control that can trigger a parachute as low as 20 and even 15 percent.

We believe that it can be in the shareholders' interests to ensure that a CEO must make every effort to work cooperatively with a substantial block holder. Making departure so painless can be a disincentive for those considering the purchase of a block of stock. This can discourage the involvement of substantial investors, who will not want to buy in knowing that the CEO can just walk out the door, taking a hefty sum from the corporate coffers on the way out.

Furthermore, these low triggers can create perverse incentives. The motivation for the recent Time Warner/AOL deal became clearer when Graef Crystal revealed in his newsletter that the deal paid out at least $1.8 billion in option profits for Time Warner executives and that this was triggered not by completion of the deal but merely by the vote of the directors in its favor.[10] Similarly, the Sprint executives received their golden parachutes for the merger with MCI, even though regulators refused to approve the deal and it was never completed. A 2003 settlement of a shareholder lawsuit against Sprint had a precedent-setting 50 governance improvements, including a commitment not to trigger future parachutes unless the transaction was completed.

An ideal contract for a chief executive should provide incentives and protections solely designed for tying compensation to the creation of shareholder value. Anything that distracts from or contradicts that goal is an indication that a company's board is not sending a clear message about its priorities to the CEO, the officers and employees, or the investment community.

Executive compensation is most important not because of what it shows us about the CEO but for what it shows us about corporate boards. Shareholders want CEOs to be aggressive and even a little greedy. But shareholders depend on directors to make sure that those qualities are directed at shareholder value. It is fine for the CEO to ask for the moon. But it is the job of the directors to say, "Sure! You can have half of the moon now, and the other half when the stock price doubles." And when the board fails to do so, it is the job of the shareholders to remind them that we demand accountability.

NOTES

This chapter is adapted from *Corporate Governance* by Robert AG Monks and Nell Minow (third edition). Oxford, England: Blackwell Publishing Ltd. (2004).

1. Thomas A. Stewart, "The King Is Dead," *Fortune,* 14 January 1993, p. 34.

2. *Forbes,* May 27, 1991.

3. Graef Crystal, *In Search of Excess* (New York: W. W. Norton, 1991).

4. See Graef Crystal's study for the United Shareholders Association, "Executive Compensation in Corporate America 1991," and Graef Crystal, "The Compensation 500: What America's Top CEOs Should Be Paid This Year," *Financial World,* 29 October 1991. For press coverage, see Michelle Osborne, "Author's Recipe for CEO Pay," *USA Today,* 9 October 1991; Robert J. McCartney, "Quote the Maven, Cut Some More," *Washington Post,* 29 January 1992; Alison Leigh Cowan, "The Gadfly CEOs Want to Swat," *New York Times,* 2 February 1992.

5. Michael C. Jensen and Kevin J. Murphy, "CEO Incentives: It's Not *How Much* You Pay, It's *How,*" *Harvard Business Review,* May/June (1990): p. 138.

6. See Towers Perrin, "XYZ Company: Weaknesses of Conventional Stock Option Plans and a Proposed Solution: An Indexed Stock Option Plan," New York, 1991.

7. Berkshire Hathaway, Inc., *Annual Report to Shareholders,* 1985, p. 12.

8. Crystal, supra, p. 134, note 4.

9. Statement of Richard Breeden, Chairman of SEC, at open meeting of the Commission, 15 October 1992.

10. We particularly appreciated Crystal's pointing out the unique provision in the Time Warner options—they became exercisable not when the deal was concluded, but as soon as the board voted to approve it.

CHAPTER 15

ACCOUNTING 101

RICK ANTLE

THE FIRST real indication that my profession had changed forever was a CNN scroll about Andersen's admissions in the Enron fiasco. During the arc of my career as a student in a traditional undergraduate accounting program, as a graduate student in business, and as an accounting professor, I had come to terms with the relative anonymity of the accounting profession. To be sure, one could expect the occasional scandal. But society's interest had always been confined to the business section of the newspaper and specialty television programs targeted only at the most desperate Wall Street news junkies. The Enron scandal had broken through to more mainstream media, but this was something different. This was a scroll about one of the five largest accounting firms in the world, one of our most prestigious partnerships, a firm that had employed me, helped me, encouraged me, and some of whose people—as trite as it sounds—had inspired me in my accounting career. And not only had that firm behaved badly, it had broken the sacred eleventh commandment for auditors: *Thou shalt not destroy documents!*

Since that day, the accounting profession has gotten more public attention than any of its members wanted. We have seen several more scandals, congressional hearings, Andersen's criminal conviction, and the establishment of a completely new body regulating the accounting profession in the United States—the Public Company Accounting Oversight Board. We are deep in the process of re-examining aspects of financial reporting and auditing.

171

Strengths of Financial Reporting

The main strength of our financial reporting system lies in its goal—to convey information about an organization's financial resources, financial commitments, and the results of the use of those resources over time. This goal gives rise to the familiar basic financial statements. A balance sheet portrays in financial terms an organization's resources and commitments at a point in time, while an income statement depicts an organization's consumption and production of resources over time.

These financial statements conform nicely to a simple view of the job of a manager of a for-profit organization: to make a profit for its owners. In assessing the manager's performance, obviously, it is important to consider the resources at the manager's disposal and the obligations he has created and discharged. That is, the most basic measure of performance is some type of return measure—net income divided by a measure of resources employed.

Another strength of financial reporting is the way it forces the depictions of resources at points in time and what happened over time to fit together. That is, it forces consistency: an income statement must fit nicely in between the beginning and ending balance sheets for the period. In accounting jargon, we call this the *articulation* of financial statements.

It is easy to underestimate the usefulness of having a system that forces consistency. At the risk of giving away my age, I am reminded of some experience with computer programming languages. Early FORTRAN had a fairly rigid set of rules about defining variables and what one could do with different classes of variables. At the cost of some overhead in the code, it forced me to carefully and methodically consider the things my program was manipulating. My FORTRAN code tended to be lengthy, but it progressed in a series of small steps that eventually led to the intended result.

The program Array Processing Language (APL), on the other hand, was an extremely flexible programming language. It had virtually no constraints on what types of things could be done to any type of variable. In theory, one could write incredibly concise code in APL. My problem was that it let me do things like multiply the list of names of state capitals by five, add a matrix of elevens, then divide the result by the letter *c*. Thus, APL was too flexible for me, and my programs too often produced nonsense. I needed more structure to discipline my work.

Our system of financial reporting provides some structure to discipline our work of depicting the stocks and flows of an organization's resources. This is a considerable strength.

Another source of discipline imposed by our system of financial reporting comes through its ties to objective facts and events. Note carefully my use of the phrase *its ties to objective facts.* Financial reports are full of estimates, which are unavoidable in anything other than a cash basis accounting system. Once we define an asset as a future benefit, for example, we have implicitly required a prediction of the future—an estimate, for example. But vital discipline is injected by an accounting system that demands that estimates eventually be *trued up* to actual events.

Consider the way we handle potentially uncollectible receivables. First, we record them at what is owed because we want to keep track of that to aid in collection. But we are also interested in how much we actually expect to collect. So we make an estimate about the amount that is likely to go uncollected, and we establish an allowance for doubtful accounts to reflect the fact that we do not expect 100 percent collection.

Having made this estimate, a vital part of the financial reporting process is the comparing of estimation to the actual collection experience. If we have overestimated collections, we add to the allowance. If we have underestimated collections, we reduce the allowance. This ongoing process of adjusting the allowance to reflect actual collections keeps the accounting from departing completely from reality.

Having some points at which the accounts are trued up to reality is handy for many reasons. Departures from reality can come from two different sources—simply bad estimates, made in good faith or outright manipulation of the financial reports. Either way, truing up is helpful because it fixes both good-faith errors and manipulation. Plus, it might deter manipulation by raising the chances that there will be a day of reckoning for the manipulator.

The main point of all this is that our system of financial reporting imposes discipline in several ways, and discipline is useful. However, the system does not completely nail things down, and that brings me to its weaknesses.

WEAKNESSES OF FINANCIAL REPORTING

The biggest weakness of our financial reporting system is that it leaves out a lot of things. We can only capture some of an organization's resources in the asset section of its balance sheet. For example, how could we determine the value of all of Microsoft's intellectual property without a ridiculous web of guesswork? The stock market implicitly estimates the value of this property but changes its mind every second.

Once we have a partial financial picture, some of the numbers we produce do not mean what we think they should mean. Suppose a piece of land that cost $100 is sold for $300. On the books, there will be a profit of $200. That appears to be a good thing. But suppose I told you that the land was sold to the CEO's brother-in-law and another buyer had offered $350. What appeared as a gain of $200 really should have been a gain of $250. The gain of $200 looks like a loss of $50 when we compare it to what should have happened.

The accounting did not keep up with changes in the value of the land. That is, before the transaction with the brother-in-law, the accounts included only a partial picture—the holding gain of $250 on the land had not been recorded.

In some ways, Enron represented the height of the partial-picture problem. Any set of financial reports has to have some organization on which it is reporting. In accounting, we call this the entity. An asset is a future benefit, but whose future benefit is it? It would not make sense to list the cash in my personal checking account as an asset of the Yale School of Management. When we make up financial statements for the Yale School of Management, the assets we list on its balance sheet should be its assets, not its assets mixed with mine.

Enron used thousands of special purpose entities. These were legally separate organizations, many of which were established by Enron and with which Enron had dealings. No doubt, there were legitimate business reasons for Enron to establish many of these special purpose entities. And the rules of financial reporting are actually fairly good about requiring that the economically meaningful entity, not just the legal entity, be the focus of financial reports. But one of the problems at Enron was that the definition of the right entity got off track. The consolidated Enron entity was not defined broadly enough, and this allowed two things to happen. First, some assets and—more importantly—liabilities were left off the balance sheet. Second, Enron recorded profits on transactions that were simply transactions with itself.

The more complex an entity gets and the more complex transactions get, the greater the danger that the financial reports will paint only a partial picture. In addition to their ability to be manipulated—which clearly, no one should do—partial pictures also can be misleading.

MANAGERIAL BEHAVIOR

There is a scene in the movie *Office Space* in which management, attempting to refocus the workforce, puts up a huge sign that reads, "Is this good for the company?" In the context of the movie, this message is used to underscore the plight of the helpless lower-echelon drones that are exploited by middle management. The sign would have an entirely different effect on the viewing audience if it were hung in the executive suite. Slightly rephrased, it might then be interpreted as a simple guidepost to executive decisions: "Is this good for the shareholders?"

Of course, the world is a complex place, and it is sometimes difficult to determine whether something is good for the shareholders. But one thing we know for sure is that the issue of whether something is good for the shareholders is not the same as whether it makes for a larger bottom line on the income statement. Everyone knows that financial reports paint a partial picture, and sometimes the bottom is lower when the right thing is done. In the 1970s, for example, many companies switched from First In, First Out (FIFO) to Last In, First Out (LIFO) to obtain tax benefits. The LIFO conformity rule imposed LIFO in the published financial reports as well. Executives had no trouble explaining why bonus plan parameters should be adjusted for the lower LIFO earnings—the action taken was good for the shareholders, but it resulted in a lower bottom line.

That is why I am especially mystified by the "I am not an accountant" defense of some executives caught up in scandals. "I am not an accountant" does justify why an executive might be unsure of the proper accounting for a transaction. Accounting, mirroring business practice, has become very complex. But "I am not an accountant" does not relieve an executive from explaining why he thought that transaction was good for the shareholders in the first place.

It may seem simplistic, but I am advocating a straightforward rule for chief executives: do what is best for shareholders and let the accounting chips fall where they may. If you feel that the partial picture painted by the financial statements is misleading about your actual performance, make your case and move on. You might end up saying, "I am not an accountant." But you will not have to say, "I was not a good CEO."

CHAPTER 16

PRINCIPLES AND BEST PRACTICES OF EXECUTIVE COMPENSATION THAT STAND THE TEST OF TIME

ROBERTA D. FOX AND MICHAEL J. POWERS

CORPORATE GOVERNANCE and executive pay critics had a heyday in 2003 as the media focused its lens on executive compensation. Suddenly, it seemed that everyone—the Securities and Exchange Commission, the stock exchanges, the Financial Accounting Standards Board, Congress, the courts, and shareholders—was demanding reforms in one way or another. Several reports were issued setting forth principles and best practices, including *The Business Roundtable's Principles of Executive Compensation, The Report of the National Association of Corporate Directors on Executive Compensation and the Role of the Compensation Committee,* and *The Breeden Report.* Large public pension funds, such as Teachers Insurance and Annuity Association–College Retirement Equities Fund (TIAA-CREF) and California Public Employees' Retirement System (CalPERS) also weighed in, establishing their own policies to determine how they will vote on proxy proposals. And if 2003 was a wild ride, 2004 will likely be even more so. Simply add "presidential candidates" to the list of those out to reform executive compensation in the United States.

However, the question remains as to whether these principles and best practices actually make sense and have what it takes to stand the test of time. Many of them do in that they are both logical and necessary. However, others are built on reaction rather than sound governance principles and business judgement.

In our view, executive compensation principles and best practices that stand the test of time are those that share the following characteristics:

- Designed in an environment focused on good corporate governance principles.
- Provide companies with flexibility to design programs that are best suited for their business and their shareholders (including complexities that are inherent in a very competitive market for retaining, motivating, and compensating executives to work for the best interests of long-term shareholders).
- Pay well only for sustained, superior financial and stock price performance.
- Designed in a cooperative, nonadversarial environment between management and an independent compensation committee.
- Provide full disclosure of the program design, the potential economic and dilutive costs to shareholders, and the processes by which independence is ensured.
- Allow shareholders to vote on key compensation arrangements for senior executives.
- Make sense regardless of whether the stock market is bull or bear.
- Do not inadvertently motivate the wrong type of behavior.

But before we discuss what we believe are executive compensation best practices, it is important to step back and look briefly at how we got to this point. What drove us to the excesses that have occurred and, ultimately, to the key principles that we advocate? Are those drivers of change likely to shift again, and, if so, what would they tell us? Which ones have staying power, and which are of a more temporary nature?

DRIVERS OF CHANGE

Let's first examine the stock market. Clearly, it is a significant driver of change, particularly with respect to executive compensation, as it all too often causes immediate, short-term reactions to plan design. In the early 1980s, the bulk of an executive's total compensation package was cash. In fact, long-term incentives—and thus the portion most directly tied to the stock market—only comprised about 20 percent of an executive's total compensation. By the beginning of the 1990s, long-term compensation comprised about one-third of an executive's total compensation package, which was just slightly more than base salary. However, this was also the beginning of the greatest bull market in recent history, and by the mid-1990s, long-term incentives accounted for more than 45 percent of an executive's total compensation. Not only did that percentage exceed what was provided to an executive in base pay, it also exceeded the combination of base pay and annual bonus. By the time the bull market peaked in 2000, long-term incentives—the majority of which were in the form of stock options—had grown to comprise almost two-thirds of an executive's total compensation package. The pay of a CEO was even more slanted toward stock options and other equity incentives.

When the stock market was rising, executives wanted stock options, and companies were willing to provide them. The reasons for this were many:

- Stock options were not accounted for as an expense on the company's financial statements.
- At that time, shareholders viewed stock options as the preferred equity vehicle because they believed stock options tied the interests of executives to the interests of shareholders and they were linked to performance. In other words, executives would gain only if shareholders also reaped benefits.
- They were highly leveraged (i.e., because they are less valuable than a full share of stock, executives receive more of them).
- Congress made them easy to qualify as deductible performance-based compensation.
- Overhang and run rates[1] were still at manageable levels.

Then, the Dow peaked at 11,723 in January 2000 and began its precipitous three-year decline to 7,416. Suddenly, companies have executives holding options that are significantly out of the money (also called underwater stock options). New option grants are made, but stocks continue to decline. Executives complain that stock options are no longer "motivating," leading them to consider replacing stock options with other vehicles. Interestingly, this is yet another example of history repeating itself. During the 1970s, when the market was virtually flat and stock options were in disfavor, long-term performance plans that focused on internal financial metrics (e.g., performance share and performance unit plans) became more prevalent.

Another driver of change included the spectacular corporate meltdowns among large Fortune 100 companies, primarily caused by fraud and financial misconduct. These have rocked the business world, and the ripple effect has been enormous. To ensure the integrity of the world's largest capital markets, a renewed and intense focus on the transparency of financial statements and the independence of board members and key committee members has emerged. The Sarbanes-Oxley Act of 2002 is all-encompassing in addressing issues of corporate governance. Though much of the focus in the corporate governance arena has been in the financial controls and audit area, executive compensation gone awry has been viewed as another key contributor to the abuses in the current system and thus a target for change.

The Financial Accounting Standards Board (FASB) is currently addressing the transparency issue and is expected to require the expensing of stock options as of 2005.[2] If this expectation becomes a reality, it will essentially level the playing field with other long-term incentive vehicles that have always had a charge to earnings associated with them. The New York Stock Exchange (NYSE) and NASDAQ also have put in place new rules on shareholder approval of equity compensation plans that generally require that shareholders approve all equity compensation plans, with some limited exceptions. The exchanges also have adopted corporate governance rules regarding the independence of the board and the operation as well as the independence of key committees, such as audit, compensation, and nominating. This helps ensure that plans are developed in an independent environment—without undue influence from the CEO and management—and should encourage companies to develop plans that are more performance based.

Shareholder activism is another important driver of change. Major institutional shareholders and vocal unions are no longer content to sit on the sidelines and be passive investors in the business. As they become more involved in determining how their shares are spent or their ownership is diluted, they, too, are influencing executive compensation design. Because of the growth in long-term incentives during the 1990s and the extensive use of stock options, shareholders have seen overhang levels increase from around 10 percent in 1997 to over 15 percent in 2003. Currently, annual run rates stand at approximately 1.7 percent, with companies in the high-technology sector approaching 3 percent. Shareholders often view these amounts as excessive. Consequently, it is increasingly difficult for companies to get strong support for plans when they go back to shareholders and ask for additional shares. Thus, companies are looking at plan designs that can conserve share usage. What's more, as a result of the new stock exchange rules that require shareholder approval of equity compensation plans, shareholders know they have a voice on plan-design issues, and they are making those views known (e.g., not supporting plans for companies with high overhang levels or plans that have unfavorable provisions, such as stock option repricing).

At this point, the dominoes have started to fall. Because excessive executive pay is a populist issue, the media gets involved and cries for change. Every year in the spring, companies publish their proxies, and the so-called Easter Parade begins. *The Wall Street Journal, Fortune,* and *Business Week* (to name just a few periodicals) publish what America's top executives are making. Disparities in pay between the CEO and the average worker are examined, revealing a huge gap. While these CEO pay ratios are not particularly useful, because there certainly is a free market for CEO pay, our data shows that the average total compensation for top executives among Fortune 100 companies has nearly doubled since 1995 (from $1.4 million to $2.5 million).

Congress also believes it can legislate change or benefit from the attempt. Why not? It has in the past. Consider these examples: incentive stock options; 162(m) dealing with the deductibility of compensation for executives; and 280G dealing with golden parachutes. None of these provisions have worked as intended. In fact, they have had the unintended consequences of driving undesired behavior and plan design. The way for companies to deal with 162(m) was not to limit pay to $1 million, but to grant lots of stock options, while the way to deal with 280G was not to limit golden parachutes but to gross-up the executives for the punitive excise tax the U.S. government imposed.

BEST PRACTICES OF EXECUTIVE COMPENSATION

Change is good as it almost always leads to better practices. However, many companies' first reaction to these forces of change is to design and implement reforms quickly. In doing so, they tend to swing to the other extreme rather than think through the long-term ramifications based on solid principles that will stand the test of time. One example we find interesting is shareholders' views on the use of stock options relative to restricted stock. Five years ago, stock options were the vehicle of choice as restricted stock was viewed as a giveaway, and its use was frowned upon. Today, some of these same shareholders are advocating the use of restricted stock and eschewing stock options. In their view, stock options lead to undesirable behavior and high overhang levels, while restricted stock more closely aligns the interests of shareholders to executives.

In contrast, the best practices we are proposing are based on a consideration of the long term, our learnings from the past, and our understanding of how the drivers of change have led to the current environment. We believe these will stand the test of time.

The Foundation: Corporate Governance and the Compensation Committee

Before we turn to a discussion of best practices in executive compensation, we first need to focus our attention on the principles for a solid foundation upon which executive compensation best practices are built. Without this foundation, there is little point to building executive compensation best practices because, like a building built on sand, they will soon crumble.

• *The compensation committee:* The compensation committee and the independence of the committee are critical to the foundation. The word *independence* is a loaded term, and there is no standard definition, even among constituents focused on corporate governance. For example, the NYSE would consider a former CEO an independent director after a three-year cooling-off period, but TIAA-CREF would argue that a former CEO can never be independent. In a recent study, The Corporate Library found that 66 percent of corporate board members are independent outsiders.[3] This does not include related outsiders who have an existing or prior relationship with the company or a family relationship with a senior officer. However, what is interesting about the study is the finding that the more independent a board is in composition, the less independent the board may actually be because of the relationships among board members that are not as transparent to shareholders. For example, 69 percent of companies combine the CEO and chairperson roles; however, 75 percent of companies with above-average independence combine the CEO and chairperson roles. This is counterintuitive because it stands to reason that a more independent board would also separate the CEO and chairperson roles. Boards that combine the CEO and chairperson roles also have greater representation of CEO-directors on the boards, and the more independent the board, the greater the incidence of board interlocks. Both of these create the potential for a conflict of interest. These findings led the Corporate Library to conclude that independence assessments should be broadened beyond the standard insider/outsider breakdowns. Although we do not necessarily agree with how far the independence assessment should be extended, we do believe a more consistent standard for independence would be useful.

Acknowledging that there is no current consistent standard for independence and recognizing that the definition should probably be broadened somewhat beyond what is contained in the stock exchange rules—for example, we are hard pressed to think of situations where a former CEO can be viewed as independent and serve on the compensation committee—our first principle is that the compensation committee should be comprised entirely of independent directors. The committee must be given ample competitive market information to make informed decisions and should set aside time to convene an executive session at every meeting. Good committee meeting practices should be followed, including advance mailings of materials and multiple meetings on important issues. The committee should also regularly perform a self-evaluation.

There has been a great deal of discussion regarding the role of the compensation consultant and whether a compensation consultant can work for both management and the compensation committee. We believe that dual consultants should be avoided because it is likely to lead to dueling consultants with little productive outcome for the company, the committee, or shareholders. Rather, the compensation committee should retain an outside compensation consultant to work cooperatively with management in the design of executive compensation pay and programs. Consultants hired by the committee may or may not have other relationships with management. If they do, however, the company should disclose to shareholders the process by which the independence of the consultant is ensured. It is also entirely appropriate for the compensation committee to periodically retain an advisory consultant to provide a broad review of the final plan designs and results.

- *Relationship of the compensation committee to the board:* Currently, under the NYSE corporate governance rules, the compensation committee is required to approve the pay of the CEO, although the CEO's pay may be discussed with the full board. We believe that with respect to actions that are controversial, may lead to litigation, or are very complicated, it is advisable that these actions be reviewed by the full board prior to final approval by the compensation committee. Such actions include—but are not limited to— CEO employment contracts, repricing underwater stock options, or putting in golden parachute agreements.

- *Establishing board pay:* Who should set board pay? This should not be a difficult question, but the fact of the matter is the right answer doesn't necessarily feel that "right." Management obviously cannot set board pay because there is an inherent conflict of interest. The full board should not set board pay because there are some insiders on the board and again, the conflict of interest issue is raised. A board that consists entirely of independent directors may make sense, but if the compensation committee is already 100 percent independent and reviews the pay with the full board—which we would recommend—an independent compensation committee should be responsible for setting the pay of the board of directors. Yes, this is setting their own pay; however, there are checks and balances. The equity compensation is required to be approved by shareholders, the pay packages are fully disclosed, and if shareholders do not approve the use of equity pay or believe directors are overpaying themselves, they have the recourse of withholding votes from the directors when they are up for reelection.

In terms of the mix of compensation for board members, we believe the majority should be in the form of equity, which must be approved by shareholders. Generally, equity compensation paid to members of the board should be in the form of full value shares, such as common stock or deferred stock, rather than stock options because holding and exercising stock options is a potential conflict of interest for directors. Director awards should not be structured identically to executive awards—directors represent shareholders, and thus their compensation should serve a different purpose. For example, in contrast to executive awards, grants to directors should be immediately vested to remove any potential conflict of interest in the event of a change in control. It is inappropriate to pay board members beyond the time period they serve on the board (e.g., pension plans or charitable award programs) or provide additional fees in the event of a change in control.

Committee chairs should be compensated fairly for any additional work, such as pre-meetings with management and/or the outside consultant.

- *Shareholder approval:* As stated previously, the major stock exchanges require shareholder approval of virtually all equity compensation plans, with some limited exceptions. We believe the compensation committee should use those exemptions on a limited and infrequent basis. For example, one exemption is for inducement awards, and thus shareholder approval is not required. An inducement award is a grant of an equity award as a material inducement to a person being hired or rehired after a bonafide period of employment interruption. The problem is that some companies are using this exemption for all new hires (referred to as *serial inducers* by some shareholder groups).

- *Transparency and disclosure:* Transparency and disclosure is a critical best practice because full disclosure, in and of itself, can cure a lot of evils. All components of director and executive compensation should be disclosed and discussed in the annual proxy statement using plain English. The required Compensation Committee Report should not be a boilerplate report but, rather, it should be comprehensive and forthright, clearly stating the relationship of compensation to the performance of the company and explaining the committee's actions of the last fiscal year. This includes areas of hidden compensation, like deferred compensation and Supplemental Executive Retirement Plans (SERPs). The cost and dilutive impact of executive compensation should be reflected in the financial statements and fully disclosed.

Executive Compensation

Once the preceding principles are implemented, the company has a solid foundation—a compensation committee focused on principles of good corporate governance—upon which executive compensation best practices can be developed. We believe these best practices are the following:

- *Pay philosophy:* The compensation committee should establish and periodically review an executive pay philosophy, which supports the company's business strategy in both the short and the long term. Included in this philosophy is the appropriate mix of pay (cash versus equity) and risk (fixed versus variable) at various employee levels.

• *Pay objective:* Generally, the pay objective and award sizes should be established at or near the median. Performance and performance alone (financial and/or stock price) should result in above- or below-market payouts. When companies establish pay objectives substantially above the median (e.g., at the 60th or 75th percentiles), it has the effect of ratcheting up executive compensation pay levels. Also, many compensation committees do not fully understand how significantly an above-median pay objective can impact the total compensation levels. For example, on average, a 75th percentile total compensation pay objective represents an increase in pay above the median of over one-third. If a company has an objective to pay long-term incentives at the 75th percentile, this can actually result in long-term award sizes that are more than double the median.

• *Peer group selection:* Selecting the right peer group is critical because most companies have an objective to pay relative to the market, and the peer group is the market. Thus, this should be a thoughtful process, and the group should be reviewed annually to determine the impact of mergers, acquisitions, and divestitures. It is not the compensation consultant's job to pick the peer group. Rather, the consultant's job is to act as a facilitator in the process. The compensation committee must be actively involved in the selection and/or approval of the peer group that is used for compensation comparison purposes. Factors that should be evaluated include size (revenue, market capitalization, number of employees), performance (e.g., total shareholder return, earnings per share, growth, return, and cash-flow measures), industry competitors, and executive talent competitors. Once an appropriate peer group has been determined, detailed financial and stock price performance information should be reviewed annually and compared to the performance of the company by the compensation committee.

• *Benchmarking:* In and of itself, benchmarking does not contribute to excessive pay. By using a near-median pay objective and selecting the appropriate peer group and matching position responsibilities, proper benchmarking—both externally and internally—can actually ensure that pay is fairly established. Valuation methodologies (e.g., Black-Scholes or binomial model for valuing stock options) for all noncash forms of pay should be sound and yield a pretax salary-equivalent figure for comparisons across different elements of pay. Regression analysis is also a useful tool in size-adjusting market data.

• *Performance measures:* There is no one-size-fits-all performance measure.

Performance measures for both short- and long-term plans should be selected based on the company's business strategy and its ability to project and measure business results. They may be qualitative or quantitative in nature and based on individual, business unit, corporate, or relative performance. Financial and stock price goals, such as total shareholder return, are also appropriate performance metrics, depending on each company's business strategy and objectives. Many companies find it very difficult to establish performance goals for three- or four-year performance periods, particularly on an absolute basis. For those companies, it may not be appropriate to put a long-term performance plan in place. Generally, performance goals should not be changed after they have been established. However, the compensation committee, operating in an environment of heightened corporate governance awareness, should always have the ability to modify performance goals in the best interests of the shareholders and the company, particularly if it is a result of an unusual and/or unforeseen event.

• *Long-term incentive plan design:* Just as there is no one-size-fits-all performance measure, there is no one-size-fits-all long-term incentive plan design. Every long-term compensation vehicle has its beauty marks and its warts. The abuse is in how they are used, not in that they are used. Stock options are not inherently evil, just as restricted stock—which was in disfavor five years ago—was not inherently evil then.

Long-term incentives should be designed to support the company's long-term business strategy, create value for shareholders, and be cost-effective. In most cases, long-term incentives should be balanced so that inappropriate behavior is not unintentionally encouraged by placing too much weight on a given incentive. When the stock market swings or there is criticism of a particular vehicle's disadvantages, care must be taken not to overreact and swing 100 percent in the opposite direction. We believe equity incentives should have vesting provisions of at least three years and stock options should not be repriced absent compelling circumstances.

• *Supplemental retirement plans and perquisites:* This is a sensitive subject with shareholders, primarily for two reasons. First, there has been some perceived abuse in the form of providing credit for years not worked or protecting benefits in the event of bankruptcy. Second, disclosure in this area is clearly inadequate, so shareholders either don't understand or distrust what they read. However, many shareholders also do not understand the extent to which an executive's secured retirement benefits are cut back by the

Internal Revenue Code. For most executives, their retirement money would disappear in an instant if the companies for which they work go into bankruptcy. This, however, would not happen for most employees because their retirement money is protected by the government.

Nevertheless, we believe that crediting additional years of service—that have not been worked—or enhancing the pay formula beyond what other executives typically receive is generally not appropriate. It is appropriate, however, for executives to have their retirement benefits based on their full pay rather than limited by the Internal Revenue Code. Unfortunately, unless the code is changed (which is unlikely), the bulk of an executive's retirement benefit must be provided in nonqualified programs and deferred compensation that are unsecured and subject to the risk of creditors.

Executives should be entitled to receive reasonable perquisites, such as a company car or allowance, financial planning assistance, first-class air travel, or membership to a country club or business club, especially if they are common in the marketplace or help them be more efficient in their role.

• *Other nonqualified deferred compensation arrangements:* Executives should be allowed to defer compensation to a later point in time, as permitted under current tax laws, provided the terms of the deferral, including investment alternatives, are reasonable.

• *Severance:* Severance is another sensitive subject for shareholders, evidenced by the fact that most shareholder proposals requesting shareholder approval of severance packages that exceed specified limits have received majority support. For example, in 2003, 18 proposals came to a vote and 15 received a majority vote. Note that even if a shareholder proposal receives a majority vote, it is nonbinding. Nevertheless, of the 15 companies that received a majority vote, nine of those companies agreed to limit the severance they pay unless shareholder approval is received.

We believe that senior executives should be entitled to reasonable severance in the event that they lose their jobs as a result of a change in control. This enables executives to stay focused on getting the best deal for shareholders without undue concern about their own job and financial situation. A double trigger (i.e., a change in control followed by a qualifying termination of employment) should be required in most instances, and cash severance should be in the range of one to three times the sum of base pay and a target bonus. Long-term incentives should not be included in calculating the cash severance as it goes beyond competitive practice and the need to bridge the executive's cash compensation until new employment is found. Rather than a single trigger on stock options and restricted stock (i.e., the change in control triggers the acceleration of vesting upon a change in control), a double trigger should be required. However, if the trigger for stock options and restricted stock is single, it should be upon consummation of the transaction rather than shareholder approval. Shareholders are particularly incensed when a change in control is triggered because shareholders have approved the transaction, the stock options and restricted stock vest, and then the deal falls through. Long-term performance plans should be prorated and not be paid at maximum performance levels. Care must be taken in drafting *good reason* termination provisions to ensure that there is not, in substance, a single trigger.

It is also appropriate to provide executive severance for a nonchange in control-involuntary or constructive termination, generally in the range of one-half to two times base pay or the sum of base pay and a target bonus. Again, long-term incentives should not be included in calculating severance. Also, equity incentives, such as stock options, restricted stock, and performance plans, should not vest upon an involuntary or constructive termination of employment. In addition to drafting good reason termination provisions, it is also critical to determine what constitutes a retirement for purposes of the company's plans and what is provided upon a retirement termination.

• *Stock ownership and holding period requirements:* Stock ownership by directors and senior executives ties their wealth directly to the interests of shareholders. Likewise, holding-period requirements tie those interests together for the long term. Therefore, as a best practice, directors and senior executives should be required to own a minimum, yet meaningful amount of company stock, with holding-period requirements put in place until those ownership levels are reached. Consequences should also follow if goals are not achieved, but both directors and executives should be given a reasonable period of time to reach them. However, there can be too much of a good thing. Companies need to be careful not to require holding periods on all stock that is received upon stock option exercise because the inability of executives to diversify can also lead to unintentional consequences that may not be in shareholders' best interests (e.g., risk-adverse behavior).

We believe that these principles and best practices are balanced and will stand the test of time. They are specific, but they do not advocate a one-size-fits-all approach. Provided the compensation committee is operating in an environment built on solid corporate governance principles and shareholders are aware of actions taken by management, companies should be permitted flexibility to develop their compensation objectives, given their specific business goals and objectives and the competition for superior executive talent.

NOTES

1. Overhang is the level of voting power that dilution shareholders would suffer from equity-based compensation plans. It is generally defined as stock options outstanding plus shares available to grant under existing plans divided by fully diluted common shares outstanding. Run rate is the amount companies spend each year in equity.

2. Note that the International Accounting Standards Board has already issued its standard with a 2005 effective date for European Union countries.

3. Jackie Cook, "Corporate and Director Interlocks in the USA: 2003," *The Corporate Library,* September 2003.

CHAPTER 17

EVOLUTION OF CORPORATE CRIMINAL LIABILITY

IMPLICATIONS FOR MANAGERS

JENNIFER ARLEN

UNTIL RECENTLY, most managers of publicly held corporations did not worry about corporate crime. Managers generally assumed that their employees (and peers) were honest. In addition, federal prosecutors generally focused on smaller corporations, with barely 3 percent of federal convictions involving publicly held firms. Those publicly held firms that were convicted rarely faced fines large enough to hurt the firm. Finally, managers had limited ability to intervene effectively to protect their firms because the extent of any corporate criminal liability depended simply on whether an employee committed the crime; managers could not necessarily reduce any corporate liability either by attempting to prevent crime or by reporting it to the government once detected.[1]

Times have changed. Today, managers of publicly held firms must recognize that both their fellow managers and their employees can, and do, commit serious crimes. Moreover, criminal activity puts public corporations at greater peril than previously. State and federal prosecutors are more willing to proceed against publicly held firms and their managers. Convicted corporations now face onerous criminal fines and civil penalties as well as intrusive government oversight and other nonmonetary sanctions.

Managers also now are more responsible for the fate of their companies should a crime occur. In contrast to the traditional approach to corporate criminal liability—under which there was little managers could do to avoid a conviction or reduce the sanction once a crime was detected—under the modern approach, managers can take actions that fully or partially insulate a company from criminal liability for its employees' wrongs. Managers can protect their firms by responding proactively with programs designed to deter crime.

Managers of publicly held firms must understand the changing landscape of federal criminal law if they are to successfully respond to the challenges presented by potential wrongdoing by managers and other employees. This chapter discusses how managers can best respond to the evolving practice of corporate criminal liability. It highlights measures that managers can take to deter crime; it also discusses what managers can do to reduce potential sanctions for any crimes that are committed. Finally, the chapter discusses problems with the current system and pitfalls that arise for managers attempting to promote good corporate compliance.

SANCTIONS FOR CONVICTED CORPORATIONS

In the last 20 years, corporations have witnessed a sea change in the magnitude of liability imposed for federal crimes. Whereas in the early 1980s, publicly held firms and their managers generally had little to fear from a federal conviction, now a federal conviction may spell corporate and personal ruin.

Federal prosecutors appear to be more willing to proceed against public corporations than in the past. Moreover, some state prosecutors—for example, New York State Attorney General Eliot Spitzer—have focused on detecting and sanctioning corporate wrongdoing.

Sanctions for corporate crime have increased dramatically over the last 10 years. As recently as the early 1980s, most criminal fines imposed on corporations convicted of federal crimes were small. Indeed, 60 percent were less than $10,000; the average fine was only $45,790.[2] Then in 1991, the U.S. Sentencing Commission promulgated guidelines designed to increase sanctions imposed on corporations, particularly the largest corporations. The guidelines had an immediate effect. Judges governed by the guidelines imposed significantly higher criminal fines. The average fine imposed on publicly held firms jumped to $19 million in the years immediately after the guidelines (1991–1996). Moreover, now corporations could face truly ruinous fines. Daiwa Bank was subject to a fine of $340 million.[3] More recently, F. Hoffman-LaRoche was required to pay a fine of $500 million.

The adoption of the guidelines not only increased criminal fines, they also heralded a dramatic increase in other sanctions imposed on convicted corporations. These sanctions include criminal restitution of gains received and remediation of the harm caused as well as substantial civil sanctions (imposed by government agencies as well as private actors). Average total sanctions imposed on publicly held firms convicted of federal crimes jumped from approximately $13.3 million preguidelines to more than $49 million under the guidelines (1996 dollars). The largest total sanction in the five years immediately after the guidelines was $646 million.[4]

The guidelines also subjected convicted corporations to more intrusive forms of sanction. Prosecutors routinely seek, and judges regularly impose corporate probation in addition to monetary penalties. At a minimum, probation exacerbates the sanction for any future wrongdoing. In addition, judges often use probation to impose more intrusive sanctions, such as ordering the adoption of a compliance program, requiring regular governmental review of the firm's operations, or insisting that the company publicize its wrongdoing.

The trend toward larger and more intrusive corporate criminal sanctions is likely to continue. Recent congressional legislation, such as the Sarbanes-Oxley Act,[5] can be expected to result in ever-higher fines and other sanctions not only in the cases they apply to directly but also in other cases.[6]

Managers facing huge criminal sanctions and prosecutors eager to impose them thus must pay greater attention to how to protect their firms from liability for criminal wrongdoing.

STANDARDS FOR LIABILITY

To tackle corporate crime, managers must recognize that corporate crime is, in the end, committed by individuals. The board need not be involved at all.

Under both state and federal law, a corporation can be held criminally liable for any crimes committed by its managerial and nonmanagerial employees in the course of performing their jobs (if ostensibly for the firm's benefit). The act of one individual is sufficient. Prosecutors need not show that the board, or even senior officers encouraged or were complicit in the crime.[7] Indeed, under common law, the corporation can be criminally liable even if the wrongful employee violated corporate policy or express instructions when she committed the crime.[8]

Although corporate crime is committed by individuals, corporate managers can take a variety of actions to deter it. Indeed, a central reason why corporations are held criminally liable is to provide them with strong financial incentives to deter their employees' wrongdoing.[9]

IMPLICATIONS FOR MANAGEMENT

To deter corporate crime, managers must understand its roots. Corporate wrongdoers are not motivated by the altruistic desire to benefit shareholders. Instead, they commit crimes to benefit themselves.[10] For example, in hard times an employee whose compensation is tied to the profitability of her division may feel impelled to boost the division's profits by cutting corners on environmental compliance or by violating the antitrust laws in order to preserve her compensation. Similarly, a manager of a financially precarious firm may commit securities fraud in a desperate effort to save her job (and her options compensation), even though this lie will injure existing shareholders (who may not only be defrauded into retaining stock but will bear the corporate liability should the fraud be detected).[11]

Thus, in order to deter crime, managers must ensure that those people within the company who are willing to break the law do not face strong incentives to do so.[12] If managers ensure crime does not pay, then employees will eschew it. If crime *does* pay, then someone is likely to commit it.[13]

Managers can reduce the benefit of crime in a variety of ways. Of particular importance, managers often can reduce the gains from crime by altering corporate compensation and promotion policies. Evidence suggests that employees are more likely to commit crimes that boost short-run profits (such as antitrust) when their compensation or promotion is based on short-run profits because a wrongful employee obtains the immediate benefit of the crime but does not bear the full effect of any firm-wide sanction (should her role remain undetected).[14] Incentive pay tied to annual profits creates a particularly high risk of crime in poor or unstable market conditions where employees cannot retain their accustomed salaries through hard work alone. By contrast, crime is less likely when pay is based on the firm's long-run profits, which includes the cost of any future criminal sanction for employee wrongdoing.

Managers seeking to reduce the threat of corporate criminal liability would be well advised to reexamine their compensation policies to ensure that they are not inadvertently encouraging wrongdoing in their effort to reward diligence and hard work. Managers must balance between their desire to provide strong incentives for employees and the recognition that the wrong type of incentives will encourage employees to seek rewards through illegal means if they are unable to do so through lawful effort.[15]

MONITORING, REPORTING, AND COOPERATION

Corporations also can deter crimes by taking actions that increase the effectiveness of government sanctions. Employees contemplating wrongdoing are less likely to violate the law if they expect to be caught and sanctioned. Managers, thus, can deter wrongdoing by implementing "policing measures"[16] that increase the likelihood that the government detects and sanctions wrongdoers. These measures include adopting effective compliance programs truly designed to detect wrongdoing and identify violators, promptly reporting wrongdoing to the government, and cooperating with any government investigation.[17]

Although effective enforcement of the criminal law depends on encouraging corporations to detect and report wrongdoing, until recently federal law did not encourage companies to do so. As previously discussed, under the federal law that traditionally governed corporate criminal liability, a corporation faced criminal liability for its employees' crimes even if it attempted to prevent them. Liability also was unaffected by other good corporate acts, such as reporting wrongdoing.

This rule did not encourage companies to monitor or report. A company that detected and investigated wrongdoing might find its own investigations used against it by the government, while a company that turned a blind eye might avoid sanction should the government be unable to obtain sufficient evidence to convict.[18] Corporations also had little reason to report wrongdoing, and every reason not to. By reporting the wrong, a manager would effectively subject the firm to criminal liability for a wrong that otherwise might remain undetected. Thus, far from encouraging reporting, traditional corporate liability actually discouraged it (and even provided incentives for firms to cover up the crime).[19]

INSULATING THE FIRM FROM PROSECUTION

Over the last 10 years, both federal and state governments have dramatically changed their approach to corporate crime in an effort to ensure that corporations that monitor, report, and cooperate fare better than those that do not.

To induce companies to monitor, report, and cooperate, firms must expect to be better off if they engage in such policing measures than if they do not. This implies that they must be confident of facing lower expected liability if they monitor, investigate, and report.

Consistent with this, current Department of Justice policy encourages prosecutors not to indict a corporation for employee wrongdoing if the corporation had an effective program to deter wrongdoing, reported detected wrongdoing to the government, and cooperated fully.[20] This promise of insulation from criminal sanctions—both fines and probation—grants a substantial benefit to corporations that adopt compliance programs to deter crime, respond proactively to reports of suspected wrongdoing, and cooperate fully with any government investigation.[21]

To benefit from this modern federal policy, boards faced with evidence of potential wrongdoing must avoid the temptation to circle the wagons in an effort to thwart unwanted government intrusion—particularly when evidence suggests managers may indeed have committed a crime. Instead, they must focus on their primary duty to the firm. This often will place directors in the uncomfortable position of cooperating with investigations that threaten long-term colleagues and friends. But current federal policy generally provides little viable alternative option. Managers that place their corporations squarely on the side of the government may protect their firms; those who refuse, do so at their firm's peril.

REDUCING CORPORATE SANCTIONS

Managers who implement effective measures to detect crime and who report wrongdoing can benefit their companies even if prosecutors do decide to indict. Under the federal sentencing guidelines, a convicted corporation faces a significantly lower criminal fine if it had an effective compliance program, reported wrongdoing promptly, and cooperated than if it did not. Moreover, a corporation whose managers follow good corporate practices in deterring crime may avoid intrusive corporate probation. By contrast, a convicted corporation that did not have an effective compliance program is likely to have one imposed (and designed) by the government.[22]

Managers cannot obtain the full benefit of these mitigation provisions if they wait to act until they suspect wrongdoing. The sentencing guidelines only provide full mitigation for reporting and cooperating to firms that had an effective compliance program at the time the crime occurred. (Prosecutors also are more likely to indict companies that did not have a compliance program.) Thus, managers who fail to institute a program designed to detect wrongdoing put their firms at much greater risk of criminal sanction even if they report any wrongdoing they detect.[23]

To insulate companies from corporate criminal liability, directors must not only institute a compliance program, they also must ensure that it is effective. Under the sentencing guidelines, a firm that reports wrongdoing is not entitled to substantial mitigation unless it had an effective compliance program (and vice versa).

The sentencing guidelines presume that a compliance program is not effective if the crime was committed by, or condoned by, senior personnel within the firm.[24] This limitation on fine mitigation for crimes by senior personnel makes it all the more important for a corporation to avoid indictment. The board can help insulate the firm by ensuring that the compliance program was, indeed, effective (notwithstanding the presumption of the guidelines). It is critical to ensure that the compliance program includes a mechanism whereby employees can report suspected managerial wrongdoing to outsiders on the board. Should evidence arise of potential wrongdoing by managers, the outside board members also need to ensure that the firm handles the matter appropriately, including reporting wrongdoing and working with the government to investigate its own officers. A company that cooperates may be insulated from criminal liability, notwithstanding failures of internal compliance; one that fails to cooperate so may be subject to enormous criminal sanctions.

POTENTIAL PITFALLS

While federal criminal policy has improved with the adoption of stronger policies encouraging reporting and cooperation, many pitfalls exist for the unwary. These pitfalls undermine the ability of federal criminal policy to provide clear incentives to companies to detect and report wrongdoing.

To encourage reporting and cooperation, public companies must be assured that they are better off if they report suspected wrongdoing. A clear policy penalizing companies that report and insulating those that do not can provide the requisite incentive to report.

Unfortunately, while existing federal policy is intended to provide this clear incentive, the total regime governing corporate crime does not. Many different agencies—at both the state and federal level—potentially can proceed against a company for wrongdoing. The existing regime is able to induce reporting only to the degree to which state and federal agencies coordinate and jointly agree to refrain from proceeding criminally against companies that report wrongdoing and cooperate with criminal investigations. Unfortunately, at present these different enforcement agencies do not necessarily cooperate with each other. Managers contemplating cooperation with one government actor must be sure to carefully negotiate with all other relevant government enforcement agencies prior to proceeding.[25]

In addition, the existing regime may discourage reporting and cooperation to the extent that the crime also presents the risk of substantial liability in private actions. A company seeking to insulate itself from criminal liability by cooperating with federal authorities may increase its potential private civil liability by doing so. Department of Justice prosecutors require full cooperation as a condition of any agreement not to prosecute the firm. To fully cooperate, a company generally must turn over all relevant materials, even materials otherwise covered by the attorney-client privilege. Failure to provide such materials may be deemed a failure to cooperate fully and may subject the firm to criminal liability, as well as a civil sanction (e.g., by the Securities and Exchange Commission). Yet problems arise because turning over such materials to a government enforcement agency—such as the

Securities and Exchange Commission—may effectively waive the firm's attorney-client privilege in many jurisdictions, thereby potentially increasing expected recovery in any private civil action.[26] This approach to privilege potentially undermines the incentives provided by the new federal mitigation regime in situations where employee wrongdoing threatens the corporations with potentially ruinous private liability.

One partial solution to this problem would be to seek reform of punitive-damages laws to insulate corporations from punitive damages if they investigate wrongdoing promptly and fully cooperate with enforcement authorities.[27] In the meantime, board members faced with credible evidence of suspected wrongdoing must consider the privilege issue when evaluating whether the firm should conduct a full internal investigation prior to reporting suspected wrongdoing to the government. Companies also should carefully tailor confidentiality agreements with the government to gain whatever protection may exist for privileged material shared with enforcement authorities.

CONCLUSION

Most people are, by and large, law abiding; so are most publicly held firms. Yet the benefits of a lawful citizenry depend in part on the government investing resources in detecting and punishing crime. So, too, good corporate behavior depends on managers being willing to invest in compliance and enforcement, even when they believe their employees would never commit a crime. To effectively deter crime, managers must not only implement formal compliance programs designed to detect wrongdoing, they also must reassess corporate compensation and promotion practices that potentially increase employees' incentives to violate the law.

Moreover, under modern federal practice, directors and officers must play a more active role in overseeing investigations of suspected wrongdoing and negotiating with prosecutors in order to ensure that the corporation follows good practices designed to avoid indictment (or reduce any fine). In particular, outside directors must exert strong oversight to ensure that the corporation investigates and reports wrongdoing and does not attempt to hide crime in order to shelter its own.

Managers who respond effectively to crime can dramatically reduce both the risks and consequences of crime for their firms. Those who remain inactive do so at both their firms' and their own[28] peril.

NOTES

1. See text accompanying notes 2 and 6–7.

2. Mark A. Cohen, "Corporate Crime and Punishment: An Update on Sentencing Practice in the Federal Courts, 1988–1990," *Boston University Law Review* 71 (1991): pp. 247, 254–256. One reason that sanctions were so low is that, prior to 1984, federal criminal statutes provided the same monetary penalties for corporations as for natural persons. Congress did not adopt fine provisions tailored to corporations until 1984. Cohen, "Corporate Crime and Punishment," pp. 254–256; see Jennifer Arlen, "The Potentially Perverse Effects of Corporate Criminal Liability," *Journal of Legal Studies* 23 (1994): pp. 833, 838–839.

3. Cindy R. Alexander, Jennifer H. Arlen, and Mark A. Cohen, "Regulating Corporate Criminal Sanctions: Federal Guidelines and the Sentencing of Public Firms," *Journal of Law and Economics* 42 (1999): pp. 393, 410.

4. Alexander, Arlen, and Cohen, "Regulating Corporate Criminal Sanctions," 410 (the preguidelines total sanction excludes the Exxon Valdez case); Cindy R. Alexander, Jennifer H. Arlen, and Mark A. Cohen, "The Effect of Federal Sentencing Guidelines on Penalties for Public Corporations," *Federal Sentencing Reporter* 12 (1999): pp. 20, 22.

5. Sarbanes-Oxley Act of 2002 (Public Company Accounting Reform and Investor Protection Act), Pub. L. 107-204, 116 Stat. 745 (July 30, 2002).

6. In addition to increasing fines for certain crimes, the renewed focus on corporate wrongdoing embodied in recent legislation may increase corporate sanctions in other cases as well. Examination of sentencing practice suggests that, following adoption of the 1991 sentencing guidelines, judges imposed higher sanctions on firms convicted of federal crimes even when not required to do so by the sentencing guidelines. See Alexander, Arlen, and Cohen, "Regulating Corporate Criminal Sanctions," pp. 411–417. This suggests that legal changes may affect sentencing indirectly by affecting prosecutors' and judges' attitudes about appropriate sanctions. If so, recent legal reforms may alter sentencing practice in ways beyond those explicitly provided for in the law.

7. Jennifer Arlen, "The Potentially Perverse Effects of Corporate Criminal Liability," pp. 833, 838–839 (summarizing federal corporate criminal law); see *New*

York Central and Hudson River Railroad Co v. U.S., 212 U.S. 481, 29 S. Ct. 304, 53 L.Ed. 613 ([1909]; establishing corporate criminal liability through the doctrine of respondeat superior). Wrongdoing by an employee in the performance of her job ostensibly to benefit the firm (for example, increase sales or reduce costs) is a sufficient basis for corporate criminal liability. The company cannot avoid liability by arguing that the wrong did not benefit the company because it threatened it with criminal sanctions. Companies can avoid liability by arguing *no benefit* when the crime actually hurts the firm as when an employee embezzles from the firm.

8. See, e.g., *United States v. Hilton Hotels Corp.,* 467 F.2d 1000, cert. denied 409 U.S. 1125, 93 S. Ct. 938, 35 L.Ed.2d 256 ([1973]; a corporation can be criminally liable for an employee's crime committed within the scope of employment even when done against corporate orders). Corporate criminal liability thus differs from individual criminal liability in an important respect: individual criminal liability generally requires a showing of fault or blame on the part of the wrongdoer (i.e., mens rea). By contrast, corporate criminal liability only requires a showing that an employee committed a crime in the course of performing her job for the firm, ostensibly on the firm's behalf.

9. In many situations, the government could not adequately deter corporate crime, absent cooperation from corporations in reducing the benefit and increasing the cost of crime, because, absent this assistance, the government may not be able to impose sufficient sanctions to ensure that crime does not pay. This is particularly true of crimes that the government would be unlikely to detect or adequately prosecute without the aid of the wrongdoer's employer. Corporate criminal law provides an important supplement to individual criminal liability by providing corporations with a direct monetary incentive to prevent and deter wrongdoing. See, e.g., Arlen, note 2 (discussing the reasons why individual liability alone may not be enough). For a further elaboration of the arguments favoring entity-level liability (in the civil context), see Jennifer Arlen and W. Bentley MacLeod, "Malpractice Liability for Physicians and Managed Care Organizations," *New York University Law Review* 78 (2003): pp. 1929, 1987–1998.

10. Consistent with this, evidence suggests that crime by managers is less likely the greater managements' ownership stake. Cindy R. Alexander and Mark A. Cohen, "New Evidence on the Origins of Corporate Crime," *Managerial and Decision Economics* 17 (1996): p. 421.

11. Jennifer Arlen and William Carney, "Vicarious Liability for Fraud on Securities Markets: Theory and Evidence," *University of Illinois Law Review* (1992): p. 691 (discussing the reasons senior officers commit securities fraud).

12. Evidence suggests that corporate crime cannot be dismissed as the result of the rare bad apple, who inadvertently slipped into the corporate barrel. Individuals

who commit corporate crimes are not somehow especially bad or immoral people. Corporate crime results from a confluence of an individual's willingness to commit crime and her incentives and ability to do so. Any large group of people (such as a publicly held corporation) contains people who will be willing to break the law if the gains from doing so are large enough.

13. Thus, adopting a strong corporate culture that disdains wrongdoing and rewards those people who obey the law (even at the expense of immediate gains) is laudable but is not sufficient. Because wrongdoers do not commit crimes to serve the firm, they will not be dissuaded by heartfelt statements that crime hurts the firm. Instead, managers must determine what incentives its employees may have to commit crimes and determine how the corporation can make crime less attractive.

14. There is empirical evidence that the incidence of certain types of corporate crimes is greater when employees' compensation or performance evaluations depend on the corporation's annual rate of return or short-run profits as opposed to long-run profits. See, e.g., Mark A. Cohen and Sally S. Simpson, "The Origins of Corporate Criminality: Rational Individual and Organizational Actors," in *Debating Corporate Crime: An Interdisciplinary Examination of the Causes and Control of Corporate Misconduct,* William S. Lofquist, Mark A. Cohen, and Gary A. Rabe eds. (Anderson Publishing, 1997), p. 33. See evidence discussed in Jennifer Arlen and Reinier Kraakman, "Controlling Corporate Misconduct: An Analysis of Corporate Liability Regimes," *New York University Law Review* 72 (1997): pp. 687, 702 n.35.

15. Corporate liability for employee wrongdoing is designed to induce managers to recognize both the positive and potentially negative sides of incentive pay in evaluating compensation and promotion policies. By forcing corporations to pay for their employees' crimes, corporate liability ensures that the corporation both bears the expected cost and obtains the benefit of short-run, or tailored, incentive pay. Moreover, by using a liability scheme instead of direct regulation, corporate liability enables each company to tailor its own compensation and promotion policies to attain the appropriate balance between the benefits resulting from providing employees strong incentives to work hard and the potential costs associated with an increased risk of certain types of corporate crimes. Arlen and Kraakman, note 14, pp. 701–705.

16. *Policing measures* are those that affect the probability that the government will detect employee wrongdoing. Jennifer Arlen and Reinier Kraakman, "Controlling Corporate Misconduct: An Analysis of Corporate Liability Regimes," *New York University Law Review* 72 (1997): pp. 687, 699.

17. Jennifer Arlen and Reinier Kraakman, "Controlling Corporate Misconduct: An Analysis of Corporate Liability Regimes," pp. 706–717.

18. Under this regime, corporations faced a dilemma: while policing measures

may reduce a corporation's expected liability by deterring crimes, such measures also potentially increase the firm's expected liability for any crimes that its employees do commit. If this latter liability enhancement effect is sufficiently strong, a firm subject to respondeat superior liability may be better off not doing anything to help detect wrongdoing. Arlen, note 2.

19. Arlen and Kraakman, note 14, pp. 712–717.

20. See generally Arlen and Kraakman, note 14, at pp. 745–746 (discussing policies governing prosecution).

21. This new federal approach to corporate crime effectively substitutes a duty-based regime for the old common law rule of absolute corporate liability for employee crimes. Under this duty-based regime, corporate criminal liability depends not only on employee behavior, but also on whether management satisfied its duties to implement an effective monitoring program, to report wrongdoing promptly and to cooperate with government investigations. This change to duty-based liability is justified by the need to ensure that corporate criminal liability accomplishes an essential goal of inducing companies to implement policing measures. The continued threat of civil liability ensures that even corporations with good policing programs retain incentives to implement measures designed to deter crime (such as appropriate compensation). See Arlen and Kraakman, note 14, pp. 726–730, 735–741 (discussing the benefits of an optimal mitigation regime).

22. See generally, Arlen and Kraakman, note 14 (discussing the guidelines). Finally, managers of publicly held firms have an additional incentive to thoroughly consider the adoption of an effective compliance program. The Delaware Chancery court has held that directors' fiduciary duty of care includes the duty to ensure that the company has an effective program to ensure "the board that appropriate information will come to its attention in a timely manner . . ." While the board retains discretion over what type of reporting system is appropriate in any given case, those boards that do not even consider the issue of internal reporting are potentially liable for breach of duty of care. In re Caremark International Inc. Derivative Litigation, 698 A.2d 959 (Del. Ch. 1996).

23. U.S. Sentencing Guidelines Manual, ch. 8. (date). See Arlen and Kraakman, note 14, pp. 745–752 (discussing these provisions).

24. While this provision appears correct when applied to closely held firms—where a compliance program is likely a sham if owner-managers commit the crime—the presumption is potentially counterproductive in the case of publicly held firms that may have instituted good faith compliance programs and yet nevertheless discover crime by senior managers.

25. The problems associated with multiple jurisdictions are not necessarily best solved by federal preemption, however. Recent events have demonstrated the im-

portance of state enforcement, particularly given the relatively small amounts spent on federal enforcement of business crimes (relative to drug offenses and immigration offenses). Nevertheless, increased attention is needed to improving coordination of state and federal enforcement to ensure that government actors are encouraging reporting and cooperation.

26. For a recent example of such a case, see *McKesson HBOC v. Superior Court of San Francisco County* 115 Cal. App. 4th 1229, 9 Cal. Rptc. 3d 812 (Cal. App. 1 Dist Feb. 20, 2004). (McKesson waived its attorney-client privilege and work product privilege by turning documents over to the SEC even though the SEC and U.S. Attorneys office signed a confidentiality agreement).

27. Although the existing rules on limited waiver may discourage companies from conducting audits, this problem should not be addressed by adoption of a self-audit privilege. A self-audit privilege would insulate the information from discovery in both an action against the firm and an action against the wrongful employees. Deterring wrongdoing requires that victims be able to prevail in tort actions against wrongdoers. Privileging corporate audits would make it harder for victims to proceed against individual wrongdoers. A better approach would be to allow the information to be used in any action where the individual wrongdoer is indeed the defendant, while exploring ways to protect the company itself from any negative effect of conducting an audit. Jennifer Arlen and Reinier Kraakman, "When Companies Come Clean: Mitigation is Better Than Environmental Audit Privileges," *Business Law Today* 46 (2000): p. 9 (arguing against environmental audit privileges).

28. See note 22 (discussing Caremark).

CHAPTER 18

CORPORATE GOVERNANCE IN EUROPE

LEONARDO SFORZA AND ALAN JUDES

CONSIDERING THE frequency with which the phrase *corporate governance* has been thrown about in recent years, one easily could assume it's a relatively new term, concocted by the media or some self-proclaimed guru seeking to cash in on the scandals rocking the business world. In reality, however, corporate governance[1]—the arrangements by which companies are directed, managed, and controlled—has deep roots. Academic literature dates back to the 1960s, but the question of ensuring proper governance as a fundamental condition for the success of the business and the market was a cause of concern as far back as the nineteenth century, both in Europe and the United States.[2] Its newfound prominence is the result of three converging factors, which are both external and internal to the corporation, even if the border between the two worlds is becoming slimmer.

First is the level of internationalization, democratization, and development of the capital markets. No longer is this a U.S.-only prerogative. Despite its current limit, the European capital market is experiencing the emergence of a new cohort of small investors and institutional investors, who claim to have better information on company performance and want to play a role in influencing the decisions of the organizations in which they have taken a financial position. Granted, this is still news in Europe, but it will become more obvious with the expansion of pension funds and the pro-

205

gressive removal of the remaining anachronistic national barriers, which, until now, have impeded the leverage of all the potentialities that an integrated financial market can offer in terms of liquidity and efficiency.

Second, the corporate governance question is no longer merely an agency[3] issue, driven by the unique efficiency criterion of maximizing shareholder value with governance arrangements designed to protect exclusively shareholder interests. There are now more widespread expectations in relation to the public role of private enterprises, which lead toward the emergence of a new business model—that of a corporate citizenship. Companies and their executives are called upon to deliver sound and sustainable financial performance while ensuring the implementation of the highest standards in relation to environmental, labor, and human rights throughout the entire organization. This directly affects the traditional concept of business leadership and the competency model that business leaders are asked to fulfill in terms of cultural background, skills, mind-sets, and behaviors.

Third is the complexity of the regulatory framework that is being set up to govern the market, address recent market failures, and, at least at the European Union level, modernize the entire corporate law system. Among the most challenging aspects is the juxtaposition of the levels of intervention—local, regional, and international. European companies, as well as those involved in cross-Atlantic transactions, live this challenge due to the increasing role of the European Union legislator that often substitutes completely or overrules the local and national regulatory authorities. Even if policy-makers succeed in setting up a coherent system of rules that is more in line with the new structure of production and of cross-border business organization, however, it would be naïve to think that it would be enough to deliver market trust and prevent frauds.

CROSS-CONTINENTAL CHALLENGE

As Enron, WorldCom, Tyco, and other U.S.-based scandals came to the fore, we Europeans initially believed that corporate governance issues were primarily an American problem. That assumption was backed up by European accountants, who looked at the Enron nonconsolidation of 97 percent owned, special-purpose vehicles and concluded that such problems could not arise in Europe. Regrettably, European companies have since demonstrated to shareholders, bond holders, and other bank creditors that corporate governance issues are present within European organizations as well. Even the United Kingdom, which prides itself on having one of the strongest corporate governance systems in the world, admits to corporate failures. Take Marconi, for example.

The European Union is challenged, therefore, with strengthening its corporate governance environment without creating an unnecessary framework of legislation that will inhibit normal commercial development. The challenge is made even more complex when one considers that Europe consists of a great many nation states, each with its own corporate governance framework, stock exchange regulations, and criminal law. The United Kingdom, for example, utilizes the single unified board structure, while Germany and the Netherlands use a supervisory board, consisting entirely of nonexecutives, charged with supervising the actual management board. Clearly, there is not going to be a one-size-fits-all solution.

What's more, it has become evident that traditional modeling of corporate governance systems is unlikely to survive the next decade. Therefore, the transition toward a new, enlarged concept of governance will rely upon four key facets:

- *Rules:* Looking at a greater coherence and interconnection of the country-specific legal frameworks
- *Values:* Adapting company culture and practices through the integration of the legitimate and evolving expectations of the society vis-à-vis of business
- *Profit:* Ensuring sound and reliable financial results, which match shareholder interests
- *Value:* Contributing to long-term sustainable financial success of the company

FROM LAW COMPLIANCE TO PRINCIPLES ENFORCEMENT

Although some aspects of corporate governance are written into the commercial law affecting European countries, others remain statements of best practice to which companies are expected either to comply or explain why they have not. In practice, of course, there will be significant pressure for compliance because that will be perceived as best practice by shareholders.

The varying nature of shareholdings across Europe helps to explain the differences. Both the Dutch and British economies have the largest percentage of listed companies in the ownership of pension funds and insurance companies. As a result, corporate governance in those countries is much more closely enforced by shareholder votes. The German corporate governance environment is very different, meanwhile, because the prevailing philosophy of German corporations tends to be family owned and financed more by bank loans than by equity investment.

The United Kingdom stands on the leading edge of European corporate governance. Every year, U.K.-listed companies are required to put their remuneration policy to a shareholder vote. Even if the constitution of the board complies fully with corporate governance best practice, a company still can find that certain aspects of the policy offend shareholders to the extent that they vote against it. In other European countries, meanwhile, the disclosure of directors' remuneration is only just beginning to take place. According to a recent Hewitt survey of Europe's top-listed companies, nine out of 10 publish the remuneration package for the board as a whole, but just half disclose the individual packages of executive board members.[4]

A similar issue arises with performance conditions for executive stock option arrangements. In Germany, such conditions are mandatory because they are written into the company law. In the United Kingdom, however, there is no requirement in law, but the major institutional investors have published guidelines, setting out their conditions for shareholder approval of such plans. What's more, a group of shareholders is in a position to enforce a performance requirement, should they decide to do so. By contrast, France generally does not have any performance conditions in its stock options arrangements, which are frequently seen as being a tax effective remuneration facility, because it is possible for both employer and employee to avoid social charges arising on gains from qualified stock options.

Italy is similarly ruled by a tax efficient structure for stock options. Recent events involving Parmalat have led to speculation that corporate governance will have an effect on a company's cost of capital. Specifically, if corporate governance does not comply with what the market thinks it should do, then the company's cost of capital will go up. If the market believes that an entire country's corporate governance is below par, then all companies located there may face a higher cost of capital. Simply put, companies incorporated elsewhere will be able to operate at better margins than companies incorporated in a country with low corporate governance standards. Thus, the invisible hand of the market should require an elevation in corporate governance standards to a best-practice level.

Many people think that corporate governance is just about compliance with guidelines and rules of control—a sort of *box-ticking* exercise to be fulfilled by those at the very top of the organization in order to contain investors' concerns and face control by supervisory agencies. They couldn't be more wrong. Without good corporate behaviors deep rooted throughout the company, it remains just a compliance exercise, an end in itself, rather than a means to achieve the company's success. The issues involved are not relevant merely at the boardroom level; it can't be dealt with just by adding a corporate governance chapter in the annual company report, rotating external auditors, and involving some independent executives from outside the company. Rather, it affects all management and employees. And all employees, no matter what their position, can have an impact on the governance of their firm and contribute to walk the talk of their board.[5]

At management level, this role is possibly most obvious, but even there, a culture of complacency and disengagement can flourish easily when internal checks and balances are missed and every level relies on the other to fulfill its own task of control.

WHAT MATTERS AND TO WHOM

Across Europe, the most urgent emerging corporate governance problems include the following:

1. The constitution of the board and how its members are appointed
2. The internal controls of the organization and whether income is properly recognized and assets and liabilities are on the balance sheet of the company
3. Whether there is a robust and transparent procedure for setting executive pay

The majority of public companies have already begun tackling these issues in anticipation of more stringent regulatory standards emerging at the national, European, and international levels. Some leading companies have even moved beyond the boundaries of legal compliance and corporate governance branding. Before this approach can be generalized throughout Europe, however, there first must emerge a new type of business culture and daily practice of management, integrating leadership, management, and control.

ANTICIPATING THE NEXT PROBLEM

While it's difficult to predict Europe's next corporate governance problem, it's likely that variations of existing issues will emerge in different companies across the region. In preparation, therefore, boards will want the following reassurances:

- There are adequate internal controls over assets and income recognition is realistic.
- Assets and liabilities of the entity are correctly disclosed on the balance sheet.
- Reasonable estimates are made for future liabilities, including those connected with employee remuneration, occupational pension, or other deferred pay arrangements.
- Pay increases that could lead to significant increases in salary-related liabilities are properly controlled and the consequences of the salary increases are considered when salary increases are prepared.
- Independent directors review the remuneration policy for the executives and the appointment of the independent audit firms.

GETTING IT RIGHT

For corporate governance to be successful, it must be modeled by top management and implemented by all employees. For example, simply stating that environmental protection is important will not mean anything if management fails to ensure that its factories do not pollute the environment.

Furthermore, statements of respect will not be treated seriously if workplace harassment takes place and the offender is not disciplined.

Corporate governance begins with a firm's objectives and mission statements as well as the way it treats its customers and other stakeholders. For European organizations, the challenge lies in giving the right leadership message without getting too bogged down by unnecessary red tape, all the while avoiding the culture of suspicion that threatens to put all business leaders into the same category as those at failed companies.

NOTES

1. Marco Becht, Patrick Bolton, and Ailsa Röell, "Corporate Governance and Control," ECGI Finance Working Paper no. 02/2002, October 2002, attribute the first use of the term to Richard Eells in *The Meaning of Modern Business: An Introduction to the Philosophy of Large Corporate Enterprise* (New York: Columbia University Press, 1960).

2. For example, see in the context of the earliest U.S. railroad corporation—Baltimore and Ohio (B&O) Railroad—that, from its inception in 1827, set up an audit function conducted by an audit committee of directors with a view to control the financial, operating, and administrative activities of B&O. An interesting analysis of the B&O case is in the study on the origin of U.S. corporate accountability, audit, and information rights made by professors G. J. Previts, W. D. Samson, and D. L. Flesher. An analysis of the origin of corporate governance practices on both sides of the Atlantic has been made by C. A. Dunlavy, "Corporate Governance in Late 19th Century Europe and the U.S.: The Case of Shareholder Voting Rights," in *Comparative Corporate Governance. The State of the Art and Emerging Research,* ed. K. J. Hopt, H. Kanda, M. J. Roe, E. Wymeersch, and S. Prigge (Oxford: Oxford University Press, 1998).

3. This is namely the structure and functioning of relations between an agent (the CEO) and different principals (the shareholders, creditors, suppliers, client, employees, and other parties with whom the CEO is in business on behalf of the company). In the middle, the intermediaries (board of directors, external auditors, employee representatives, etc.) are due to represent the respective interests of the principals. See Becht, Bolton, and Röell, "Corporate Governance and Control" for an analysis of the agency problem, its origin, and evolution.

4. Hewitt, *Corporate Governance and Executive Remuneration—A European Perspective,* November 2003, p. 12.

5. An inspiring analysis about emerging corporate governance models and their scope is included in L. van Den Berghe, *Corporate Governance in a Globalizing World: Convergence or Divergence? A European Perspective* (Boston: Kluwer Academic Publishers, 2002).

CHAPTER 19

DEVELOPING LEADERS
OF CHARACTER

LESSONS FROM WEST POINT

RAKESH KHURANA AND SCOTT A. SNOOK

THE RECENT rash of corporate scandals has sparked an important debate about the process by which we produce business leaders. For those of us who teach in business schools, the unprincipled behavior by some of our former students has been particularly troublesome, raising questions about how well we prepared them for their roles as leaders in society. For others, particularly corporate directors, the lack of integrity exhibited by so many senior executives has caused us to reconsider the qualities we look for in business leaders and how to both cultivate and screen for them. As a result, everyone involved in the process of developing leaders is now facing a rare window of opportunity.

Fortunately—or unfortunately, depending on one's perspective—such windows don't remain open for very long. The only real question is, what will we do with it? Will we simply throw another course at it? Or will we engage in those often-painful conversations that address fundamental questions of institutional identity and responsibility? Will we respond by doing what we're most comfortable with? Or will we make the most of this opportunity and learn?

These questions are particularly relevant to both of us. Scott spent much of his career as an army officer on the faculty of the United States Military Academy at West Point. There, he helped lead a 10-year *institutional conversation* during which one of America's oldest and most respected institutions

213

reconsidered its fundamental purpose, basic assumptions, and, ultimately, how it went about the task of producing leaders. He later moved on to the Harvard Business School, which was in the midst of its own institutional conversation in response to the corporate scandals of the last few years. There, he became a colleague of Rakesh, who had recently completed a body of research critiquing the leadership criteria and CEO selection process of many large corporations.[1] Through numerous conversations, we have become aware of significant parallels between the challenges currently facing business schools and those that West Point encountered following the end of the cold war. As a result, we believe that West Point's recent experience has much to offer other institutions as they reconsider both their conceptions of effective leaders and the processes by which they are developed.

THE CASE OF WEST POINT

In this section we will examine the changes that took place at West Point.[2]

A New Environment

In 1989, the world changed. The Berlin Wall came down, the Soviet Union collapsed, and the cold war ended. Gone was the relatively stable and predictable bipolar world that had dominated our geopolitical landscape and shaped American military structure, policy, and identity for nearly half a century. What would take its place? And what were the implications for West Point?

As the Soviet military threat dissolved, many thought our security problems were behind us.[3] In search of a *peace dividend,* Americans took one of the largest organizations in the free world—the U.S. military—and cut it by a third. Before long, however, it became apparent that without the order imposed by the dominance of two relatively rational nation-states, the world was a much more complicated and unstable place. In the first decade of the post–cold war period, a much leaner U.S. Army found itself chasing drug lords in Central America, conducting humanitarian relief operations in Somalia, fighting a conventional war in the Persian Gulf, and supporting protracted multinational peacekeeping and nation-building efforts in the Balkans.

One thing was clear: The workplace for American soldiers was changing dramatically. Gone was the relatively linear, conventional, and symmetric battlefield of the cold war. In its place emerged a future described by army leaders as VUCCA—Volatile, Uncertain, Chaotic, Complex, and Ambiguous. Amid their seclusion along the peaceful banks of the Hudson River, not even West Point's leaders could escape the impact of such sweeping change. As a result, the academy found itself asking some very fundamental questions:

- What are the implications of VUCCA for future army leaders?
- How should the academy prepare its graduates to lead in such an unpredictable and increasingly hostile world?

But change does not come easy to an institution like West Point. As the joke among academy graduates goes, "Ah, West Point—200 years of tradition, untouched by progress!" Fortunately, every so often an unusual mix of circumstances combines to create the conditions where even the stodgiest of institutions can change. Such was the case at West Point during the final decade of the twentieth century.

Starting the Conversation

In 1989, the shock of the cold war ending combined with the fortuitous timing of a decennial Middle States Accreditation process to create the impetus and structure for serious introspection. Add to this mix a senior leader—in this case, the academy's superintendent—who had an unusually keen eye for sensing important historical moments as well as the personal courage to ask difficult questions,[4] and West Point was ready for change. As part of a broader strategic review sweeping the army—characterized by initiatives like the "Army After Next" and doctrinal debates like the "Revolution in Military Affairs"—the military academy entered an unprecedented period of reflection.[5]

What would turn out to be a decade-long institutional conversation[6] began to unfold. Hard questions were asked, not the least of which was, what is the purpose of the academy? As a military organization, West Point had always had an explicit mission statement clearly detailing exactly what was expected of the institution.[7] However, it had been a long time since the academy had addressed more fundamental questions of institutional identity: why have a military academy in the first place? What is its broader purpose in society?

One of the first products to come out of this conversation was an answer to these fundamental questions of identity:

> The purpose of the United States Military Academy was to provide the nation with leaders of character who serve the common defense.

While these leaders were initially developed for the army, in the long run, academy graduates by and large served the nation as leaders not just in the military but also in their communities, in nonprofits, in churches, and in business.[8] Over time, the academy began to think of itself as one of the world's premiere leader-development institutions.[9]

With a new identity came new questions. If West Point's raison d'être was to produce leaders of character, then it had to be able to answer some fundamental questions about what that entailed. Exactly what is a *leader of character*?[10] How do you develop leadership? How do you develop character?

Like any good military organization, the academy looked first to its mission statement. As approved by the Department of the Army, it read:

> The mission of the United States Military Academy is to educate, train, and inspire the Corps of Cadets, so that each graduate is a commissioned leader of character committed to the values of Duty, Honor, Country; professional growth throughout a career as an officer in the United States Army; and a lifetime of selfless service to the Nation.

As later summarized in the academy's *Cadet Leader Development System* (CLDS) handbook, a close analysis of this mission statement revealed two crucial elements:

> First, there is an objective, the target of our [West Point's] efforts—a "commissioned leader of character." To become a commissioned leader of character requires adopting a unique identity or self-concept, one that is consistent with our Nation's expectations of what it means to be an Army officer. Second, there are the verbs—"educate, train, and inspire." Taken together, these three verbs define development, the holistic means by which USMA accomplishes its mission, the process by which cadets internalize the defining fundamentals of officership. Officership and development, directly derived from our mission statement, are the two conceptual lenses through which we view CLDS.[11]

Given this understanding, two fundamental questions remained:

- What does it mean to be a "commissioned leader of character"? (A question of identity.)
- How do cadets acquire the self-concept of *officership*? (A question of development.)

Let us consider, in turn, how the conversation at West Point addressed each of these two questions.

Identity

As the conversation evolved, maintaining credibility and legitimacy were critical concerns. Once again, academy leaders turned to an institutionally vetted document for guidance. In addition to its formal mission statement, West Point also had a strategic vision. *USMA Strategic Vision—2010* envisioned future academy graduates as

> [o]fficers prepared for the uncertainty and ambiguity of military service . . . because they will have reflected upon and developed a personal understanding of the unique characteristics of their chosen profession.[12]

Based on this guidance, the following logic ensued: West Point is charged with graduating army officers, and army officers are commissioned leaders of character inspired by a unique professional identity. Therefore, understanding the concept of *professional identity* was central to accomplishing the academy's mission. But there was one problem. The concept itself was not very well understood, let alone clearly defined. Perhaps even more troubling was the growing sense that somewhere along the way, the army as an institution had lost its collective identity as a profession.

To address this shortcoming, West Point commissioned a formal study to better understand the army as a profession. This ambitious two-year initiative was the first major study of the army as a profession in over 30 years. It involved a diverse group of senior officers from across the army as well as leading civilian scholars from the academic community. Results largely validated their initial concerns. While the U.S. Army had long considered itself to be a profession,[13] over time its members had lost their sense of what it truly meant to *be* a member of a profession.[14] As a result of extensive interviews, it became clear that most army officers no longer even had the language to discuss their vocation as a profession. When asked to describe their professional identity, they struggled.[15]

If West Point's mission boiled down to developing in its graduates a unique professional identity, then it was necessary for the institution to clearly articulate exactly what such a self-concept might look like. After lengthy discussions and extensive reflection throughout not only West Point, but also the army as a whole, the following working definition of *officership* was adopted:

> The practice of being a commissioned Army leader, inspired by a unique professional identity, that is shaped by what an officer must *know* and *do,* but most importantly, by a deeply held understanding and acceptance of what an officer must *be.* This unique self-concept incorporates four interrelated roles: Warfighter, Servant of the Nation, Member of a Profession, and Leader of Character.[16]

According to West Point's leader-development handbook, "Cadets must adopt all four components of Officership to construct a professional identity robust enough to meet the complex demands of the 21st Century."[17]

After additional study, it became increasingly clear that one of these four components needed some serious work. Most academy graduates saw themselves as warriors, selfless servants, and leaders of character. However, few, if any, saw being a member of a profession as an important component of their professional identity. Similar to officers in the broader army, cadets, too, were largely unfamiliar with the language of professions.

Drawing lessons from the Army Professions study, the academy adopted the following description of the fourth component of officership—what it means to be a *member of a profession:*

> The self-concept of officership has no meaning in American society absent its context within the military profession . . . democratic nations create professions to do what they cannot do for themselves. But it is the profession, with its inherent expertise that provides the client—the Nation—with what it needs. [This component of professional identity] describes the nature of the Army Officer Corps as a corporate body [with the following characteristics]: unique competence or expertise (warfighting), authority delegated by the Nation (servants), distinct culture, ethically based (leaders of character), and a life-long calling (not a job).[18]

By this point in the conversation, West Point was well on its way to discerning a clearer picture of its target—a commissioned leader of character with a professional identity shaped by the self-concept of officership. Still missing, however, was an equally clear and shared understanding about how to go about inculcating such a professional identity. How do cadets internalize the self-concept of officership? Institutional emphasis shifted to focus on the process of leader development.

Development

One of the most startling revelations to come out of this decade-long self-examination emerged relatively early in the process. Not long after the academy started thinking of itself as a leader-development institution, an embarrassing problem arose. It seemed that, after all these years, West Point had never clearly articulated its theory of leader development. Anecdotes, myths, and legends abounded, but there was no shared understanding or set of basic assumptions about how they went about developing leaders or shaping character.

When asked "How does West Point develop commissioned leaders of character?" most members of the faculty typically listed the three major developmental programs: Physical, Military, and Academic. When pushed a little harder, "No, I mean how does *it* [leader development/character development] really happen?" most people would then describe specific components or various activities of the *West Point experience*. However, if really pushed, few, if any, could clearly answer the more fundamental questions: how does *it* really happen? How do you develop character? How do you develop leadership? What is West Point's collective understanding about how to develop a self-concept or professional identity?

Like any institution of higher education, the academy generally understood its core competency to be *planned change*—systematically transforming people and fundamentally shaping who they are, what they know, and what they can do. But exactly what it was that was being *transformed and shaped* and how the underlying mechanisms worked to bring about those changes was less clear.

While not exactly a theory, embedded in the broader army was an already well-established and widely accepted leadership doctrine. According to the army's leadership manual,[19] to be a competent leader there are certain things that you must *be, know,* and *do*. This simple model, as illustrated in Figure

Figure 19.1
West Point's Model of Leader Development

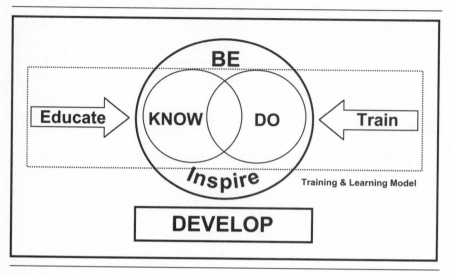

19.1, provided the conceptual framework for a more detailed analysis of the various components of leader development.

After some reflection, academy leaders concluded that they were relatively effective on the *know* and the *do* but weak on the *be*. As a top-tier university, West Point felt that it was at least on the right track when it came to the *know* part. They had a fairly sophisticated theory about how to educate cadets as well as a set of mechanisms to continuously assess and make refinements in this area. Senior officers were even more confident about the *do* piece. They knew how to train. The army was one of the most benchmarked training institutions in the world. With over 200 years of accumulated experience, the army had developed a robust system for taking large numbers of people and quickly training them to standard in a wide range of technical skills.

What caught West Point's attention was the *be* component—who you are, your identity, your character, how you know what you know, your worldview, and your values. Clearly, knowledge and skills are important components of a professional identity. Equally important, however, is the realization that professionals are much more than the accumulated sum of what they *know* and what they can *do*.

In fact, the more academy leaders thought about the relative importance of these three components, the more they suspected that, if anything, they had historically overestimated the relative impact of training and education on the long-term development of officers. After all, explicit knowledge and skills are largely perishable. What you learn today, if not regularly applied, is easily gone tomorrow. And with the current pace of change in the world, much of what you learn today is likely to be irrelevant tomorrow. Perhaps the real leverage for developing leaders was found in their identity—the *be* component of *be, know,* and *do.*

As a result of this assessment, West Point reaffirmed that it indeed did care deeply about the *be* piece. "Give me someone who has that piece right, and I can teach them to do anything" was the common sentiment among officers. However, if character and professional identity were so highly valued, then West Point should have an equally clear theory about how to go about developing the *be* component in cadets. What was the analog of *education and training*—the traditional learning model—when it came to the *be* component? As an institution, West Point knew how to *in*form but had never clearly articulated its basic underlying assumptions and beliefs about how to *trans*form, about how to take over a thousand incoming cadets each year from all walks of life and somehow shape them into commissioned leaders of character for the nation.

By simply reframing the question in this manner—with a focus on the *be* component of development—leaders at West Point became much more intentional about the way they designed and implemented every aspect of cadets' 47-month *experience.* Each major activity, training event, organizational system, and structure was reexamined in terms of its potential impact on cadets' evolving self-concept. If an activity was deemed inconsistent with the four components of officership or if it didn't increase the likelihood of cadets affirming a stronger sense of their professional identity, then it was either changed or eliminated.

As a result of this review, leaders at West Point learned that developing the *be* component is in many ways a fundamentally different task, based on a fundamentally different set of assumptions than the ones that they followed to educate and train cadets

Figure 19.2 summarizes several salient differences between West Point's traditional training and learning model and a more holistic developmental perspective. Simply recognizing these differences led to significant changes in how the academy approaches its mission.

Figure 19.2
Contrasting Classical "Training and Learning" Model with a
"Developmental Perspective"

	Training & Learning	Developmental Perspective
Outcomes	Behavioral Changes; Gradual accumulation of Knowledge & Skills	Changes in understanding; Discontinuous & qualitative
Process	Assess the job & fill the gap	Assess the learner & create a gap
Motivation	Learner success	Learner failure
Our Role	Provide structure; impart knowledge & demonstrate; provide immediate feedback & reinforcement	Challenges & seeks learner point of view; mentors by sharing perspective & supporting learner
Cadets' Role	Practices desired responses	Provides structure to the experience; applies new ways of understanding; provides self-assessment
Time	Short-term	Long-term

One example of a powerful experience designed specifically to target cadets' evolving professional identity is an exercise called *The Cemetery Walk*. Cadets are given the names of academy graduates who made the ultimate sacrifice for their profession and who were buried in the cemetery at West Point. Each student is provided with a name and obituary. Cadets are then required to find the gravesite, reflect on the dead soldier's contribution and sacrifice, and then write a short reflective essay capturing what they learned from this experience as it pertained to their joining the profession of arms.

The Cemetery Walk is only one example of many initiatives and curriculum design changes made as a direct result of West Point's increased appreciation for the *be* component of professional development. Many of these novel interventions contain several common characteristics. First, explicitly recognizing the third verb (inspire) in West Point's mission statement, some of these experiences are intentionally designed to elicit emotional responses from cadets. Second, getting cadets out of their comfort zone is another goal of many of these exercises. Third, West Point faculty have come to recognize the value of structured reflection and meaning-making when it comes to influencing cadets' identity and commitment to the profession. No longer is the emphasis solely on the experience; now it is also on what cadets do with the experience.

Character development is one area where the implications of adopting a more developmental model raised important questions and led to some significant changes at the academy. After years of experimenting and thinking deeply about how to develop character, West Point noticed that there seemed to be three types of challenges faced by its graduates when it came to *leading with character,* defined simply as doing the right thing consistently over time.

The first challenge is to frame an issue as one with moral or ethical implications—moral sensitivity. The second challenge is to decide what is right—moral judgment. And finally, the third requirement for leading with character is to confidently act in accordance with what one knows to be right, often in the face of great difficulties. At West Point, such action is called "doing the harder right instead of the easier wrong." The challenge is one of moral courage.

It turns out that all three of these components—sensitivity, judgment, and courage—appear to be largely independent and orthogonal variables when it comes to predicting ethical behavior in professionals.[20] As a result, each component calls for a different kind of developmental intervention. While classroom discussions might work for moral judgment, for example, they may have little impact on developing students' moral courage. Clearly, West Point needed to think more broadly and creatively about how it developed character.

Not too surprisingly, perhaps, the academy found itself doing what it was most comfortable with—investing heavily in traditional classroom courses to influence cadets' character development. Faculty also realized that they were spending a disproportionate amount of time focusing on the second component—moral judgment—perhaps at the expense of the other two. Clearly it takes all three—sensitivity, judgment, and courage—to produce consistently ethical behavior. And yet, it seemed that even West Point, with its honor code and immense institutional emphasis on character development, had been seduced into relying too much on standard classroom experiences in hopes of developing all three.

In sum, perhaps the most fundamental insight from West Point's institutional conversation is that a professional calling is as much about the *be* as it is about the *know* and the *do*. On the one hand, it should be obvious to all of us that a professional education entails much more than simply conveying technical knowledge and skills. On the other hand, however, we shouldn't be too surprised to learn that most universities tend to focus on what they do best, which is to offer traditional classroom-based experiences that primarily target the *know* and the *do*. At a minimum, West Point's experience should draw our attention to the *be* because developing a strong professional identity goes to the very heart of developing leaders of character for society.

QUESTIONS FOR INSTITUTIONS EDUCATING LEADERS

What are the lessons for business schools? As mentioned earlier, this chapter was in part motivated by Scott's retirement from West Point to join the faculty at the Harvard Business School. As luck would have it, he arrived just in time to join another institutional conversation, this time at a different institution but one that was struggling with many of the very same questions.

The mission of the Harvard Business School is to educate leaders who make a difference in the world.

The barrage of corporate scandals involving business executives—not to mention the accountants, investment bankers, stock market analysts, lawyers, and money managers— was nothing like any of us had experienced in our lifetimes. The level of greed and societal contempt displayed by many of these leaders gave pause to us all, especially those of us involved in educating business leaders. Not surprisingly, in the midst of these revelations, many of us were not completely satisfied with the kind of difference that some of our graduates were making in the business world. And, similar to West Point, many business schools, including our own, launched an institutional conversation to examine their role—as a faculty, as a school, and as an institution—in the derailment of these fallen leaders. Is there a way that we can do better? we asked.

In the immediate wake of these scandals, business schools responded in two ways. Some schools launched a discussion about the relationship between business and society, with a particular emphasis on social responsibility. Often relying on a multidisciplinary and multistakeholder approach that emphasizes corporate responsibility, corporate governance, and legal frameworks, this approach aims to educate students about the social roles that corporations should play. It emphasizes that addressing societal concerns about corporations has important consequences for both the vitality and public legitimacy of the business sector.

Other schools have responded by fine tuning existing elements of their curriculum. Accounting departments, for example, have pushed a greater emphasis on transparency, accountability, and the role of auditors and audit committees. Behavioral finance, which recognizes the role of psychology and sociology in creating speculative bubbles, has helped create a climate of credulity around hyperrational economic theories, such as the efficient-market hypothesis. Organizational behavior and general management departments have reconsidered the role for charismatic leadership and the extent to which it contributed to conditions in the boardroom that inhibited candid discussions about a CEO's performance and executive compensation. Business schools around the country are introducing new—and sometimes required—courses on ethics and social responsibility.

Reconsidering the role of business in society and refining the curriculum are important responses. They represent a serious recognition of the powerful role that business schools play in educating and diffusing ideas that are then implemented in a broader business context. Our concern is that these changes may be insufficient to prompt the larger questions of institutional purpose, mission, and professional identity. Many of these initiatives merely respond to the specific problem areas uncovered in the most recent rash of scandals. While helping students understand the specific issues behind current headlines is helpful, such a focus may blind us to more general problems with the way we go about preparing future leaders.

One of the lessons illustrated by the West Point case is that a broader and more deliberate institutional conversation about educating leaders can have a lasting and potentially powerful influence on our students' development and for discussing the more serious issues of institutional identity and commitment in this area. The West Point experience suggests that institutions charged with educating and developing leaders need to get to the roots of professional identity, specifically the *be* component. What's more, getting to the *be* component of professional identity cannot be done through classroom work alone. The *be,* as highlighted by both West Point's experience and academic research on professions, is largely what distinguishes a professional from others who simply leverage and act upon technical knowledge.

However, directly addressing the *"be"* component and, more specifically, "character development in professional schools inevitably generates heated debate. In our experience, these debates tend to cluster around the following four fundamental questions:

1. *The Question of Appropriateness (Should We?):* The leader of the Protestant reformation, Martin Luther, described a teacher's calling as akin to that of a minister's. An educator's role was to explicitly affect students' beliefs and to do so in a planned and goal-directed manner. Owing to the secularization of our society, mainstream higher educational institutions have been reluctant to introduce values-based education. This tension introduces the first set of fundamental questions concerning appropriateness:

- Should schools explicitly tackle the subjects of ethics and character development?
- Doesn't this more appropriately belong in the home, synagogue, chapel, or mosque?
- How many of us would include as part of our school's mission the responsibility to inspire students to a calling in addition to training and educating them to be competent practitioners?
- Is this an appropriate role for modern institutions of higher learning or should we stick to safer, more objective, value-neutral topics?

2. *The Question of Realism (Can We?):* Simply asking this question presupposes that education may have little impact on the beliefs and attitudes of young adults. Even if we decided that this was an appropriate challenge for us to take on, how realistic is it for us to believe that we can have an impact on our students in this area? This is a difficult question, one that has been perennially debated in the *nature versus nurture* and *born versus made* arguments of human development.

- Can we really have much of an impact on our students' identities after they've reached adolescence?

- Can we have a significant impact on this area if students are not open to being influenced along these dimensions? After all, many students tell us that this is not what they are paying us for in the first place.

3. *The Question of Content (What Should We?):* This question begs those of us who teach future leaders to make educational knowledge itself problematic. Several scholars argue that values-free education is a social fiction.[21] There is a hidden curriculum built into the educational process itself. It is conveyed to students in the form of norms, values, and dispositions that are created simply by living in and responding to institutional expectations and the routines of school. This perspective argues that regardless of whether educators want to be in the role of shaping students' identity and beliefs, they already are. It asks educators to pay much greater attention to the messages conveyed by the curriculum—where this knowledge comes from, whose knowledge it is, what interests this knowledge supports, and so on. Such an acknowledgment requires educators to explicitly consider the ideological and epistemological commitments they are conveying to students by supporting certain models and pedagogical traditions. Without an understanding of these dimensions, one cannot seriously connect the content of the work with how it shapes students' beliefs, attitudes, and subsequent behaviors.

- So even if we agree that "yes, this is important" and "yes, we can still have an impact on our students' development in this area," what then is the specific content of the message that we would like them to take away in this area?
- What is the unique character of our students' professional identities that we would like them to construct?
- Could we ever come up with a consensus among the faculty as to a set of shared values that we would all agree to intentionally pass along to our students?

4. *The Question of Process (How?):* A model to replace industrial age education has not yet fully emerged. However, the idea that a centralized authority communicating asymmetrically to sentient adults is coming under scrutiny. Traditional habits are designed to create a fixed, standardized student body to make students who are alike in many ways. Standardization

reduces uncertainty and creates predictability. Business schools have traditionally taught individuals to work effectively in fixed organizational roles. In recent years, however, there has been a concerted effort to transform them into leaders and creative thinkers. Moreover, even if we agree that the goal is to create a transformative experience for our students to fundamentally affect their identity, it will require rethinking and realigning the structure of the classroom and the pedagogical tools available to support such changes.

- Even if we decide that we are serious about this endeavor as a part of our professional responsibilities, that we are confident that we can make a difference in their lives, and we come up with a list of shared values, how then do you go about teaching ethics or developing character? Is it the same as teaching marketing or strategy?
- How creative and sophisticated are we at designing and offering developmental experiences that intentionally target character, self-concepts, and worldviews?

Intelligent and well-meaning people can and do disagree about each of these questions, which is all the more reason to raise them in open debate. Several institutions have already begun this process and are moving toward answering them. Yet many have not. Why?

Research on how organizations respond to threatening events suggests that when under pressure to do something—typically in the wake of periodic, highly visible failings—they tend to leap immediately to visible steps to appease constituents as well as take actions that organizational members are most comfortable with. Such external threats and the questions they raise tend to send organizations into defensive routines and dominant responses. As a result, many institutions elect to short circuit the process and go directly to the fourth question. In most educational settings, this means throwing a course at the problem or making minor revisions to their current curriculum. Most educators are comfortable debating issues of pedagogy and curriculum design.

We have few pivotal moments to transform institutions of professional education, and we should exploit those moments. Much as the end of the cold war provided West Point with such an opportunity, so too does the spate of recent scandals for business schools. West Point's experience suggests that directly addressing fundamental questions of institutional purpose, professional identity, and development can lead to significant improvements in the processes by which we develop leaders of character for society.

Notes

1. R. Khurana, *Searching for a Corporate Savior: The Irrational Quest for Charismatic CEOs* (Princeton, N.J.: Princeton University Press, 2002).

2. Writing a case study combining personal observation with archival data presents the author (in this case Scott) with some difficult editorial challenges. Not only does the process of distilling 10 years of history into a few pages necessitate leaving out significant parts of the story, but there are also thorny issues of objectivity and retrospective sense-making at play. No doubt the institutional conversation described here appears to make much more sense in retrospect than during the middle of it. And no doubt countless others experienced this same conversation differently and might offer an entirely different account. Anyone who has spent some time in the military comes to understand these fundamental problems of telling war stories:

> War stories present two problems to authors striving for The Truth. First of all, if you live long enough to tell them and have enough of an audience to practice telling them to through the years, war stories become just that—stories. Just as time distances the storyteller from the events themselves, so do the repeated tellings. Gradually the stories are embellished in places, honed down in others until they are perfect tales, even if they bear little resemblance to what actually happened. Yet the storyteller is completely unaware of how far he may have strayed from the facts. Those countless tellings have made the stories The Truth.
>
> The second problem with war stories is they have their genesis in the fog of war. In battle, your perception is often only as wide as your battle sights. Five participants in the same action, fighting side by side, will often tell entirely different stories of what happened, even within hours of the fight. The story each man tells might be virtually unrecognizable to the others. But that does not make it any less true. (D. H. Hackworth, *About Face* [New York: Simon & Schuster, 1990], p. 9)

With these cautions in mind, what we offer here is one soldier's war story of an institutional conversation—battle—that he and countless others participated in and fought at West Point during the final years of the twentieth century.

3. This argument is most notably credited to Francis Fukuyama's controversial book *The End of History and the Last Man* (Los Angeles: Avon Books, 1992).

4. Lieutenant General Dave Palmer was West Point's Superintendent from 1986–1991. Not only was he the academy's college president but he was also a trained historian with an eye for recognizing a historic moment and the personal courage to make the most of it. For a detailed summary of the strategic initiatives launched during General Palmer's tenure, see L. Donnithorne, *Preparing for West Point's Third Century: A Summary of the Years of Affirmation and Change 1986–1991,* http://www.west-point.org/publications/PWPTC2.html (accessed February 8, 2004).

5. The "Army After Next" (AAN) was an ambitious long-range planning project charged with conducting "broad studies of warfare to about the year 2025 to frame issues vital to the development of the U.S. Army after about 2010 . . ." (AAN Mission Statement). Following the end of the Cold War, the term *revolution in military affairs* emerged as a catch-all phrase to describe how the innovative application of new technologies (digitized battlefields, smart munitions, unmanned drones, etc.) combined with dramatic changes in military doctrine and operational and organizational concepts (information, net centric, and asymmetric warfare) was fundamentally altering the nature of modern warfare.

6. The phrase *institutional conversation* refers to a series of wide-ranging discussions—both formal and informal—that took place over a decade at all levels both within West Point and across a wide range of external constituencies. While 1989 makes for a good starting point, no doubt the seeds for this conversation were planted over many years. While this essay focuses primarily on those conversations that culminated in revising the academy's *CLDS* in 2002, such discussions are never complete and we're certain that the conversation continues today. U.S. Military Academy, *Cadet Leader Development System,* USMA Circular-101 (West Point, NY: U.S. Military Academy, 2002).

7. Prior to this time, West Point relied on a single document for strategic guidance—its mission statement. Out of this decade of institutional discussions, however, emerged a hierarchical family of strategic documents, each written to address specific design questions. The most fundamental question, *Why* West Point? is addressed with a *purpose* statement, first articulated during General Palmer's tenure. The future or end state for the institution is captured in a *vision* statement, first published in 2000. Next in line comes the academy's traditional *mission* statement, crafted specifically to answer the question, *What* does West Point do (to fulfill its purpose and attain its vision)? Finally, the *CLDS* was written as an operational level document to answer the question, *How* does the academy accomplish its mission? See U.S. Military Academy, *Cadet Leader Development System.*

8. All academy graduates are required to serve as commissioned officers in the

army for a minimum of five years. For those who choose to make the army a career, they may remain on active duty for up to 30 years. As a general rule, however, all officers are required to retire at the end of 30 years. This purpose statement was written to reflect the belief that, even after they take off their uniforms, academy graduates continue to serve the nation as leaders of character in other walks of life.

9. This notion was first articulated when the academy published a formal vision statement in 2000. As captured in the U.S. Military Academy's *Strategic Vision for USMA—2010* (West Point, NY: U.S. Military Academy, 2000), the institution's vision was to be the "Nation's Premiere Leader Development Institution" and a "Wellspring of Values for the Army and Nation."

10. As defined in the *CLDS,* a *leader of character* is someone who "seeks to discover the truth, decide what is right, and demonstrate the courage to act accordingly . . . always" (U.S. Military Academy, *Cadet Leader Development System,* p. 16).

11. U.S. Military Academy, *Cadet Leader Development System,* p. 3.

12. U.S. Military Academy, *Strategic Vision for USMA—2010,* p. 7.

13. See S. P. Huntington, *The Soldier and the State* (Cambridge, MA: Harvard University Press, 1957); M. Janowitz, *The Professional Soldier* (Glencoe, IL: Free Press, 1960).

14. The army was not unique in this sense. During this period of history, all professions seemed to be under attack by multiple forces. See A. Abbott, "Status and Status Strain in the Professions," *American Journal of Sociology* 86 (1981): pp. 828–829; D. Snider and G. Watkins, "Introduction," in *The Future of Army Professionalism: A Need for Renewal and Redefinition,* ed. D. Snider and G. Watkins (Boston: McGraw-Hill, 2002), pp. 6–8.

One outcome or symptom of this general weakening of professions is the loss of professional identities—what it means to be a member of a particular profession, as opposed to alternative vocational structures.

15. See D. Snider and G. Watkins, "Introduction," pp. 6–8.

16. See U.S. Military Academy, *Cadet Leader Development System,* p. 8.

17. See U.S. Military Academy. *Cadet Leader Development System,* p. 8.

18. See U.S. Military Academy, *Cadet Leader Development System,* p. 13.

19. See U.S. Army, *Army Leadership: Be, Know, Do,* Field Manual 22-100 (Washington, D.C.: Department of the Army, Headquarters, 1999).

20. For a detailed treatment of a similar four component model, see D. Narváez and J. Rest, "The Four Components of Acting Morally," in *Moral Behavior and Moral Development: An Introduction,* ed. W. Kurtines and J. Gerwitz (New York: McGraw-Hill, 1995). For examples of how to construct educational interventions targeting each of these components in professional education programs, see M. J. Bebeau, "Influencing the Moral Dimensions of Dental Practice," in *Moral Development in the Professions,* ed. J. Rest and D. Narváez (Hillsdale, NJ: Lawrence Erlbaum, 1994); L. J.

Duckett and M. B. Ryden, "Education for Ethical Nursing Practice," in *Moral Development in the Professions: Psychology and Applied Ethics,* ed. J. Rest and D. Narváez (Hillsdale, NJ: Lawrence Erlbaum, 1994).

21. See S. Bowles and H. Gintis, *Schooling in Capitalist America* (New York: Basic Books, 1976); J. Meyer, "The Effects of Education as an Institution," *American Journal of Sociology,* 83, 55–77 (1977): p. 64; P. Bourdieu and J. C. Passeron, *Reproduction in Education, Society, and Culture* (London: Sage, 1977).

CHAPTER 20

SPEECH BY SEC CHAIRMAN

REMARKS AT THE 2003 WASHINGTON ECONOMIC POLICY CONFERENCE

WILLIAM H. DONALDSON

THANKS, COMMISSIONER Glassman, for your generous introduction, and thanks to National Association for Business Economics for inviting me to speak before your highly regarded organization. The economics profession should be very proud indeed that one of your own, Cynthia Glassman, is making such a profound contribution to the vital work of the Securities and Exchange Commission. Before I go any further, I feel obliged to make the standard disclaimer that the views I express today are my own and not necessarily those of the Commission or its staff.

As Commissioner Glassman noted, this is one of my first public appearances since my swearing in as Chairman of the SEC. I have to admit that when I heard "an audience of economists," I got a little nervous. Economists? How would I ever speak inspiringly about the latest theoretical developments or forecasting techniques? I knew that if I attempted to sound like an economist, I'd only make matters worse!

But to my relief, I was told that you were interested in hearing a few thoughts about corporate governance. I believe that the inattention to good corporate governance practices over the past decade or more is at the heart of what has gone so terribly wrong in corporate America in the past few years. If significant steps are not taken to revisit and remodel corporate governance practices, corporate America will continue to attract the anger and animosity not only of disillusioned shareholders, but also of a much broader cross-section of American society.

Corporate governance is, for sure, a hot topic these days. We have all seen countless articles in newspapers and magazines discussing the subject. We've heard numerous proposals from the exchanges, public policy think tanks, shareholder advocacy groups, and individual scholars. Congress, leaders of the Administration, and the SEC have put forth their own proposals related to corporate governance as well. It's no understatement to say that there are plenty of ideas out there, almost a cottage industry, and no shortage of opinions.

For the most part, this has all contributed to a healthy dialogue about what companies can and should do to ensure that they are living up to the expectations of investors and serving as respectable participants in America's business environment.

The intense discussion of corporate governance and increased scrutiny of business has already led to changes in corporate behavior and philosophy that go beyond the new laws and regulations. The most fundamental, almost seismic, change has been the growing recognition that for the protection of investors, the primary responsibility for guardianship of corporate governance practices must reside with the board of directors and must not be diluted by the power of the chief executive.

Over the past decade or more, at too many companies, the chief executive position has steadily increased in power and influence. In some cases, the CEO had become more of a monarch than a manager. Many boards have become gradually more deferential to the opinions, judgments and decisions of the CEO and senior management team. This deference has been an obstacle to directors' ability to satisfy the responsibility that the owners—the shareholders—have delegated and entrusted to them.

The need for such a change has, of course, been driven by a distressing array of corporate malfeasance that is all too apparent. The corporate scandals have exacerbated the roughly $7 trillion collapse in the aggregate market value of American corporations over the past few years. We are all aware of the bubble that burst, led by dot-com mania, the explosive overexpansion of the telecommunications industry, and the availability of cheap capital due to historically low interest rates and historically high equity valuations.

The names from the recent big corporate scandals are by now infamous. The SEC's enforcement division, along with the Department of Justice and other members of the President's Corporate Fraud Task Force, continue to work double time to bring wrongdoers to justice— as demonstrated by new allegations of massive fraud uncovered just last week. While over 15,000 companies report to the SEC, and the vast majority of them have sound, honest management and dedicated directors, the malfeasance that has occurred makes it apparent that reforms were and still are needed.

Millions of Americans have lost their jobs, much of their savings, or both. Such devastation goes beyond just a missed paycheck or decreased balance in a 401(k) account. Their loss is profound, and public outrage should not be underestimated. It is, of course, exacerbated not just by corporate malfeasance, but also by the perception, and in many cases the reality, that those at the top have not shared in their loss; that those at the top have continued to enjoy massive salaries, bonuses, and perks unrelated to performance. The modest compensation cutbacks currently underway have seemed, to many, rather underwhelming.

A central point that I would like to make is that over the past decade, even many of the most well-intentioned companies that were consistently mindful of corporate governance got caught up in the boom times. Frequently, conceptions of responsible corporate governance were adjusted to accommodate the temptations of a runaway bull market. As the band played faster and faster, standards began to erode throughout the business community.

Corporate America developed a short-term focus, fueled by an obsession with quarter-to-quarter earnings and the pervasive temptation inherent in stock options. The game of earnings projections, and analysts who focused on achieving self-forecasted results (or a firm's failure to achieve those results) created an atmosphere in which "hitting the numbers" became the objective, rather than sound, long-term strength and performance. The perception that uninterrupted earnings growth was the hallmark of sound corporate progress made it irresistible for far too many managers to make little adjustments in financial reports to meet targeted results. Many times, such bad or questionable business decisions were rewarded with the aforementioned compensation packages that often bore no relationship to what I would call "real management performance."

Of course, it was not only corporate boards and executive management that allowed their standards to devolve. The gatekeepers who operate within and work for corporate America were very much a part of the problem. As the markets grew steadily higher, the appeal of getting in the game was irresistible. Suddenly, professional accounting firms and legal and financial advisors were offering new services designed to offer "value-added" services for enhanced compensation where rigorous professional and ethical standards were tested, strained and sometimes broken.

When the steady market increases came to a halt, and the dishonesty of some in corporate America came to light, shareholders were often left holding the bag.

As a result of all this, as your conference program suggests, we may be on the verge of another activist economic policy regime similar to that of the 1930s, which resulted in the founding of the SEC and the 1933 and 1934 securities and exchange acts. My only amendment to the program's statement would be that in response to the events and revelations of the past few years, we have already entered such an activist policy regime. Sweeping new legislation has been enacted and expectations of corporate America and Wall Street have changed.

As we move forward, companies, their management, their directors and the gatekeepers who serve them must look beyond just conforming to the letter of the new laws and regulations. They must redefine corporate governance with practices that go beyond mere adherence to new rules and demonstrate ethics, integrity, honesty, and transparency. The recent shifting of primary corporate governance responsibilities to the Board of Directors demands that directors be the true stewards of corporate governance, and their actions must demonstrate their dedication to this stewardship without interference from the CEO.

Corporate governance means different things to different people, and it is in this philosophical area that I would like to direct a few thoughts.

Now, I don't want to beat up lawyers. In my new job, I'm more dependent on lawyers than I have ever been, and I have to be careful what I say or I could be in big trouble when I get to the office! But several weeks ago, I saw an ad in the pages of a daily newspaper that exemplified the possible risk of asking directors to simply comply with a static set of governance criteria. The ad was for a law firm offering its expertise to navigate the new corporate governance landscape. Among other things, the law firm promised to increase shareholder confidence, improve public perception, and reduce the likelihood of litigation and . . . SEC investigation.

Such a "check the box" approach to good corporate governance will not inspire a true sense of ethical obligation. It could merely lead to an array of inhibiting, "politically correct" dictates. If this was the case, ultimately corporations would not strive to meet higher standards, they would only strain under new costs associated with fulfilling a mandated process that could produce little of the desired effect. They would lose the freedom to make innovative decisions that an ethically sound entrepreneurial culture requires.

As the board properly exercises its power, representing all stakeholders, I would suggest that the board members define the culture of ethics that they expect all aspects of the company to embrace. The philosophy that they articulate must pertain not only the board's selection of a chief executive officer, but also the spirit and very DNA of the corporate body itself—from top to bottom and from bottom to top. Only after the board meets this fundamental obligation to define the culture and ethics of the corporation—and for that matter of the board itself—can it go on and make its own decisions about the implementation of this culture.

This definition of culture—of what kind of company they want to be—will influence all their decisions, including what criteria they use when selecting a CEO, what criteria the CEO will use to select other management, how the board will function, what characteristics new directors should demonstrate, what the committees or instruments of the board should be, and what kind of leadership structure should be installed. This is, in my view, not a one-size-fits-all exercise.

Some practices and determinations are imperative in all cases. For example, it must be clear by now that boards of directors must demand the highest standards of integrity and dedication to investor interests in any candidate for chief executive. The tone at the top of an organization is perhaps more vital than anything else, and the chief executive will set that tone under the oversight of the board.

Sarbanes-Oxley addressed another absolutely essential aspect of good corporate governance when it mandated that all audit committees be composed entirely of independent directors. There is no doubt in my mind that the mandate of independence and the defined responsibility of the audit committee are essential to the new central role of the board.

Beyond this requirement, I believe we should go slowly in mandating specific structures and committees for all corporations. I applaud the work of many institutions, organizations and individuals, including the exchanges and other commentators on issues related to board structure in particular. Independence is a vital feature on boards and on the important components that carry out board responsibilities, such as nominating and compensation committees. We should be seeking clear assurances of independence without excessive rigidity. There are vast differences in the function, structure and business mandate of the thousands of corporations struggling with the issues of good corporate governance. I believe that these differences dictate that once the board determines the ethical culture that is to prevail, each company board should be afforded a level of flexibility to create their own approach to its structure.

Let me illustrate a few priority issues that a board might consider as early steps in a review of its organization. On the matter of board leadership—should the Chairman be nonexecutive; should the CEO be prohibited from being Chairman too; should there be a lead director? I would say that there is no one answer to these hotly debated questions for the single reason that at any particular point in the development of a corporation, one or another of these approaches may be appropriate. To insist on one rule for all belies the dynamics of the fast changing business and corporate environs and the nature of varied business situations. In particular, we must all remember that the honest and dedicated chief executives must have the freedom to run the corporation under the oversight of the board, and do so in a way that permits leadership, entrepreneurship and the taking and management of risks that have been characteristic of successful American business.

I mentioned compensation a moment ago. In my view, compensation is a key area where strong corporate governance is now essential. Directors should examine their dependence on management and compensation consultants when making decisions about compensation for the chief executive and other senior management. The conventional wisdom of many corporate boards these days has become that in order to remain competitive, executive compensation must be in the top quarter of companies in their industry. But we don't live in Lake Wobegon, where as Garrison Keillor says, "All the women are strong, all the men are good looking and all the children are above average." Such a description makes you think long and hard about moving to Minnesota. But obviously, it's literally impossible for everyone to be above average or, in this context, for every company to be in the top quarter. It is the job of the board to set appropriate compensation that is related to the goals and performance of top management, not the pressure to meet an artificial standard informed by outside consultants who do not share the responsibility of being board members.

In addition, each director and the board as a whole must make an honest assessment of how many boards and committees he or she and, for that matter, board candidates can serve on while maintaining the dedication and responsibility that is demanded of them these days. Anything less would be a disservice to other board members, company employees and, of course, the shareholders and stakeholders.

If such an assessment by all sitting directors limits their availability to serve as directors or audit committee members for as many companies as in the past, there will be vacated board seats to fill. For a long time, corporate America has depended on many of the same sorts of people to fill director slots: CEOs called on other CEOs, friends called upon friends. I understand that well over a majority of directors of New York Stock Exchange companies are CEOs. In my view, that represents excessive reliance on one model of outside director. Finding good, qualified directors is no small task, but it is time that we expand the talent pool and create a new generation of directors.

In this regard I have been pleased to see the growth of new efforts to educate new potential directors through training programs around the country. I commend business schools, law schools and organizations such as the New York Stock Exchange and others for their commitment to establishing these programs, and I encourage them all to be creative in their approaches. SEC Commissioners and staff have been involved in a number of these programs, and I pledge that the SEC will help in any way possible to accelerate these efforts.

Just as there is no one prescription for corporate governance, there is no one correct way to train a new cohort of directors. I encourage those who conduct director training programs to look beyond the traditional methodologies and include not only a study of law and business practices, but also an examination of the interpersonal human dynamics that influence a board and its decision making. One of the most interesting evaluations of a board that I ever read was not done by a lawyer or an MBA, but by an organizational behaviorist.

As business economists, your interest in corporate governance likely goes well beyond the few ideas I've discussed today. Your interest probably lies in the economic effects that new corporate governance practices will have on your individual companies. I hope that you might, as time goes on, add your voices to the debate underway and your analytical expertise in evaluating the actual results of the different approaches that will be taken.

Let me conclude by saying that the American financial system and our markets are the strongest in the world. I am proud to have been a participant in American business for most of my professional life. Although we are in a period of economic stress and uncertainty, the fact that we are undergoing the type of open and positive approach to rectifying the mistakes of the past is the hallmark and strength of our system. Taking further steps to strengthen business by reaffirming our commitment to transparency, accountability and shareholder interests is essential to restoring investor confidence and can only make us stronger. It's true, there may be costs associated with doing so, but the costs of turning a blind eye will be far greater in the long run.

I hope that you will agree that the most important first step for a board grappling with the issues of corporate governance is not debating the issues of structure. Rather, it is defining the parameters of an inviolate corporate culture by answering simple questions: "What kind of moral compass do we want guiding this corporation? What ethical standard do we want embedded in this corporation's DNA? How will we demonstrate it in our every action? How can we protect the long term interests of our investors?"

CHAPTER 21

CORPORATE GOVERNANCE AND THE CULTURE OF SEDUCTION

ARTHUR LEVITT

EVER SINCE I owned my first Macintosh in 1984, I have been addicted to Apple computers. I now have six Macintoshes and an iPod digital music player, and I occasionally go to conventions of Mac users. I guess I might be called an Apple junkie. You can imagine my delight when Apple CEO Steve Jobs invited me to join his board once I left the SEC in February 2001. At least I was under the impression that he invited me.

I flew to San Jose to meet Jobs for breakfast in mid-January. We then went to Apple headquarters, where he introduced me to his management team. After a series of meetings with department heads, Chief Financial Officer Fred Anderson briefed me on the company's finances, the responsibilities of various board members, and the dates of upcoming meetings. As I was leaving, I gave Anderson a copy of a speech I had recently made on corporate governance. I thought it might be useful to the company as it planned the board's agenda for the coming year. The next day I was Apple's guest at the annual Macworld trade show in San Francisco, where, with his rock-star presence, Jobs unveils new Apple products. By the time I left, I considered myself part of the Apple family and looked forward to my first directors' meeting with enthusiasm.

It was not to be. The very next day, Jobs disinvited me. "Arthur, I don't think you'd be happy on our board, and I think it best if we not invite you," he said over the phone. "I read your speech and, frankly, I think some of the issues you raised, while appropriate for some companies, really don't apply to Apple's culture."

I was floored. What radical ideas in that speech had set him off? Turns out, Apple's board did not meet a number of the good governance litmus tests I had highlighted. It did not, for example, have a separate compensation committee (although it does now). Instead, important executive pay issues were referred to the full board, which could hardly give them the attention they deserved or be as objective as a subcommittee of independent directors. One director, Oracle CEO Larry Ellison—Jobs's close friend—was invited to join the board in 1997, even though he warned the company that he would not attend most meetings. Since joining, Ellison has attended a little less than half of Apple's formal board meetings, an abysmal record.

One member of Apple's audit committee, Jerome York, is the CEO of MicroWarehouse Inc., whose Mac Warehouse catalog was responsible for nearly $150 million of Apple's $5.4 billion in 2001 sales. York is eminently qualified to sit on Apple's board: he is a former chief financial officer of both IBM and Chrysler. And when he joined Apple's board in August 1997, he was not involved with the Mac catalog. But when he became CEO of Micro-Warehouse in 2000, York's relationship as a major reseller of Apple products meant that he could no longer be considered an independent board member. And yet he is one of three directors on Apple's audit committee, despite a Nasdaq rule that requires audit committee panelists to be independent. Apple gets away with this because the Nasdaq rules have a loophole: one nonindependent audit committee member is allowed "under exceptional and limited circumstances." If a company invokes the exception, the board must disclose in the proxy statement why it's in the best interest of the company and its shareholders to have a nonindependent on the audit committee. Apple's explanation? Its proxy statement says only that, considering York's accounting and financial expertise, the board had determined that his service on the audit committee "is in the best interest" of Apple and its shareholders.

To me, the Apple board has even more flaws. The chairman of Apple's audit committee is former Intuit CEO Bill Campbell. Not only is Campbell a former Apple marketing and sales executive, but Apple in 1990 bought out the software company, Claris Corp., that Campbell started after leaving Apple. Under the current stock exchange listing standards, Campbell qualifies as an independent director because his Apple ties ended more than three years ago. But no matter how conscientious a director is, it's difficult to switch loyalties from one's former colleagues to shareholders. It's even more difficult not to feel beholden to the acquirer of your own company. Campbell and York, along with Genentech CEO Arthur Levinson, not only make up the audit committee, but they also are the only three members of Apple's compensation committee—the two panels that most governance experts agree should be truly independent of management.

None of this would matter were it not for the fact that Apple's tight-knit board has only six members, one of whom is Jobs. Because Ellison misses more than half the meetings, only four outside directors are regular attendees, and one of them clearly is not independent, while a second arguably is not. Mickey Drexler, the CEO of Gap Inc. until he announced his resignation in May 2002, is also among the six. But Jobs sits on Gap's board in an arrangement, called interlocking directorships, that governance gurus frown upon. What board member is going to second guess a CEO who happens to sit on his own board?

Like many CEOs, Jobs had carefully handpicked his own board. His directors are highly qualified, prominent members of corporate America. But it's plain to me that Apple's board is not designed to act independently of the CEO. Clearly, my speech signaled that I would not fit that mold.

To his credit, Jobs has turned Apple around since his 1997 return to the company he founded two decades earlier. He has restored the company's image through innovation and cost cutting. Today, Apple's product lineup is on the cutting edge technologically and aesthetically. And despite the audit committee structure, Apple has never had to restate its results or been subject to a Securities and Exchange Commission probe.

So what's the problem? Small, insular boards lack the outside perspective that is necessary in case a company finds itself in trouble. Especially when the CEO is as charismatic as Jobs, it's crucial to have independent thinkers who do not act as an extension of management.

Not surprisingly, Jobs disagrees. He says that when there was no compensation committee, the full board found the time to have "vigorous and full discussions" about pay packages. Despite Ellison's failure to show up for more than half the board meetings, Jobs insists that his friend's informal consultations are so valuable that his absences are tolerable. To me, that relationship makes Ellison more of a management consultant than an independent overseer. Jobs also says that his board members have a "stunning amount of experience, judgment, and concern for Apple." No argument there. But if something goes wrong with the company's strategy or its execution, it seems to me that this board would not buck Jobs and insist on a midcourse correction.

As you can probably tell, independent boards are a passion of mine. I have sat on many, both before I came to the SEC and now. I don't think it's proper for the CEO to make important decisions, such as the choice of his successor, how much compensation he and his management team will receive, and whether the financial statements reflect the company's true status, without vigorous board discussion and approval. Nor am I comfortable when matters that have been decided prior to a board meeting come up for the directors' rubber-stamp approval. What may have passed muster several years ago is no longer acceptable in a post-Enron environment. Investors have lost faith in corporate managers and boards, and that means companies must work harder to prove that their boards provide the strongest possible checks and balances. It is essential that CEOs recognize that they do not own the companies they run and that they are ultimately responsible to shareholders. The past few decades have brought dramatic improvements in most boards, and the seriousness with which they take their jobs, but, as recent corporate failures make clear, much work remains to be done.

What Is a Board of Directors?

A board of directors is usually composed of well-educated, accomplished individuals, elected by the shareholders annually or every few years. One of its responsibilities is to advise the CEO and the top executive team with impartial common sense and various kinds of expertise. The board should meet regularly to discuss such issues as the ongoing health of the business, the current management team and its performance, the compensation of the top executives, and the future outlook of the company. A board's most important job is to make sure the company has the best CEO it can find. Corporate boards should have a nominating committee, composed of independent directors, to review candidates to replace the CEO in case of retirement or resignation, and to help choose new board members.

If problems arise, it's the board's responsibility to address them before the situation spins out of control—ideally before investors take a beating. After all, in a bankruptcy, shareholders get what's left after everyone else gets paid. And that's usually nothing.

At major public companies, boards are made up of a combination of insiders—senior executives at the company—and others from outside the company, such as other chief executives, scientists, educators, and civic leaders. At smaller companies, boards often include the venture capitalists who funded the company or other financiers, such as the local banker.

The board's mandate is to oversee management as a representative of the shareholders. The board is not the same as the management and does not have the same responsibilities. Management makes most of the company's day-to-day operating decisions, but major strategic issues, such as whether or not to buy another company or to enter a new line of business, require the board's participation and approval.

Most boards are subdivided into committees, each of which focuses more directly on parts of the business. Some of them, such as a corporate governance committee, are optional. But stock exchange rules require publicly traded companies to have an audit committee to oversee how the management team prepares the company's financial statements and to make sure that internal controls are working properly. Most companies also have a compensation committee to determine the salaries and bonuses of top management.

A board's makeup is vital. If you think a director is not doing her job or if you feel a director's business interests could create a conflict, it's your right—your duty, really—to vote against her, using the ballot that comes with your proxy statement. Unfortunately, removing unacceptable directors from a board isn't easy. Large shareholders, such as pension and mutual funds, tend to vote with management unless the company's share price has plummeted. Boards of directors also are often presented as one slate: you vote for all or none. But as activist shareholder groups and the financial media frown on this practice as a management-protection ploy, companies increasingly are putting individual directors up for annual reelection by shareholders.

WHY SHOULD YOU CARE?

I believe a company's corporate governance is one of the most important factors to consider before investing in a company. Put simply, corporate governance is the relationship between the investor, the management team, and the board of directors of a company. Each of these groups has different rights and responsibilities. When the three groups are able to communicate openly and independently, we can say that a company is exhibiting good corporate governance.

This does not mean that the board second-guesses every decision made by the top executives of a company. Rather, a board should provide careful oversight of a company's activities, drawing on its members' expertise in areas such as marketing, finance, or technology. A board can help solve problems by sharing its own experiences with similar matters. A board should add value to an already strong executive team.

How can you recognize a good board from a bad board? Outside board members should be free of connections or business interests that make them feel beholden to the CEO or undermine their responsibility to make decisions in the interests of shareholders. Ideally, fewer than half the directors should be employed by the company or have other connections that hinder independence. And I use the most rigorous definition of "independence": those directors should not be family members, former employees, the company lawyer or investment banker, or even someone who represents an institution that has received donations from the company. They should not be paid consulting fees or receive exorbitant perks. All board members should have a hefty stake of their own in the company. A bad decision should sock them in the wallet, too.

Caring about governance does not guarantee that a company will outperform others in its industry, but there is ample evidence that paying attention to governance issues leads to better financial results. One study, by Wilshire Associates, examined the performance over five years of 62 companies named by the California Public Employees' Retirement System (CalPERS) as poor performers. While the stocks of these companies trailed the S&P 500 by 89 percent in the five-year period before CalPERS singled out the companies, the same stocks outperformed the index by 23 percent in the following five years.

That's not to say that companies will fail unless they have a model board of directors. Take Warren Buffett's Berkshire Hathaway Inc. Among the seven directors are his wife, his son, longtime business partner Charlie Munger, a partner at his company's law firm, and a coinvestor with Berkshire Hathaway in another company.

When a corporation is in trouble, it often becomes clear that the board failed in some way. A landmark case brought by the SEC in 1998 against chemical company W. R. Grace illustrates my point. As the company foundered, the board allowed CEO J. Peter Grace to negotiate a retirement package that included such generous perquisites as the use of a corporate jet and a company-owned apartment. The perks were valued at $3.6 million. W. R. Grace was also planning to sell a small subsidiary to the ex-chairman's son.

Clearly, good corporate governance means not letting a former CEO walk away with a private jet when the company has hit the skids. Yet it wasn't strictly illegal. What got Grace's board in trouble was its failure to disclose these and other matters to shareholders in its 10-K annual report and proxy statement. Although one member of the board led the negotiations for the retirement package and another was aware of the negotiations for the subsidiary's sale, neither required Grace to inform its shareholders. The negotiations were not fully disclosed or described, as the law requires, in any SEC filing. Indeed, the company's filings contained only the briefest description of the retirement perks, and never mentioned any proposal to sell a subsidiary.

After reviewing the case, the commission concluded that not only the company, but also several W. R. Grace directors bore responsibility for these failures. Each of them knew about the deals and should have known that such sensitive matters would not sit well with shareholders. The company settled the SEC case, without admitting or denying guilt, by consenting not to further violate securities laws.

What is obvious in hindsight can be avoided through foresight. In practice, this simply means that boards must be equipped with an effective system to monitor management. But directors can't stop there. If they have reason to know something doesn't seem right, they cannot avert their gaze. Every time directors demand a tough disclosure or ask a difficult financial question, thousands of shareholders benefit. So there must be an atmosphere that encourages directors to be active—to avoid the trap of believing that they must go along to get along.

Sometimes boards make sensible decisions, but wait far too long. In November 2001 the board of apparel company Warnaco replaced longtime CEO Linda Wachner, who had driven the company into bankruptcy while still managing to be one of the nation's better-compensated executives with a salary exceeding $2 million, plus generous stock options. But for years the board had tolerated Wachner's poor management skills. Under Wachner,

Warnaco became mired in litigation with its biggest licensor, Calvin Klein, for trademark violations. And at one point Wachner spun off a company, Authentic Fitness, but remained its CEO while also serving as Warnaco's CEO. Later, she sold the company back to Warnaco. She made millions, but Warnaco's shareholders lost money in the transaction. Warnaco's share price slid 92 percent between 1995 and 2001, leading the company to declare bankruptcy in June 2001. But even then the board did not remove Wachner for five more months.

Such governance failures have led to calls for increased board accountability and caused quite a bit of upheaval as directors second-guess management and shareholders second-guess directors. At company annual meetings, for example, shareholders increasingly are turning to shareholder resolutions, which also appear in the proxy, to force change. To bring a shareholder proposal to a vote, there must be some logical relationship between the proposal and the company's business. Proposals can't involve "ordinary business," or issues considered part of a company's normal day-to-day affairs. If a company wants to disqualify a proposal as ordinary business, it must notify the SEC, which makes the final decision.

To offer a proposal, a shareholder must have owned $2,000 worth of a company's stock for the past year. If a resolution fails, it must have received at least 3 percent of the votes cast to be eligible for the ballot the next year. You can find more detail on shareholder proposals at the SEC's website, *www .sec.gov*. Once there, click on the "Division of Corporation Finance," then "Staff Legal Bulletins," then "SLB 14."

Shareholder proposals are now a favorite tool of governance activists. Pension funds, mutual funds, labor unions, social activists, corporate gadflies, and ordinary investors use the shareholder proposal system hundreds of times each year to promote their view of good governance. After the Enron calamity, one popular cause is auditor independence. Consider how this issue played out at Disney's February 2002 annual meeting. A union-owned mutual fund pushed for a shareholder vote on a resolution directing Disney to stop awarding consulting contracts to PricewaterhouseCoopers, its auditor. Disney was vulnerable on this point: the previous year it had paid PwC $7 million in audit fees, but more than four times that for such services as financial systems design and tax preparation.

Disney management fought to keep the resolution off its proxy statement.

It asked the SEC to strike the proposal because, Disney claimed, it dealt with "ordinary business" and, therefore, was in violation of SEC rules. But the SEC disagreed and allowed the resolution to be put to a vote at the annual meeting. CEO Michael Eisner then had a change of heart—or else he wanted to avoid an embarrassing loss. Weeks prior to the meeting, he pre-empted the resolution and announced that Disney would no longer use PwC's consulting services. By then it was too late to remove the resolution from the proxy; it won 43 percent of the vote—not enough to force Disney's hand, but a powerful sign of shareholder resolve. Rarely do resolutions garner more than 20 percent of the vote the first time around.

Another popular shareholder concern is the overuse of stock options as compensation. What began as an incentive to keep or reward extraordinary talent has now become routine. Dot-com executives especially made eye-popping sums of money from their options in the late 1990s. Cisco Systems CEO John Chambers received $150 million on top of his base pay and bonus of $1.3 million in 2000.

As generous as that seems, it doesn't compare to Steve Jobs's options and bonus awards that year. In January 2000, Apple's board awarded Jobs 20 million shares, worth $550 million if the share price increased just 5 percent a year over ten years. The board also authorized the company to spend $90 million to buy Jobs a Gulfstream V corporate jet. When Apple's share price declined the next year—pushing Jobs's options underwater (that's when the exercise price exceeds the current market price)—the board simply granted him 7.5 million more options at a much lower exercise price. At the time, Apple shares were underperforming other computer hardware stocks by 28 percent—hardly a ringing endorsement. When boards reprice stock options or, as Apple's board did, issue new ones at a lower price, they undercut the use of stock options as an incentive for management to try harder. By lowering the bar, boards send a clear signal that management will not be held accountable.

Pension funds and other institutional investors are taking umbrage at stock option abuses and are turning to the proxy system for relief. When a board approves stock option grants, the company often must issue new stock to cover the grant, thus watering down, or diluting, the outstanding shares. Like it or not, that means that your shares lose value every time a stock option is awarded. And academic studies have begun to cast doubt on just how much retention and incentivizing power stock options really have. This is where the shareholder proposal process enters the picture. Shareholders have begun to offer resolutions that, if approved, would require companies to obtain their approval for new option grants or to reprice options that are underwater. Many investors are registering their disapproval of new option grants. In 2000, 22 percent of shareholders who voted said no to stock option plans, according to the Investor Responsibility Research Center, a Washington, D.C.-based corporate governance research outfit.

The backslapping, smoke-filled, fraternal boardroom is hard to find these days, in large part because of a series of corporate meltdowns and the outcry they caused. The first corporate disaster to really strike a chord with the public came after the merger of two railroads, New York Central and Pennsylvania Railroad, in 1968. The resulting company, Penn Central, was the corporate equivalent of the *Titanic:* it hit an iceberg because its captains, the directors, weren't paying attention. Actually, it was worse than the *Titanic* because Penn Central's captains effectively stole away on the lifeboats and left the rest of the company to a watery grave. While debt soared and working capital deteriorated, Penn Central's board was busy enriching itself and approving dividend payments of more than $100 million. Everyone and everything associated with that company sank in 1970, when Penn Central, one of the country's largest companies, declared bankruptcy.

Penn Central's board was not unique. A Harvard Business School study at the time concluded that the modern firm's board of directors had ceased to function as a meaningful check on the CEO. A senior partner in a consulting group reported in the same study that he didn't know of a single board that really dug into the strategy of the business or held management accountable for results. Remember that word: *accountable.* The job of a board member is to monitor management and hold it accountable for its decisions. At Penn Central and thousands of other corporations, no one was doing this.

Slowly, investors began to realize they could do something. In the 1970s and 1980s, activist religious and political groups began using company annual meetings to push shareholder proposals that denounced investment in apartheid South Africa, as well as companies dealing in weapons and tobacco. Shareholder groups also began invoking federal securities laws in place since the 1930s to support their corporate governance struggles.

CORPORATE RAIDERS AND POISON PILLS

The biggest boost for corporate governance, however, came in the 1980s, when corporate raiders and leveraged buyout firms vied for control of struggling corporations. Many companies resisted being taken over, and enacted protections, such as special share-voting devices and poison pills. The share-voting devices block hostile takeovers by, for example, providing for super-voting rights to be cast in favor of management when an unwanted suitor appears on the scene. Poison pills are slightly different in that they grant existing shareholders (but not the unwanted suitor) rights to buy additional shares at a deep discount, thus diluting any potential acquirer's ownership stake and thwarting his efforts to control the company. These takeover defenses are not shareholder-friendly. They entrench the current management, even when it's doing a poor job. They water down shareholders' votes and deprive them of a meaningful voice in corporate affairs. And they deprive investors of a contest for their shares—and the possibility that they will receive a premium price from a new owner.

Numerous courtroom battles were waged over poison pills and other anti-takeover measures. The corporate raider era shook up many complacent management teams and corporate boards, which often were smack in the middle of these legal dramas. The mergers-and-acquisitions divisions of Wall Street firms became more profitable than their brokerage departments. But overall, the 1980s "was a mixed bag" for governance, says Harvey Gold-schmid, a securities law professor at Columbia University. "There was increased pressure on management to look after the interests of shareholders because a raider could come along if the stock was too low," says Gold-schmid, who would later become the SEC's general counsel. "On the other hand, there was a lot of funny money going around, and a lot of questionable people and motives involved."

The raiders—people such as Carl Icahn, T. Boone Pickens, and Saul Steinberg—caused much bitterness, and not just among unhappy managers turned out of their corner offices. Dozens of acquired companies were broken up and sold in pieces, thousands of people were laid off, suppliers and customers were disrupted, and local communities were torn apart.

The corporate raider movement caused governance experts to look for better ways to improve corporate performance, but with far less turmoil.

Goldschmid and others focused on forcing directors to switch their allegiance from management to shareholders. And that gave rise to a new and powerful special interest group: activist shareholders. Institutional pension funds began to use their considerable leverage to pressure companies to get rid of poison pills and take other steps to improve performance. Among the most active were TIAA-CREF (the country's largest private pension fund, formally called the Teachers Insurance and Annuity Association—College Retirement Equities Fund) and CalPERS (the nation's largest public pension fund). Together, they manage hundreds of billions of dollars' worth of retirement and savings funds on behalf of teachers and state employees. The pension funds became empowered and soon realized that they could change corporate practices that weren't in the interests of investors.

AWAKE, SLUMBERING BOARDS

In the 1990s, the idea that a board of directors should be an independent and active steward of investors' money really began to take hold. The business press also began exposing the clubbiness of some boards—in a quite unflattering way. Then, just before I joined the SEC in 1993, the agency required companies to make public more information in executive pay packages. The SEC also made it easier for shareholder groups to communicate with each other by liberalizing the rules governing the proxy system. This is the process by which a company informs shareholders of its performance over the past year and solicits shareholder approval of changes to its bylaws, board slate, and any proposals.

All this information is contained in a proxy statement, an important document that companies must send to every shareholder annually. More than any other filing, the proxy statement reveals the inner workings of a company. It lists each board member, along with a short biographical sketch. It says which directors serve on which committees, such as compensation and audit, and if they attended 75 percent of board meetings. It must say whether management has reviewed the company's financial statements with those board members who serve on the audit committee. The proxy statement also discusses the stock's performance over the past five years and compares the share price to a relevant index, such as the Standard & Poor's 500. It must reveal the compensation of the five top corporate officers. And it must explain any proposals that shareholders will be asked to vote on at the annual meeting. A ballot is provided, so that shareholders can vote without having to attend the annual meeting in person.

When added up, the charges that took place in the 1980s and 1990s were sweeping. Directors knew that shareholders could, in effect, gang up against underperforming CEOs—and the boards that protected them—so they had to act before the shareholders did. Corporate boards suddenly began ousting longtime CEOs. In quick succession, board putsches ended the careers of IBM chairman John Akers, Westinghouse Electric chairman Paul Lego, and General Motors chairman Robert Stempel. At the time, all three companies were losing money.

Then, in February 1993, the board of American Express (AmEx) shocked corporate America when it forced out CEO James Robinson III. Robinson had been chairman and chief executive for 15 years, and had appointed 15 of the 17 outside board members. These included close personal friends Henry Kissinger, the former U.S. secretary of state; Drew Lewis, the CEO of Union Pacific Corp., on whose board Robinson sat; and superlawyer Vernon Jordan, Jr., who stretched himself thin by sitting on nine other boards. These individuals had ties to AmEx that could conflict with their role as shareholder advocate. Robinson awarded Jordan's law firm a retainer, for example. Kissinger's international consulting firm received $350,000 in annual fees to advise Robinson and a brokerage subsidiary, Shearson Lehman Brothers, on overseas matters. Not only did Drew Lewis once run AmEx's cable-TV business, he also employed Robinson's wife while there. AmEx had invested $1 million in a partnership in which Lewis's son owned a major interest. At Union Pacific, Robinson sat on Lewis's compensation committee, helping to determine his pay. What director would revolt against the guy who sets his pay? The icing on the cake: all AmEx directors were eligible for retirement and life insurance benefits after serving five years. This board personified the culture of seduction.

During Robinson's reign, however, American Express's financial condition deteriorated because of numerous strategic errors. Robinson tried, but failed to merge AmEx with Disney, the Book-of-the-Month Club, and McGraw-Hill. He sold off companies, such as the cable-TV business, just before cable company prices shot through the roof. And in 1989, AmEx had to apologize publicly to international banker Edmond Safra, as well as give $8 million to charities he named, as compensation for allegedly engaging in dirty tricks to discredit Safra as he tried to set up a bank to compete with American Express. Altogether, AmEx lost some $4 billion in shareholder value under Robinson.

Shareholder protests at first fell on deaf ears until a small handful of dissident board members began pressuring Robinson to step down. Robinson finally agreed to give up the CEO position. But rather than step down entirely, he tried to maneuver himself into the chairman's office—a ploy that had worked for many a disgraced CEO in the past. Not this time. Institutional investors and even some of Robinson's own management team protested. The board had no choice but to force Robinson out completely. An era of greater board vigilance was beginning.

Sprinting for Options

Shareholders of Sprint Corp., the long-distance and wireless telephone company, used the shareholder process to register their disapproval when company executives awarded themselves millions of stock options. In 1997, Sprint's shareholders approved a stock option plan that allowed company executives to exercise all their options as a form of severance payment if the company changed hands. Sprint's board, however, quietly approved an amendment to the plan the next year that allowed executives to exercise options once shareholders approved a merger, rather than when a merger was actually completed. The company filed a notice about this seemingly minor change with the SEC, but few people noticed. Now fast-forward to 2000: Sprint shareholders approved a merger with telecom rival WorldCom Inc. But months later, regulators at the Justice Department and in Europe blocked the deal for antitrust reasons. The company's stock crashed from $61.50 in April to $25 by December. Now here's the catch: even though the WorldCom merger had to be called off, the board amendment allowed $1 billion in Sprint stock options to vest right away. Numerous top managers took advantage of the loophole by cashing in their options and resigning from the company.

Angry shareholders reacted by filing lawsuits alleging that the Sprint board and chairman William Esrey violated their fiduciary duty to shareholders and unjustly enriched themselves. While Esrey did not cash in his options, valued at $400 million, the board granted him three million more options in Sprint stock and its wireless tracking stock, Sprint PCS, in exchange for not doing so.

Rubbing salt in shareholders' wounds, the Sprint board in October 2000 also approved a plan that would allow thousands of employees to turn in their underwater stock options, only to have them reissued by the company six months and one day later. By doing so, Sprint was helping employees out of a pickle. Their options were originally priced at an average of $59 and, thus, were worthless. The "six-months-plus-one-day" ploy also lets Sprint skirt an accounting rule that requires companies to treat repriced options as an expense, if those options existed anytime in the last six months. Since Sprint launched its faux repricing plan, numerous other companies have copied the six-months-plus-one-day scheme. At all these companies, the employees now have an incentive to keep the share price as low as possible, in opposition to shareholder interests. Why? When the options are returned to them in six months, it's in the workers' interest to have a new exercise price that is as low as possible.

No wonder Sprint shareholders are unhappy. To register their dissatisfaction, they offered two resolutions at Sprint's 2001 annual meeting. One, offered by Amalgamated Bank of New York, which is the trustee for some 600,000 Sprint shares held in labor union pension funds, called on Sprint to seek shareholder approval for any future severance agreements such as the one that allowed Sprint managers to cash in their options early. It won 48 percent of the votes cast. The other resolution, sponsored by the New York State Retirement Fund and the International Brotherhood of Electrical Workers, called on the board not to reprice (or terminate and regrant) options without the prior approval of a majority of stockholders. It got 36 percent. Most shareholder resolutions fail in the first year they are offered, but can pick up steam when proposed in subsequent years. At least that's what the sponsors of the Sprint resolutions are hoping.

BOLSTERING THE AUDIT COMMITTEE

Although many boards of directors continued to improve, scandals involving overstated earnings and accounting chicanery at such companies as Waste Management, Sunbeam, and Cendant kept cropping up throughout the late 1990s. Some even involved allegations of fraud on the part of management. Something was wrong with the way companies were reporting their earnings, and it was natural to look to the board of directors for answers.

It didn't take much research to realize that there was a gaping lack of oversight on many boards, and it was right in the middle of the most important committee—the audit committee. Many of them had directors with some connection to management, such as a consulting contract. Still others had members who didn't know how to read a balance sheet. How could an audit committee spot a problem if it didn't even know the right questions to ask? Most audit committees rarely met with the outside auditors, and if they did, the CEO or other top executives were usually present to discourage any probing questions. I felt strongly that audit committees needed to be reinvigorated. These committees should be able to question auditors not only on the acceptability of a company's financial reporting, but on its quality as well. That means directors must always be ready to ask simple—but sometimes unsettling—questions. They must ask whether management's approach to a particular accounting principle is aggressive or conservative, compared to best practice. Directors also must understand the quality of financial reporting and disclosure practices so they can influence those practices when, in their judgment, they fall short of meeting investors' needs.

In the summer of 1998, the senior staff of the SEC went on a retreat and decided that one of the best things the agency could do to put an end to earnings manipulation was to reform the audit committee. The staff felt that audit committee members at least had to be financially literate and had to have the kind of independence that could challenge management in constructive ways.

Rather than decreeing this ourselves, we decided that new rules would be more widely accepted if the private sector came up with them and the stock exchanges enforced them as one of their listing requirements. So in September 1998, I gave a speech at New York University's Stern School of Business. Called "The Numbers Game," this address brought all of these brewing issues to a boil. I called for the establishment of a blue-ribbon committee to evaluate the effectiveness of corporate audit committees and to recommend changes to the listing requirements of the stock exchange.

The Numbers Game speech brought a hailstorm of criticism from some of corporate America's top executives: a phone call from Disney CEO Eisner and a letter from IBM CEO Lou Gerstner saying I was misguided. And my former business partner, Sandy Weill, now CEO of Citigroup, cornered me at a meeting of the Business Roundtable, a trade association of the country's top corporate leaders, and gave me an earful. But I found their arguments unpersuasive. At first, I wasn't certain that the blue-ribbon committee idea would fly. So I asked to speak to the Business Roundtable. I made my pitch by explaining that audit committees had become paper tigers, and warned that the capital markets were losing faith in company financial statements. I thought I would get frosty stares from this elite group—after all, I was attacking their boards. But soon after, I learned that more than half the group favored my proposal—perhaps knowing that strong, independent boards inspire investor confidence. I knew I was on to something.

We set to work putting together the panel with Dick Grasso and Frank Zarb, the chairmen, respectively, of the New York Stock Exchange and the National Association of Securities Dealers, overseer of Nasdaq. With some cajoling, they agreed to sponsor the group. Blue-ribbon committees succeed only if they include well-respected members of the profession whose behavior you're trying to influence. To that end, I invited Philip Laskawy and Jim Schiro, the CEOs of accounting firms Ernst & Young and PricewaterhouseCoopers, respectively. If there was any industry I hoped to change, it was accounting, so I was elated when they agreed to participate. The panel was led by Ira Millstein, a governance expert and a senior partner at the law firm Weil, Gotshal and Manges, and John Whitehead, the retired co-chairman of the investment bank Goldman Sachs.

After three months of deliberation, the panel recommended that audit committees be composed solely of independent directors. It also said the audit committee must have at least three people, all of whom should be considered financially literate, but one of them must have specific expertise in accounting and finance. The panel also urged audit committees to have a formal written charter that explains their purpose. The outside auditor, the panel recommended, should be accountable to the board and the audit committee, and replaceable at their discretion. The proxy statement should include a section saying whether the audit committee has reviewed the company's financial statements and other key areas, such as the independence of the outside auditor. The committee should analyze not just the numbers, but also the quality of the accounting. It should ask, for example, if the company is abusing the spirit of the accounting rules, even if it's not technically in violation. These were bold ideas.

On December 14, 1999, the stock exchanges adopted the panel's recommended listing requirements almost to the letter. I believe the blue-ribbon
committee did more to change the culture of corporate governance than almost anything else we did at the SEC. Since the report, I have seen a shift of
responsibility to the audit committee. Today, most committees have members
with financial experience who ask smart, probing questions. They don't have
to be CPAs, but they do have to know enough to understand where problems may exist. A July 2001 study published by CFO magazine found that audit committees were meeting an average of 4.6 times a year, up from 3.5 in
1998. And while 28 percent of companies in 1998 had at least one audit pan-
elist who was not independent, that number fell to 13 percent in 2001.

By now that number should be zero because of the June 2001 effective
date of the requirement that all audit committee members be fully independent. But the stock exchanges, which set many of the corporate governance
rules that companies must follow, aren't as tough about enforcing the rules
as their public relations literature implies. For example, the listing standards
allow companies to have one nonindependent audit committee member
"under exceptional and limited circumstances, provided that the board determines it to be in the best interests of the corporation and its shareholders" and discloses the reasons in the company's next annual proxy statement.
All a company need do is declare that retaining a particular nonindependent
director is in the "best interests of the company and its shareholders."

Such hubris is generally met with silence at the exchanges. As you can see,
tough new listing standards are only as good as the body that enforces them.
But Nasdaq and the New York Stock Exchange have the ultimate conflict
of interest. They are in cutthroat competition against one another and overseas exchanges for company listings, and the revenues they bring, and are
loath to tell companies to comply or leave. At a time when strict enforcement and tighter rules are needed, the exchanges must resist giving a free pass
to companies whose corporate governance fails to meet minimum standards. In response to the crisis of confidence spawned by the Enron/Arthur
Andersen debacle and many other corporate meltdowns due to accounting
irregularities, the exchanges in mid-2002, to their credit, put out for com-
ment new rules that far exceed anything done before.

Now that my SEC term is over, I've been asked to sit on several boards. I
currently serve as a director at Bloomberg L.P.; M&T Bank of Buffalo,

New York; fund management company Neuberger Berman; and U.S. Investigation Services. I take my corporate governance duties seriously.

How Do I Find Out Whether a Company Has Good Corporate Governance?

You, too, should care deeply about the governance of the companies in which you invest. But how do you know whether a company practices what I preach?

It's easier than you think, because the most important information about the board is in the annual proxy statement. This document must be mailed to every current shareholder. It tells you which items, such as the slate of directors, require investor approval, and gives instructions on how to vote your shares.

You may not think this is important, but it is. Investor groups are banding together to oppose certain corporate decisions, and they can make a difference. I think it's your responsibility as an owner of a company's shares to express your opinion whether or not you support the company's actions. Like democracy, corporate governance works only when you exercise your right to vote.

You may also think that as an individual investor, there's little you can do to change corporate governance. Yet you have powerful allies in the form of large pension funds and mutual funds, known as institutional investors. They collectively vote the shares of millions of people who, like you, have invested in these funds through their company pensions and 401(k) retirement accounts. Not all institutional investors care about corporate governance, but some of the very biggest ones are passionate about it—and can flex a lot of muscle. Among the most active, besides TIAA-CREF and CalPERS, is the AFL-CIO's Office of Investment, which sets voting guidelines for $450 billion in union pension fund investments. For the labor federation, the treatment of workers and executive pay are critical issues, in addition to increasing return on investment. The AFL-CIO has spoken out publicly against the governance practices of many companies and has won several victories that would have been unimaginable a short time ago. In 2001, 32 labor-backed shareholder proposals received an average of 34 percent of the votes cast—a far cry from the 1 percent that dissident groups typically were able to muster just a decade ago.

Different groups have different objectives. For CalPERS, increasing shareholder returns, and thus improving the standard of living for California state retirees, is paramount. In 1993, CalPERS began pressuring underperforming companies to change their board composition, but soon became more directly involved in removing poor managers. They were instrumental, for example, in persuading the board of General Motors to oust its CEO in 1992, the year GM lost $7 billion. Based on that success, CalPERS created a list of governance principles, and asked 200 other companies in which it had invested to adopt similar standards. Among the principles: a majority of directors should be from outside the company, and they should meet separately from the CEO three times a year; the board should perform an annual assessment of its own performance; and directors should have access to senior executives beyond the CEO.

Every year, CalPERS identifies companies in its portfolio that have underperformed the market for the past three years. Then its executives meet with the directors of each of those companies to talk about performance and governance issues. Those companies that also have poor governance end up on what is called the CalPERS Focus List, which can be found at *www .calpers-governance.org.*

TIAA-CREF spends over $2 million a year on governance issues. It, too, draws up an annual list of poor-performing companies and the governance changes it would like to see. But TIAA-CREF prefers to work behind the scenes before resorting to the more shame-oriented tactics of CalPERS, as by discreetly sending one or two retired CEOs on its staff to meet with the company and present its viewpoint. That's when most changes are made, says TIAA-CREF chairman John Biggs.

If you do not already own shares in a company, you can still access its proxy statement on the Internet at the SEC's website, *www.sec.gov.* Once there, click on "EDGAR," then select "DEF" (for Definitive Proxy Statement) in the box marked "form type." Then enter the company name and the year, and press "search." The proxy statement comes out in preliminary form (PRE 14A) and final form (DEF 14A) once a year. Look for the most recent filing; it usually appears in the spring for companies with a calendar fiscal year. You can also have any proxy statement sent to you by calling the company's investor relations number.

A number of other websites devoted to corporate governance are worth investigating. They'll give you a sense of how governance activists are voting on various proxy proposals, and point out egregious conflicts of interest in some companies or great governance examples in others. I recommend *www.thecorporatelibrary.com,* an overall resource on CEO contracts, pay, director independence, and other issues; and *www.iss.cda.com,* the website of Institutional Shareholder Services, a proxy monitoring organization that recommends how its clients—major investment firms—should vote. I also like the site of the Council on Institutional Investors, *www.cii.org,* which represents pension and mutual funds. Then there are the sites of TIAA-CREF, *www.tiaa-cref.org;* CalPERS, *www.calpers.org;* and the AFL-CIO, *www.aflcio.org/paywatch,* all of which have loads of helpful info on compensation, current issues, shareholder proposals, and much more. The AFL-CIO site has a handy executive compensation worksheet that can help you calculate how much a CEO is paid, including stock options. Sprint Corp. chairman and CEO Esrey, for example, took in $109.5 million in salary, bonus, and stock options, according to the site, in 2000.

A Good Board: Transparency Is Part of the Culture at Pfizer

If you're looking for an example of a company practicing good corporate governance, consider Pfizer Corp., a pharmaceutical company that has really pushed the envelope. In 1992, Pfizer became the first company to name a vice president for corporate governance, and today remains one of the few companies with such a position. It also has a corporate governance committee, in addition to the standard audit, compensation, and executive committees. And its proxy statement lists the company's corporate governance principles. Companies don't have to do this, says Peggy Foran, the company's current vice president for corporate governance. "But Pfizer makes an extra effort to be open, in the belief that it leads to better investor relations," she says.

The job of the corporate governance committee, according to Pfizer's 2001 proxy statement is to "make recommendations to the board concerning the appropriate size and needs of the board." Like the audit and compensation committees, the corporate governance committee is made up entirely of independent directors.

Pfizer's proxy statement has another advantage: it's written in clear, basic English. Most other companies' proxy statements are written in confusing legalese, making it difficult for shareholders to understand what's really going on. That's just the way some companies like it. "Transparency is part of our culture," says Foran. "I do this for a living and I can't understand a lot of [corporate material] on the first read. We believe in plain English and we give a lot of information that's not required. Pfizer tries to put itself in the shoes of the investors."

Now let's take a look at Pfizer's board. In 2000 it met twelve times. That's three times the number I recommend as a minimum, although it's worth noting that Pfizer has had plenty of business to discuss since it acquired Warner Lambert in 2000. The recent merger also explains why it has 19 directors, which is more than the ideal number but understandable considering that two companies were bolted together. All of the directors attended at least 75 percent of the full board and committee meetings during 2000—another sign that the board really cares. And the audit committee alone met six times. Five of the six audit committee members are current or former CEOs. That's a good sign that they actually understand numbers.

Each committee has a charter, which appears in the proxy statement. Only the audit committee is required to do this under SEC rules. The charter explains each panel's specific responsibilities. Again, this is unusual and worth reading to see how a committed board conducts its affairs. The corporate governance committee explicitly says it works on succession issues—a key matter for any board, but one that many ignore until it's too late.

Directors at Pfizer are paid in a combination of cash and a form of restricted stock. I would prefer to see them paid in stock alone, which would give them more of a stake in the company's performance. Pfizer doesn't require its directors to own Pfizer stock, as some campaigns do, but it expects them to hold a significant amount.

Only three of the nineteen board members are current or former executives: Bill Steere, the former CEO; Hank McKinnell, the current CEO; and John Niblack, who would succeed McKinnell in an emergency situation and therefore must be comfortable with Pfizer's board. This means that only 15 percent of the board are insiders—below the average of 22 percent.

Pfizer's board is extremely involved in the company's affairs. It regularly takes trips to Pfizer facilities in other parts of the world, such as Latin America and Asia, to meet with the executives there and understand all parts of Pfizer's business.

Yet Pfizer also monitors its directors to make sure they're not sitting on too many other boards. Each time a member is invited to join another board, he or she must submit an application to the corporate governance committee, which makes sure there are no overlaps or conflicts of interest before giving its approval. Also, when board members change jobs, they must resign from the board. The corporate governance committee then has the option to retain them or find new ones.

Although Pfizer could make improvements, such as not staggering director's terms and beefing up the stock ownership of some directors, the company is an example of what good governance is all about. I urge you to read Pfizer's proxy statement. It's also worth noting that $100 invested in Pfizer stock in 1995 would have returned $450 by the end of 2000, a 450 percent return compared to the 300 percent of Pfizer's peer group over the same period.

A GOVERNANCE CHECKLIST: WHAT TO LOOK FOR

• *Board Independence:* Who's on the board? How many are outsiders (meaning people who don't work at the company) and how many are insiders? According to Spencer Stuart, the average board in 2001 had 77 percent outside members and 23 percent insiders. Even if your company matches this profile, take a closer look. Read the proxy statement to see how many of the outsiders are actually independent. I think that the majority of the board should have no ties of any sort to the company. The only connection to the company should be their board service. If you see any commercial relationships, such as real estate deals, legal fees, or consulting contracts, that means a director is not truly independent.

Also be wary of family relationships that could compromise the independence of outsiders. At Hillenbrand Industries, for example, five of the 11 board members are Hillenbrand family members, and another is related by marriage. And watch out for interlocking directorates, or when CEOs serve on each other's boards. This could be an indication of mutual back-scratching.

Look carefully at the audit committee. Did any audit committee members ever work at the accounting firm that's been chosen to do the audit? This is a danger sign, because an audit committee member must question whether the auditor is doing a good job—yet it's human nature to give your former colleagues some slack.

Is there any mention of the board meeting periodically without the CEO present? If so, this is a true sign of independence. If the CEO is always around, it's a safe bet that no one's really conducting a no-holds-barred review. Another positive sign: boards that have lead directors who can call all the others together without the CEO's permission.

• *Board Overcommitment:* How often does the board meet? It should meet four times a year at a minimum, and preferably more often. The average S&P 500 company met eight times in 2000. The various committees should meet at least as often as the full board, particularly the audit committee. Did the members attend at least 90 percent of the meetings? The proxy statement must list the directors who attended less than 75 percent of the scheduled meetings. If some didn't, that's a possible sign that they are not paying close attention.

Make sure that the directors aren't so busy serving on other corporate boards that they don't have time for the company whose shares you own.

Vernon Jordan, for example, now serves on 11 different boards. Former Senate Majority Leader George Mitchell, a Democrat, sits on 12 boards. But Jack Kemp, the 1996 Republican vice-presidential candidate, takes the cake: he sits on 21 boards. If a board member has a demanding job, such as the CEO of a separate company, he should serve on no more than two or three other boards. The Council of Institutional Investors recommends five boards as the maximum that any one person can serve on properly.

• *Board Size:* According to executive search company Spencer Stuart, the average board today has 11 members. The Council of Institutional Investors recommends that boards have between five and 15 members. Too large a board can be unwieldy, while too small a board robs a company of the different perspectives and skills it needs. During the dot-com craze, many start-up companies, such as Yahoo!, insisted on iconoclastic boards with six to eight members, preferably with some tie to management. As we've seen from the performance of numerous dot-coms, they were misguided.

• *Board Compensation:* In 2001, according to Spencer Stuart, the average board member was paid $92,452 in a combination of cash and stock. Is your company's board paid considerably more than the average? If so, is there a good reason why? (Some companies, such as General Electric, pay their directors more because they meet more often—10 times in 2000—and must understand numerous industries.) Small companies with revenues under $500 million should pay their boards less. Keep an eye out for any extreme variations from the average. It could signal a fat and complacent board, or, at the other extreme, one that isn't paid enough money to take its role seriously. Make sure that board members get at least a portion of their compensation in stock. Like you, they should be at risk if the share price plummets.

• *Board Perks:* Remember my term "the culture of seduction"? In the old days, it was common for directors to collect a goody bag of perquisites in addition to their salaries. It once was common for a company to offer its directors a pension after retirement—despite the fact that most directors already have a handsome pension from serving as a top executive at another company. Ten years ago, more than three-quarters of S&P 500 companies offered director retirement plans. Now only 6 percent of companies offer this perk. If you see it in the proxy statement, beware.

The same goes for board meetings held at deluxe resorts and other "sweetheart deals" that may compromise directors' independence. Read your proxy statement to find out whether directors get perks such as free use of the company jet, or whether philanthropic contributions are made to their pet causes. Companies may not report all of this information, but the governance websites mentioned previously often have information about these enticements.

• *Succession Planning:* A board's most important duty is choosing the CEO. Every board should make sure there is a succession plan in place should something happen to the chief executive. Johnson & Johnson is an example of a company that makes succession planning an explicit part of the board's responsibility. Read the board's description of its duties carefully and look twice at any company whose board doesn't take an active role in succession. It could mean that the CEO has cowed the board into submission.

• *Executive Pay:* One of the most critical issues in governance is how executive compensation is determined. Read the compensation committee's report to make sure that it uses a clear, performance-driven standard for paying the chief executive. Simply put, the CEO should be paid generously only if he deserves it. If the company's share price is sinking or long-term performance targets are repeatedly missed, he should take a hit, with smaller stock option grants, a reduced or no bonus, or some other penalty. Look for any indication that the board decided to pay the CEO the full compensation package despite not meeting the agreed-to goals.

Stock options are another sensitive issue. They are a popular way to pay executives because they tie the performance of the company to the share price. That's good, in principle. Yet if a CEO is awarded too many stock options, he can become wealthy beyond all justification if the stock moves up just a dollar or two. Too many options allow managers to underperform their peer group and still make a hefty profit when they cash in their stock options. Stock options also create more shares of stock over time, which waters down the value of your shares. Remember: it is shareholder money that officers and directors are using to pay themselves. Look for a compensation committee that understands this.

• *Annual Board Elections:* In my view, it's best for the investor if the entire board is elected once a year. But about 60 percent of company boards have staggered terms. Usually this means that each year, one-third of the directors are elected to three-year terms. In the era of hostile takeovers, this made it easier for companies to deny predators the opportunity to replace a board all at once. But it also means that shareholders have far less control over who represents them. Look for companies whose boards are elected annually. In 1998, Disney ended the staggered terms of its directors and required them to stand for election as a single slate every year. Staggered boards aren't always bad. Pfizer, for example, has a staggered board, and its governance practices are otherwise exemplary. But it's a good rule of thumb to support companies that give shareholders more control over choosing directors.

• *Poison Pills:* Poison pills were of most concern in the 1980s and early '90s, when hostile takeovers were hot. But be on the lookout, because poison pills are making a comeback now that share prices are depressed. Silicon Valley execs are especially keen on having poison pills in their arsenal now that their shrunken share prices have left them vulnerable. Poison pills make it easier for incumbent management to retain control. But they also prevent shareholders, and the overall market, from exercising their right to discipline management by turning it out. I think the market should have its say. Look in the proxy statement to see whether there are any proposals to adopt a pill. If so, and you think the company might do better under new management, you might want to skip this stock.

A BAD BOARD: THE POWER FAILURE AT ENRON

Look for a train wreck of a company and chances are the vital checks and balances that active boards provide are missing. That appears to be the case at Enron.

Enron's finances, especially its many off-balance-sheet partnerships, were incomprehensible even to the smartest analysts on Wall Street, who recommended Enron's stock anyway. Why? Because it delivered glowing results: revenues in 2000 came to $101 billion, and its stock market value topped $75 billion. In early 2001, its future looked bright, too.

But almost at once, everything came unglued. Enron's overseas projects were losing money, as was a $1.2 billion investment in a fiber-optic network, which came online just as the country faced a glut of fiber-optic capacity. Enron's stock, too, suffered along with most other companies' in the recession that began in March 2001. But the biggest blow resulted from Enron's use of accounting tricks, which auditors at Arthur Andersen and the board of directors should have known about and stopped.

Why didn't the board act? Sadly, the directors appear not to have asked the right questions, and accepted Enron's financial alchemy without really understanding it. Twice in 1999, the board waived the company's code of ethics, which normally would have prohibited CFO Andrew Fastow from managing partnerships that placed his personal financial interest above Enron's. The audit committee was especially remiss in not noticing that Fastow and other employees were enriching themselves at Enron's expense. Fastow alone got at least $30 million through the off-balance-sheet deals. The audit committee also failed to notice that many of the partnerships were designed to make the financial statements look good, not to achieve bona fide economic objectives.

A report by a special investigative committee of the Enron board said that the entire board, despite its financial sophistication, had failed in its oversight duties. It especially failed to make sure that Fastow followed procedures set up to protect Enron from potential conflicts. In essence, Fastow was allowed to sit on both sides of the table without anyone looking over his shoulder, while negotiating over huge sums of money that passed back and forth between Enron and the partnerships he managed. The special committee wrote that the board "can and should be faulted for failing to demand more information, and for failing to probe and understand the information that did come to it." For example, although the board compensation committee was supposed to review the money Fastow received from the partnership deals, no such reviews ever took place. And on May 5, 2000, when the board was told that one transaction with a Fastow partnership raised the risk of "accounting scrutiny," the board never acted. Instead, it relied on assurances that auditor Arthur Andersen was comfortable with the deal.

Robert Jaedicke, the retired Stanford University accounting professor who led the audit committee, defended his stewardship of Enron before Congress: "We do not manage the company. We do not do the auditing. We are not detectives." In other words, he should be able to rely on the word of Enron management and its auditor. If only that were so. When a company's dealings are as complex as Enron's were, the board should seek outside advice, at the very least. In Enron's case, it should also have required Fastow to back up his claims about the merits of the off-balance-sheet entities and to report back each quarter on how they were performing. The board should not have accepted at face value what Enron management told them. If the board, for example, had demanded to see the paperwork for the partnership transactions, they would have spotted suspicious activities, such as the movement of assets back and forth, that would have raised many questions about financial manipulation.

Michael Miles, who was chairman and CEO of Philip Morris Cos. from 1991 to 1994, names four attributes all board members must have. They should be engaged, meaning they should be willing to commit their time and energy. They should know how the "game" is played, and by that he means the best directors are former CEOs with a sophisticated understanding of the dynamics of business. Directors should not be shy; they should ask inconvenient questions and not worry whether the CEO considers them polite or likable. And finally, directors should have a very keen bullshit detector so they know when someone is selling them a bill of goods. "My sense is these characteristics were missing at Enron," says Miles.

Conflicts of interest among board members may also have played a role in the board's lack of vigilance. Two Enron directors, one of whom sat on the audit committee, had consulting contracts with the company. Two other audit committee panelists worked for institutions that received substantial donations from Enron. One of those institutions, the University of Texas M.D.

Anderson Cancer Center alone received $1.8 million from Enron and related foundations over an eight-year period.

And where were the institutional investors and other shareholder advocates? Even the most activist of shareholder groups did not oppose Enron's opaque financial reports or its board structure. Indeed, one of Enron's biggest shareholders was CalPERS, the California pension fund whose $146 billion in assets now includes 3.5 million nearly worthless Enron shares. CalPERS also was a partner in two of Enron's off-balance-sheet deals, a transaction that produced a handsome gain of 62 percent a year for CalPERS over eight years. When Enron sought CalPERS's participation in a later off-balance-sheet deal, the pension fund balked when advisers warned it about Fastow's controlling fiduciary relationships—exactly the conflict that Enron's board did not see. But CalPERS did not publicize the problems at Enron, nor did it complain to Enron's board, even though CalPERS was also a major Enron shareholder. Why not? "We cannot read tea leaves," CalPERS director of corporate governance, Ted White, told a House committee. "It's impossible for anybody to have forecast that those relationships would mushroom and that Enron basically would commit fraud." True enough, hindsight is always 20/20. But I can't help feeling that CalPERS could have used its corporate governance expertise and its credibility to make sure Enron stopped its risky practices. Sometimes even watchdogs fall asleep.

CHAPTER 22

IF I ONLY KNEW THEN
WHAT I KNOW NOW

SUSAN C. KEATING

THE LAST several years have been a period of personal enlightenment—
a journey where risk in its broadest sense has taken on new multilevel and
multifaceted meanings. Today, we are operating in a world changing at an
unprecedented pace with risks and new threats taking us outside past experiences and testing the very best of our knowledge bases.

In the new world in which we live, everyone's job is to be a corporate risk
manager. And the roles of chief executive officers (CEOs) and other executives is to insure a robust risk framework within the organization, marrying
business strategy to operating practices while assessing risk versus rewards,
and making decisions relative to risk tolerances. Senior leadership must be
actively engaged in the development of risk *awareness,* analysis, and reporting. With the complexity of global business and expanded geographies,
technological advancements and new business ventures, *defining*—much less
managing—risk at a corporate or divisional level is more challenging than
ever.

Today's geopolitical realities, the possibility of war and bioterror events,
and a floundering economy make a comprehensive definition of risk even
more elusive. The potential impact and consequences associated with these
diverse threats are enormous. We can't eliminate those threats, but we must
factor them into our risk management approaches.

Senior leadership must be intimately involved in assessing and managing risk and must utilize people, process, and technology in a more structured and integrated way—forgetting department compartmentalization and the silo management of the past. Most important, senior leadership must not assume that risk is for *others* to deal with—such as auditing, compliance and credit policy. The only way to eliminate risk is to stop operating a business. But with senior level understanding and commitment, we can develop best-in-class processes and a culture that will reduce our vulnerabilities.

The objective has to be to create an environment that minimizes opportunities for a breach or failure. But because a failure can or will still occur, a process must be in place to allow problems to be identified early and elevated appropriately to senior management and oversight committees. The ability to move quickly to a well-developed crisis or contingency plan is crucial.

Top management understands that a key mission of every organization is to protect its assets and ensure safety and soundness on behalf of the stakeholders, but that concept must also be understood and owned by *every member of the company.* When assets are mismanaged, institutional credibility, reputation, and survival are at issue—and each and every employee is impacted. It starts at the top, but it must be part of the culture of the organization and written into job descriptions of every employee.

So you will understand why these issues are burned into my psyche, let me now describe a day in my life as CEO one year ago. I had just reaffirmed the strategic direction of Allfirst[1] with our U.S. and parent company boards; been commended by the boards for the positive double-digit year-end earnings; talked through the revenue challenges for 2002—given the weak economy; laid out specific plans for aggressively managing credit risks in some key sectors, such as communications; and described plans for significantly cutting costs to offset projected revenue shortfalls

I was headed out of the office to meet with one of our top customers when my assistant called. She had received a call from our head of risk, who insisted he meet immediately with me and our chief legal officer and the executive responsible for treasury. In my 29 years in the business, I have managed through many problems and crisis situations, but *this phone call chilled me to the bone.*

It was an extraordinary event that occurred at Allfirst Financial one year ago last February. We were defrauded in the amount of $691 million. It was a complex and intricate scheme, perpetrated by one individual over a five-year period. Unbelievable? Absolutely. Incomprehensible? Yes. Tragic? Incredibly. One rogue, foreign exchange trader seriously violated a 150-year-old, well-respected, $18 billion financial services institution, precipitating a crisis that will forever tarnish the company and the lives of many people employed by or associated with it.

As Eugene Ludwig, former controller of the currency, responsible for conducting the independent investigation into the circumstances of the fraud, said to me—"Susan, you were mugged." We were. And by an incredibly bright, creative, masterful, and arrogant employee. Hindsight and the results of the investigation reveal that there was *situational opportunity* and systemic weaknesses to our risk structure that the perpetrator recognized and capitalized on. (And, by the way, I believe that this possibility exists within every financial institution everywhere.) The rogue trader, John Rusnak,[2] successfully operated beneath the radar screen of policies and controls, breaching and manipulating them to his benefit, and intimidating and bullying employees in other areas that questioned some of his unorthodox practices.

This experience taught me a lot. Here's what I learned:

• *Conclusion #1: Management at the U.S. subsidiary and at the parent company underestimated the risk associated with the hedge-fraud style foreign exchange (FX) trading activity.* The Ludwig Report[3] noted, "The small size of the operation, and the style of trading, produced potential risk that far exceeded the potential reward."

From a management perspective, the area was small in terms of expected profits and formal risk limits and because not a part of the core business activities, was not given the top-level scrutiny it deserved.

The point is that periodic strategic reviews by business and the incorporation of a thorough risk assessment of business activities has to be mandatory within every one of our organizations. What is the nature and future of each business? How is it changing? What is the revenue contribution and potential? What are the potential risks? How can those risks be mitigated? Is the business core? If not, it should be flagged and put through even more rigorous examination.

• *Conclusion #2: The control processes in place intended to prevent such a fraud failed.* This was primarily human error resulting from manipulation by a bright and clever individual who had a firm grasp and influence over the bank's systems and procedures. The perpetrator was able to devise devious ways to obscure his risk positions and profit and loss. Further from the Ludwig Report, "He took advantage of weak and inexperienced employees with aggressive and intimidating behavior," *and that was accepted and encouraged by his supervisor.*

Structured and careful analysis and review of each element of the business might have uncovered some of the failures.

Again, an activity flagged as a noncore high-risk business should require that internal and external audits are more comprehensive and detailed and conducted more frequently.

• *Conclusion #3: Information gathered and reported was not at a level commensurate with the risk.* This is alarming when considering that the loss potential was growing as time passed.

Actually, the Asset Liability Management Committees of both the parent company and Allfirst were relatively advanced, and reporting was considered to be in the best-in-practice category in a number of respects. However, the *right* information wasn't being reported with respect to the foreign exchange trading. None of us recognized it, including two well-regarded CFOs.

• *Conclusion #4: The treasury division was organizationally siloed and matrix managed between Ireland and the United States.* This situation created an information vacuum outside of treasury and a unique operating culture within, with management accountability and oversight not up to the same standard as elsewhere within the company. Add to that a misplaced reliance on the competency of the treasury executive. He had extensive experience with foreign exchange trading, in particular, and was sent to the United States by the parent company many years prior. Substantive competency does not necessarily translate into effective risk management.

There are several key points here. No division, and I repeat, no division can be an island within a company. Integration and uniform practice simply has to occur.

Further, most financial services companies practice some form of matrix management that in its own right, can be very effective. However, and this is *big,* accountability and supervisory responsibilities must be absolutely clear.

• *Conclusion #5: Treasury audits and exams were inadequate.* Diligence in reviewing and later following through and elevating problematic issues was spotty. Part of the problem was that the auditors lacked sufficient understanding of the business to do the analysis required for these sensitive areas.

Relative to control deficiencies, no single control deficiency can be said to have caused the entire loss. It was a series of lapses and weaknesses. Interestingly, the investigation proved that had the auditors included even just a few more transactions, the probability of detecting a bogus one would have increased dramatically.

Given the growing complexity and nature of businesses that the financial services sector is conducting, the proper hiring and training of audit and compliance personnel is absolutely as critical as the hiring of the people with the expertise to run those businesses. Auditors well trained in the new specialties and detailed and thorough in their analysis and reporting are a requirement for the future.

• *Conclusion #6: The boards, audit and risk committees, and management assumed that the review and control processes were sufficiently robust.* The top-down strategic business and risk review that I described earlier simply *must* get done. Further, it needs to be *seriously* reviewed and challenged by the board, risk committees, and executives. In other words, corporate governance *has* to rise to new levels.

Support for business activities and agreement on risk tolerances are important. Reporting and consideration of identified hot spots, as well as active dialogue about emerging trends and new risks, should be standard agenda items.

• *Conclusion #7: The culture in the division was unique.* In treasury, a top-down management style of command and control—that could be intimidating and abusive—became a breeding ground for the likes of John Rusnak.

Ensuring open communication throughout the organization and among all levels is not just good business, it's an imperative. Despite tenure, experience, and contribution on the part of any one individual, intimidation and bullying *cannot* be tolerated.

If a healthy, progressive risk culture were in place, where every employee understood his or her role in being corporate risk managers, someone might have reported and elevated some of John Rusnak's unusual activities. Suspicious activities must be surfaced and all employees must be empowered to do that. And I really believe that this kind of environment can be achieved without creating an aura of mistrust among colleagues.

Allfirst came through the event, still deemed as well capitalized by definition, and in the quarter following recognition of the fraud was reporting earnings—which have continued to improve by quarter. The final chapter is still being written, however, as Allfirst has been acquired and will become a part of a larger U.S. company.[4]

The strength and resiliency of the company, an obsessive focus on holding on to customers and employees, and the support of the parent company got Allfirst through, but no one living through the experience will ever think about risk in the same old way. I certainly won't.

Senior executives everywhere must consider the new requirements and thinking relative to managing operational risk. New legislation and regulations have set the stage. Now, it's really up to *us* as leaders.

As leaders we have the privilege of working on behalf of our stakeholders. There is no room for complacency or taking anything for granted. Given the new world in which we live, we have a choice between value destruction and scandal, on the one hand, or protecting and increasing shareholder value on the other. Sounds pretty extreme, doesn't it? The real success stories within financial services in the future will be companies that have been able to strike the optimum balance between growth and risk taking. It's about strategy, business practice, and risk versus reward and making the right calls. It is thinking broadly and creatively about the future—considering the people dimension, implementing appropriate processes with a vengeance, *and* investing in technology and better information systems. Information is key—and although expense management is high on everyone's agenda today, any costs saved can be quickly consumed with one event or business failure.

The world is changing, my friends, and we must too.

NOTES

1. Allfirst was a regional bank owned by Allied Irish Bank, once the 43rd largest U.S. bank holding company.

2. John Rusnak was a lone wolf currency trader at Allfirst. He engineered Ireland's largest banking scandal and the fourth largest banking fraud in the world. In January 2003, Rusnak was sentenced to seven and a half years in federal prison.

3. From Eugene Ludwig, *The Ludwig Report,* April 2002.

4. In early 2003, Baltimore-based Allfirst financial was acquired by M&T Bank Corporation.

About the Contributors

Rick Antle, Ph.D.

Rick is senior associate dean and William S. Beinecke Professor of Accounting at the Yale School of Management. An expert in topics related to the interface of accounting and economics, his consulting engagements have involved valuation, auditing standards, auditor independence, and capital budgeting. Formerly a faculty member at the University of Chicago, Rick's widely published research has focused on such topics as auditor independence, auditors' incentives, audit fees, financial reporting, fees for nonaudit services, and the economics of accounting firms, managerial compensation and performance evaluation, revenue recognition, capital investment decisions, and transfer pricing. In addition to coauthoring *Financial Accounting,* a textbook used at all levels for the first course in accounting, Rick has served as associate editor of *Contemporary Accounting Research* and on the editorial boards of *The Accounting Review, Journal of Accounting Research, Review of Accounting Studies, The British Accounting Review,* and the *Journal of Business Finance and Accounting.*

Jennifer Arlen, Ph.D., J.D.

Jennifer is the Norma Z. Paige Professor of Law at New York University School of Law, where she teaches corporations, securities fraud litigation, and business crime. Jennifer's scholarship focuses on organizational liability, both criminal and civil. She has been published in numerous journals such as the *Yale Law Journal, Journal of Legal Studies, Journal of Law and Economics,* and the *New York University Law Review,* and currently is coauthoring a casebook on business crime. Prior to joining the NYU faculty, she was the Ivadelle and Theodore Johnson Professor of Law and Business at the University of Southern California Law School and a founding director of the USC Center in Law, Economics, and Organization. She also has been a visiting professor of law at Yale Law School and the California Institute of Technology, and an Olin Fellow at Boalt Hall School of Law, University of

California, Berkeley. She currently is the editor of the *Experimental and Empirical Studies* series on the Legal Scholarship Network and is on the editorial board of the *International Review of Law and Economics.* She has served on the board of directors of the American Law and Economics Association and chaired the Remedies, Torts, and Law and Economics sections of the Association of American Law Schools.

Norman R. Augustine

Norman has had a long and distinguished career, formerly serving as president, CEO, vice chairman and chairman of Lockheed Martin Corporation. Currently, he is chairman of the company's executive committee. He began his career at Douglas Aircraft, leaving to serve at the Pentagon in the Office of the Secretary of Defense and later as undersecretary of the army. In industry, he worked for LTV Missiles and Space Company and Martin Marietta Corporation, the latter as chairman and CEO. In the charitable world he has served as president of the Boy Scouts of America and as chairman of the American Red Cross. In recent years he served as lecturer with the rank of professor on the faculty of Princeton University School of Engineering and Applied Science. He has served on the boards of numerous organizations, including ConocoPhillips, Black and Decker, Procter and Gamble, Lockheed Martin, and the Ethics Resource Center. He has also served as a trustee of Princeton, MIT, Johns Hopkins, and the Colonial Williamsburg Foundation. He is a director of the National Association of Corporate Directors and is a member of the President's Council of Advisors on Science and Technology. He has served as chairman of the National Academy of Engineering and as president of the American Institute of Aeronautics and Astronautics and has been awarded the National Medal of Technology by the President of the United States and has received the Department of Defense's Distinguished Service Medal on five occasions. He is the coauthor of two books, *The Defense Revolution* and *Shakespeare in Charge* and the author of *Augustine's Laws* and *Augustine's Travels.*

Katharina Balazs

Katharina is associate professor of strategy and organization at ESCP-EAP, Paris. She also has worked as a strategic management consultant in Scandinavia, France, Austria, Germany, and Hungary, specializing in executive development and cross-cultural management issues in international mergers and acquisitions. Her current organizational interests include leadership, entrepreneurship, cross-cultural management, innovation and organizational excellence, and she has written several books and articles on these and other topics.

Warren Bennis, Ph.D.

Warren is university professor and distinguished professor of business administration and founding chairman of the Leadership Institute at the University of Southern California. He also serves as the chairman of the Advisory Board of the Center for Public Leadership at Harvard University's Kennedy School and is the Thomas S. Murphy Distinguished Research Fellow at the Harvard Business School. He is visiting professor of leadership at the University of Exeter (United Kingdom) and a fellow of the Royal Society of the Arts (United Kingdom). He has written or edited 26 books, including the best selling *Leaders* and *On Becoming a Leader,* both translated into 21 languages. The *Financial Times* recently named *Leaders* as one of the top 50 business books of all time. In 1993, Addison-Wesley published a book of his essays, *An Invented Life: Reflections on Leadership and Change,* which was nominated for a Pulitzer Prize. In 1998, Jossey-Bass republished his 1968 path-breaking book, *The Temporary Society,* coauthored with Philip Slater. His recent books, *Organizing Genius* (1997), *Co-Leaders* (1999), and *Managing the Dream* (2000), summarize Bennis's major interests: leadership, change, great groups, and powerful partnerships. Bennis's latest book, *Geeks and Geezers* (2002), examines the differences and similarities between leaders 30 years old and younger and leaders 70 years old and older. Bennis has served on the faculty of MIT's Sloan School of Management, where he was chairman of the organizational studies department. He is a former faculty member of Harvard and Boston University, former provost and executive vice president of the State University of New York, Buffalo, and former president of the University of Cincinnati from 1971 to 1978. He has received 11 honorary degrees and has served on numerous boards of advisers, including Claremont University, American Leadership Forum, the American Chamber of Commerce, and the Salk Institute. He has served on four U.S. presidential advisory boards and has consulted for many Fortune 500 companies, including G.E., Ford, and Starbucks. The *Wall Street Journal* named him as one of the top 10 speakers on management in 1993, and in 1996, *Forbes* magazine referred to him as the "Dean of Leadership Gurus." Bennis is proud of the four years he served in the U.S. Army, 1943–1947; he was one of the youngest infantry commanders and was awarded the Purple Heart and Bronze Star.

John Clifton Bogle

John is founder of The Vanguard Group, Inc. and president of the Bogle Financial Markets Research Center. He serves as chairman of the board of the National Constitution Center, as director of Instinet Corporation, on the Investment Committee of the Phi Beta Kappa Society, and as a member of the Conference Board's Commission on Public Trust and Private Enterprise. In 1997, U.S. Securities and Exchange Commission Chairman Arthur Levitt handpicked him to serve on the Independence Standards Board. Numerous financial organizations have lauded John with awards. The Financial Analysts of Philadelphia presented him with the lifetime "Award of Distinction;" the Association for Investment Management and Research gave him its "Award for Professional Excellence;" and the Commonwealth's Chamber of Commerce named him Pennsylvania's "Business Leader of the Year for 2000." He has been inducted into the Hall of Fame of the Fixed Income Analysts Society, Inc., named one of the "Financial Leaders of the 20th Century" in *Leadership in Financial Services,* and dubbed "Fund Leader of the Year" by *Fund Action* magazine. In 1999, John received the Woodrow Wilson Award from Princeton University for "distinguished achievement in the Nation's service." Later that year, he was named by *Fortune* magazine as one of the investment industry's four "giants of the 20th century." John has authored several books, including *Bogle on Mutual Funds: New Perspectives for the Intelligent Investor; Common Sense on Mutual Funds: New Imperatives for the Intelligent Investor; John Bogle on Investing: The First 50 Years;* and *Character Counts: The Creation and Building of The Vanguard Group.*

William H. Donaldson

William became the 27th chairman of the U.S. Securities and Exchange Commission on February 18, 2003, after being confirmed by the United States Senate. As SEC Chairman, Mr. Donaldson is the chief regulator of America's securities markets and the chief enforcer of America's securities laws. A graduate of Yale and Harvard Business School and a Marine Corps veteran, Mr. Donaldson has spent more than 40 years at the highest levels of business, government, and academia. He was a cofounder and CEO of the international investment bank and stock research firm Donaldson, Lufkin & Jenrette; the founder of Yale University's School of Management, where he served as dean and professor of management studies; an undersecretary of state in the Nixon administration and, later, counsel and special adviser to Vice President Rockefeller; the chairman and CEO of the New York Stock Exchange; and chairman, president, and CEO of Aetna. Mr. Donaldson's career reflects an interest in nurturing and managing human and financial resources through strategies that enhance productivity by encouraging mutual respect and cooperation between employees. As SEC chairman, Donaldson is dedicated to holding accountable all those who have violated the public trust, demanding responsible corporate governance throughout the business and financial world, and strengthening America's market structure—making the securities markets more efficient, more transparent, and friendlier to all investors, particularly small investors.

Charles M. Elson

Charles is the Edgar S. Woolard Jr. Chair in Corporate Governance and the director of the John L. Weinberg Center for Corporate Governance at the University of Delaware. A former professor of law at Stetson University College of Law in St. Petersburg, Charles practiced for several years with the New York law firm of Sullivan & Cromwell; worked as a law clerk to the United States Court of Appeals for the Fourth and Eleventh Circuits; and served as a visiting professor at the University of Illinois College of Law, the Cornell Law School, and the University of Maryland School of Law. Currently, he is "Of Counsel" to the Tampa law firm of Holland & Knight, a Salvatori Fellow at the Heritage Foundation in Washington, D.C., and a member of the American Law Institute. He is also vice chairman of the ABA Business Law Section's Committee on Corporate Governance and a member of its Committee on Corporate Laws. A frequent contributor on corporate governance issues to various scholarly and popular publications, Charles has written extensively on the subject of boards of directors and specifically on board compensation.

Roberta D. Fox

Roberta is a consultant with Hewitt Associates' Talent and Organization Consulting (TOC) line of business. She consults in all aspects of director and executive compensation, specializing in technical areas impacting executive and director compensation, and compensation issues associated with business restructuring transactions, such as initial public offerings, spin-offs, and change in control. Roberta heads the TOC Center for Technical Expertise, which has global responsibility for technical areas impacting compensation, corporate restructuring and change, and global equity issues. She manages the eGuide to Global Stock Option Plans, an Internet-based source of information on the feasibility of granting global stock options and stock purchase awards outside the United States. Prior to joining Hewitt, Roberta, a certified public accountant, was a tax manager with a Big Six public accounting firm. A frequent lecturer at numerous legal and business seminars, she also has written a number of articles for publications such as *Directorship*, *ACA Journal*, *WorldatWork Journal*, *Journal of Compensation and Benefits*, and *Directors & Boards*.

Robert P. Gandossy

Robert is a global practice leader for Talent and Organization Consulting for Hewitt Associates. He has special expertise in improving organizational effectiveness, human resource strategy, leadership, managing large-scale change, M&A, and increasing growth through innovation. Bob was coproject manager of a major research effort, *The Changing American Workforce*, and has written more than three dozen articles and five books on subjects including HR strategy, M&A, pay-for-performance, productivity improvement, innovation and change, and business ethics. His book *Bad Business* was deemed a "masterful job" by Tom Peters and "high drama and a fascinating story" by Rosabeth Moss Kanter. Bob also coauthored *Leading the Way: Three Truths from the Top Companies for Leaders* and coedited *HR in the 21st Century*, featuring chapters by the world's thought leaders in human resources and leadership. He has been a speaker for Harvard Business School, Human Resources Planning Society, The Wharton School, Tom Peters Group, Yale Law School, Yale's School of Organization and Management, World at Work, SHRM, American Management Association, and The Conference Board.

William W. George

Bill is senior lecturer at the Harvard Business School, where he is teaching "Leadership and Corporate Accountability." He is the author of *Authentic Leadership: Rediscovering the Secrets to Creating Lasting Value* and was recently named one of "The 25 Most Influential Business People of the Last 25 Years" by PBS Nightly News. Prior to joining the Harvard faculty in January 2004, Mr. George was professor of leadership and governance at IMD International in Lausanne, Switzerland and executive-in-residence at Yale University's School of Management. Mr. George is the former chairman and chief executive officer of Medtronic. He joined Medtronic in 1989 as president and chief operating officer and was elected chief executive officer in 1991, serving in that capacity through 2001. He was chairman of the board from 1996 to 2002. Under his leadership, Medtronic's market capitalization grew from $1.1 billion to $60 billion, averaging 35 percent a year. Prior to joining Medtronic, he spent 10 years as an executive with Honeywell, serving as president of Space & Aviation Systems and Honeywell Europe; and 10 years with Litton Industries, primarily as president of Litton Microwave Cooking. Mr. George serves as a director of Goldman Sachs, Novartis, and Target Corporation, is on the boards of National Association of Corporate Directors, Harvard Business School Board of Dean's Advisors, Carnegie Endowment for International Peace, the Minneapolis Institute of Arts, and is chair of Minnesota Thunder Pro Soccer. Mr. George received his BSIE with high honors from Georgia Tech and his M.B.A. with high distinction from Harvard University, where he was a Baker Scholar. He has been named Executive-of-the-Year by the Academy of Management (2001) and Director-of-the-Year by NACD (2001–2002). He has received the Legend in Leadership Award from Yale University and the Alumni Achievement Award from Harvard Business School.

Marshall Goldsmith

Marshall is a founding director of A4SL—The Alliance for Strategic Leadership. Recently, Marshall was named by the American Management Association as one of 50 great thought leaders and business executives that have influenced the field of management. He has been listed in *The Wall Street Journal* as one of the top 10 executive educators, in *Forbes* as one of five most respected executive coaches, in the *Economist* as one of the most credible thought leaders in the new era of business, and in *Fast Company* as America's preeminent executive coach. Marshall's 18 books include *The Leader of the Future, Coaching for Leadership,* and *Global Leadership: The Next Generation.* He teaches in executive education programs for major corporations and at Dartmouth and Michigan Universities.

Alan Judes

Alan is a remuneration consultant in the London office of Hewitt Bacon & Woodrow, leading the European executive compensation practice. He works with U.K., North American, European, Australian, and South African clients on their international business and reward strategy. Alan has been responsible for the development of a number of innovative services, including phantom share incentives, restricted share plans, option pricing models, total shareholder return incentives, and group unapproved funded final salary pensions. Prior to joining Hewitt, he worked in the London office of Peat, Marwick, Mitchell & Co. and the Johannesburg office of Louis E. Kaplan & Co. He was also a member of faculty for WorldatWork and the Institute of Personnel & Development, teaching in their executive remuneration program. In addition to writing the taxation chapter for numerous manuals on compensation practice, he is the author of *Transactions: Share Incentives for Employees.*

Rosabeth Moss Kanter

Rosabeth is the Ernest L. Arbuckle Professor of Business Administration at Harvard Business School. Rosabeth conceived and led the Business Leadership in the Social Sector (BLSS) project, under the auspices of the Harvard Business School's Initiative on Social Enterprise. Currently, she is researching the development of new leadership for the digital age. In addition to serving as editor of the *Harvard Business Review,* she is the author or coauthor of 16 books, including her forthcoming book, *Confidence: How Winning Streaks and Losing Streaks Begin and End* (September 2004); *Evolve! Succeeding in the Digital Culture of Tomorrow;* and *Men & Women of the Corporation.* Other award-winning bestsellers include *The Change Masters; When Giants Learn to Dance;* and *World Class: Thriving Locally in the Global Economy.* She joined the Harvard Business School faculty in 1986 from Yale University, where she held a tenured professorship from 1977 to 1986; previously, she was a fellow in law and social science at Harvard Law School. Professor Kanter has received 21 honorary doctoral degrees and over a dozen leadership awards, and has been named to lists of the "50 most influential business thinkers in the world" (ranked in the top 10), the "100 most important women in America," and the "50 most powerful women in the world." She cofounded Goodmeasure Inc., a consulting group, and also serves as a director or adviser for other companies. Her consulting clients include some of the world's most prominent companies, and she has delivered keynote addresses for major events in the United States and dozens of other countries, sharing the platform with prime ministers and presidents. A keynote speaker for major events throughout the world, she appears often on radio and television.

Susan C. Keating

Susan is the president and chief executive officer for the National Foundation for Credit Counseling, Inc. (NFCC). Through its member agencies, NFCC sets the standard for quality credit counseling, debt reduction services, and education for financial wellness. The NFCC is the nation's largest and longest-serving national nonprofit credit counseling organization. Prior to joining NFCC, Susan spent more than 29 years in the commercial banking industry. She was formerly president and chief executive officer of Allfirst Financial Inc., once the 43rd-largest bank holding company. In that role she was the highest-ranking woman CEO in banking in the United States. She served on the board of the Financial Services Roundtable and chaired their Consumer Issues Committee. Keating served as cochair of the governor's Economic Development Policy Committee in Maryland and banking chair for the U.S. Savings Bond National Volunteer Committee. In 2002, the *Daily Record* honored Keating with her induction into the Top 100 Women of Maryland Circle of Excellence. She was presented an Honorary Doctorate of Humane Letters in 2000 by Towson University. Keating was named one of the "Magnificent Seven" by Business and Professional Women/ USA in 1994 and is also a member of the Council of One Hundred, a select group of professional women graduates of Northwestern University.

Manfred F. R. Kets de Vries

Manfred holds the Raoul de Vitry d'Avaucourt Chair of Leadership Development at INSEAD, Fontainebleau, France and Singapore. He is the director of INSEAD's Global Leadership Center. He is also serving as program director of its top management seminar, "The Challenge of Leadership: Developing Your Emotional Intelligence" and the program "Mastering Change: Developing Your Coaching and Consulting Skills." He is also a certified psychoanalyst and a member of the International Psychoanalytic Association. He is a consultant on organizational design/transformation and strategic human resource management to leading U.S., Canadian, European,

African, and Asian companies. A clinical professor of leadership development, he scrutinizes the interface between international management, psy-
choanalysis, psychotherapy, and dynamic psychiatry. Specific areas of interest
include leadership, career dynamics, executive stress, entrepreneurship,
family business, succession planning, cross-cultural management, and the
dynamics of corporate transformation and change. A founding member of
the International Society for the Psychoanalytic Study of Organizations,
Manfred has held professorships at McGill University; the Ecole des Hautes
Etudes Commerciales, Montreal; and the Harvard Business School. He is the
author, coauthor, or editor of 20 books, including *The Neurotic Organization,
Organizations on the Couch, The Leadership Mystique,* and the prize-winning
*Life and Death in the Executive Fast Lane: Essays on Organizations and Leader-
ship.* In addition, he has published more than 200 scientific papers, many of
which have appeared in such journals as *Behavioral Science, Organizational Dynamics, Harvard Business Review, Sloan Management Review, Human Relations,
Harper's,* and *Psychology Today.*

Rakesh Khurana, Ph.D.

Rakesh is an assistant professor of business administration at Harvard Business School, teaching leadership and organizational behavior in the M.B.A.
program. His current research focuses on the CEO labor market, with a particular interest on the factors that lead to vacancies in the CEO position; the
factors that affect the choice of successor; the role of market intermediaries,
such as executive search firms in CEO search; and the consequences of CEO
succession and selection decisions for subsequent firm performance and
strategic choices. A founding member of Cambridge Technology Partners in
Sales and Marketing, he also taught at MIT's Sloan School of Management.
He consults with corporations and executive search firms to help improve
their CEO succession, governance, and executive development practices. He
has authored a book, *Searching for a Corporate Savior: The Irrational Quest for
Charismatic CEOs,* and his articles have appeared in numerous publications,
including *Harvard Business Review* and *Sloan Management Review.*

Robert W. Lane

Bob is chief executive officer and chairman of the board of Deere & Company, posts he has held since 2000. He has served the company in a number

of high-level positions, including president and chief operating officer, chief financial officer, and president of John Deere's Worldwide Agricultural Equipment Division. He was also president of Deere Credit, Inc., and has directed most of John Deere's operations around the world. Bob joined John Deere in 1982, following a career in corporate banking that included management assignments in Europe. In addition to his duties at Deere, Bob is a member of the board of directors of Verizon Communications Inc. He also serves as a trustee for the Committee for Economic Development and is a member of The Business Roundtable and Business Council. His civic activities include being a member of the boards of the Lincoln Park Zoo and the Lyric Opera of Chicago.

Arthur Levitt

Arthur is senior advisor to The Carlyle Group and a member of the American Academy of Arts and Sciences. He was the longest serving chairman of the United States Securities and Exchange Commission, from his appointment in July 1993 to February 2001. During that time, he created the Office of Investor Education and Assistance and established a website (www.sec.gov), which allows the public free and easy access to corporate filings and investor education materials. Other hallmarks of his tenure include improving the quality of the financial reporting process; maintaining the independence of auditors; saving investors billions of dollars by reducing spreads in the Nasdaq market; promoting the use of plain English; requiring that important information be released to all investors simultaneously; fighting Internet fraud; and cleaning up the municipal bond market. Before joining the commission, Arthur served as chairman of both the New York City Economic Development Corporation and the American Stock Exchange. Prior to that, he spent 16 years working on Wall Street. He is the author of the bestselling book *Take On The Street: What Wall Street and Corporate America Don't Want You to Know/What You Can Do to Fight Back*.

Nell Minow

Nell is editor of thecorporatelibrary.com, an Internet site that compiles research, study, and critical thinking about the nature of the modern global corporation, with a special emphasis on best practices and standards. She is a former principal of LENS, a $100 million investment firm that buys stock in underperforming companies and uses shareholder activism to increase their value. Before that, she served as president of Institutional Shareholder Services, Inc., a firm that advises institutional investors on issues of corporate governance and as an attorney at the Environmental Protection Agency, the Office of Management and Budget, and the Department of Justice. Coauthor of three books and author of over 200 articles about corporate governance, Nell was named one of the 30 most influential investors of 2002 by *Smart Money* magazine.

Michael J. Powers

Michael is Global Practice Leader for executive compensation and corporate governance consulting at Hewitt Associates. Michael has significant experience consulting on executive compensation design issues. He has been responsible for Hewitt's Total Compensation Measurement™ services and the Midwest region talent and organization consulting practice. Michael consults actively with compensation committees of boards of major companies. An attorney and certified public accountant, Michael was a tax manager with a major public accounting firm prior to joining Hewitt. He is a frequent lecturer at national conferences, and his many articles have been published in magazines, such as *The WorldatWork Journal* and *Directors & Boards* magazine.

Leonardo Sforza

Leonardo is head of research and European Union affairs at Hewitt Associates' European Headquarters in Brussels, where he assists the firm and Hewitt's global clients on European Union (EU) policies and their implications for business, particularly in the fields of financial services, corporate restructuring, labor law, and corporate governance. Prior to joining Hewitt, he spent a decade working with the European Commission, where he launched and coordinated numerous initiatives for improving the European business environment. Leonardo has published numerous articles and position papers on EU legislative and policy developments affecting business strategies and is regarded as an influential opinion leader in this area. He serves as a columnist for the *Financial Times* magazine *European Investment and Pension News* and as a keynote speaker at numerous conferences, including the European Association of Labor Lawyers in Vienna, the International Pension and Employment Benefit Lawyers Association in San Diego, and the U.S. National Foreign Trade Council in New York, Houston, Dallas, and San Francisco.

Scott A. Snook

Scott is an associate professor at the Harvard Business School, where his research and consulting activities include leadership, leader development, leading change, organizational systems, and culture. Previously, he served as an academy professor in the behavioral sciences and leadership department at the United States Military Academy and directed West Point's Center for Leadership and Organizations Research, as well as its joint Master's Program in leader development. Scott spent 22 years in the U.S. Army Corps of Engineers, serving in various command and staff positions, leading soldiers into combat, and earning the rank of colonel. His military decorations include the Legion of Merit, Bronze Star, Purple Heart, and Master Parachutist badge. He was also awarded the Sage-Louis Pondy Best Dissertation Award from the Academy of Management for his study of the friendly fire shootdown in northern Iraq. Scott is the author of *Friendly Fire* and the coauthor of *Practical Intelligence in Everyday Life*.

Barbara Ley Toffler

Barbara advises, teaches, and consults in the areas of leadership, managerial decision-making, responsible business practices, and organizational ethics. A founding principal of Resources for Responsible Management, Inc., a Boston-based consulting firm, Barbara has consulted to over 60 companies in the United States, United Kingdom, and Asia. She also has served on the faculty of the Boston University School of Management and the Harvard Business School and as a lecturer at the Yale School of Management. Barbara is the author of *Managers Talk Ethics: Making Tough Choices in a Competitive Business World* and *Final Accounting: Ambition, Greed, and the Fall of Arthur Andersen,* a study of Andersen's culture, based on her experiences as the founder and partner-in-charge of the firm's Ethics and Responsible Business Practices Consulting Services. The book has been described as "a fascinating insider exposé" that "may be the most important analysis coming out of the corporate disasters of 2001 and 2002." She also has authored numerous articles, including the coauthored *Managing Ethics and Legal Com-*

pliance, What Works and What Hurts, the first scientific study of the behavioral and attitudinal effects of corporate ethics programs.

Michael Useem

Michael is professor of management and director of the Center for Leadership and Change Management at the Wharton School of the University of Pennsylvania, where he teaches M.B.A. and executive-M.B.A. courses on management and leadership. He also works on leadership development with numerous organizations in the private, public and nonprofit sectors, offering programs on leadership and change for managers in the United States, Asia, Europe, and Latin America. Michael is the author of *The Leadership Moment: Nine True Stories of Triumph and Disaster and Their Lessons for Us All* and *Leading Up: How to Lead Your Boss So You Both Win.* He also coauthored and coedited *Upward Bound: Nine Original Accounts of How Business Leaders Reached Their Summits.*

Sherron S. Watkins

Sherron is the former vice president of Enron Corporation, who alerted then-CEO Kenneth Lay to accounting irregularities within the company in August 2001. In the months that followed, she testified before congressional committees from both the House and the Senate and, along with two other whistle-blowers, received *TIME* magazine's prestigious Person of the Year award. She has received numerous honors, including *Court TV*'s Scales of Justice Award, the National Academy of Management's Distinguished Executive Award, and the Women's Economic Round Table's Rolfe Award for Educating the Public about Business and Finance. A certified public accountant, Sherron previously worked as the portfolio manager of MG Trade Finance Corp.'s commodity-backed financial assets in New York City and in the auditing group of both the New York and Houston offices of Arthur Andersen. Currently an independent consultant and speaker on the subject of Enron and the erosion of trust in the U.S. capitalist system, she is coauthor of *Power Failure, the Inside Story of the Collapse of Enron.*

INDEX